CRITICAL ETHNOGRAPHY AND EDUCATION

In this book, Fitzpatrick and May make the case for a reimagined approach to critical ethnography in education. Working with an expansive understanding of *critical*, they argue that many researchers already do the kind of critical ethnography suggested in this book, whether they call their studies critical or not.

Drawing on a wide range of educational studies, the authors demonstrate that a methodology that is lived, embodied, and personal—and fundamentally connected to notions of power—is essential to exploring and understanding the many social and political issues facing education today. By grounding studies in work that reimagines, troubles, and questions notions of power, injustice, inequity, and marginalization, such studies engage with the tenets of critical ethnography.

Offering a wide-ranging and insightful commentary on the influences of critical ethnography over time, Fitzpatrick and May interrogate the ongoing theoretical developments, including poststructuralism, postcolonialism, and posthumanism. With extensive examples, excerpts, and personal discussions, the book thus repositions critical ethnography as an expansive, eclectic, and inclusive methodology that has a great deal to offer educational inquiries. Overviewing theoretical and methodological arguments, the book provides insight into issues of ethics and positionality as well as an in-depth focus on how ethnographic research illuminates such topics as racism, language, gender and sexuality in educational settings. It is essential reading for students, scholars, and researchers in qualitative inquiry, ethnography, educational anthropology, educational research methods, sociology of education, and philosophy of education.

Katie Fitzpatrick is Associate Professor and Head of School in the Faculty of Education and Social Work at the University of Auckland, New Zealand. Her research and teaching are focused on health education, physical education, and sexuality education, as well as critical ethnographic and poetic research methods.

Stephen May is Professor of Education in Te Puna Wānanga (School of Māori and Indigenous Education) at the University of Auckland, New Zealand. He is an international authority on language rights, language policy, bilingual education, and critical multiculturalism, as well as having a longstanding interest in critical ethnography.

CRITICAL ETHNOGRAPHY AND EDUCATION

Theory, Methodology, and Ethics

Katie Fitzpatrick and Stephen May

Routledge
Taylor & Francis Group

NEW YORK AND LONDON

Cover image: © 'Tomorrow' (2019) by Lucy Davidson.
Reproduced courtesy of the artist: https://lucydavidson.nz

First published 2022
by Routledge
605 Third Avenue, New York, NY 10158

and by Routledge
2 Park Square, Milton Park, Abingdon, Oxon, OX14 4RN

Routledge is an imprint of the Taylor & Francis Group, an informa business

Library of Congress Cataloging-in-Publication Data
A catalog record for this book has been requested

ISBN: 978-1-138-63195-3 (hbk)
ISBN: 978-1-138-63196-0 (pbk)
ISBN: 978-1-315-20851-0 (ebk)

DOI: 10.4324/9781315208510

Typeset in Bembo
by Apex CoVantage, LLC

CONTENTS

ACKNOWLEDGMENTS

Katie

My work on this book was supported by a Rutherford Discovery Fellowship from Te Apārangi, The Royal Society of New Zealand. I wish to acknowledge Contemporary Ethnography Across the Disciplines (CEAD), an academic association and conference initiated by Bob Rinehart, which has been so central to the development of my ethnographic imagination. I am also indebted to the Qualitative Inquiry conference and the work of all the scholars who attend and are part of the discussions and academic work connected with that gathering. The feedback I have received on this work from colleagues at the European Conference on Educational Research (ECER) has, likewise, been invaluable as is the support of my friends and colleagues in the field of health education, especially Deana Leahy, Peter Aggleton, Jan Wright, John Evans, Richard Tinning, Symeon Dagkas, and many others. I wish to acknowledge the Faculty of Education and Social Work at the University of Auckland and the support of the Dean, Mark Barrow, who has provided both encouragement and writing leave for me to finish this book. Likewise, my deputy head of school, Paul Neveldsen, without whom I could not hope to continue academic writing while also being head of school. And to Monica Bland for her invaluable research support throughout. Thanks to Bob Rinehart, Jonathan Wyatt, Marek Tesar and Mary Lou Rasmussen, who generously provided feedback on earlier versions of specific chapters. I am also immensely grateful for my other friends and colleagues at the University of Auckland (past and present), many of whom have shared their ethnographic ideas and research practices, and who are all so wonderful, supportive, and intellectually curious: Jean Allen, Toni Bruce, John Fenaughty, Esther Fitzpatrick,

Te Kawehau Hoskins, Fetaui Iosefo, Dillon Landi, Alys Longley, Hayley McGlashan, Peter O'Connor, Darren Powell, Rachel Riedel, Melinda Webber, and Analosa Veukiso-Ulugia. Finally, I am ever mindful of those who have done the very hard work of developing, troubling, and re-working ethnographic theory-methodology in ways that have impacted my own work in profound ways, and whose scholarship is strongly threaded through this book: Jessica Fields, Michelle Fine, Alison Jones, Patti Lather, and D. Soyini Madison. Finally, thank you to Stephen for collaborating on this book and on many other things.

Stephen

My thanks to my legendary former editor, Naomi Silverman, who was responsible for publishing all my previous books with Routledge, for first commissioning this book, and for (sensibly) deciding to retire rather than wait for its completion! My thanks too to Karen Adler for taking over the reins so ably and, most of all, for her inestimable patience in successfully shepherding this to print. My thanks to Katie for thinking this was an important book to write in the first place, for including me in it, and for persevering with it to completion. While it took longer to write than we hoped, it is the better for it. Thanks too to Sara Delamont and Paul Atkinson for their encouragement early on to pursue this project, along with their wonderful hospitality when we first visited them in Cardiff. To Blanca Caldas and Deborah Palmer for reconnecting me directly with exciting current critical ethnographic work in language education in North America. Closer to home, thanks to my Dean, Mark Barrow, for providing me with writing leave to complete the book (writing by the sea making all the difference). To my colleagues in Te Puna Wānanga (School of Māori and Indigenous Education), especially Melinda Webber and Lincoln Dam, for their āwhina and tautoko, and to the faculty members at Te Papa Ako o Tai Tokerau (Tai Tokerau Campus) whom I have had the pleasure to work with over the last few years. To Richard Hill for our collaborative ethnographic work (and friendship) over the years. To Giselle Martinez Negrette who, on her international research internship to New Zealand in 2018 (funded by University of Wisconsin-Madison), provided me with invaluable research support with my most recent ethnographic work in Richmond Road Primary School and Te Kōpuku High School. To my children, Ella, Grace, Tomas, and Luke, whom I can now finally tell that this writing project is done, and to Olive and Jethro, troopers to (and through) the end.

AUTHOR BIOGRAPHIES

Katie Fitzpatrick is Associate Professor and Head of School in the Faculty of Education and Social Work at the University of Auckland. Her research and teaching are focused on health education, physical education, and sexuality education, as well as critical ethnographic and poetic research methods. She has a background teaching in New Zealand high schools and has led national curriculum policy in sexuality education and mental health education. Katie has published 5 books, over 50 articles, and book chapters, and is the lead coeditor of the book series *Critical Studies in Health and Education* (Routledge, New York). Her 2013 critical ethnography – *Critical pedagogy, physical education and urban schooling* (Peter Lang) – won the North American Society for Sports Sociology (NASSS) outstanding book award. Katie was also a recipient of a five-year Rutherford Discovery Fellowship from Te Apārangi, the Royal Society of New Zealand. Her homepage is http://www.education.auckland.ac.nz/uoa/katie-fitzpatrick

Stephen May is Professor of Education in Te Puna Wānanga (School of Māori and Indigenous Education) at the University of Auckland, New Zealand. Stephen is an international authority on language rights, language policy, bilingual education, and critical multicultural approaches to education. He also has longstanding research interests in critical ethnography, social theory (particularly the work of Bourdieu), and sociolinguistics.

Stephen has published over 100 articles and book chapters, along with numerous books, in these areas, including *The Multilingual Turn* (2014) and *Language and Minority Rights* (2nd ed., 2012). He is Editor-in-Chief of the 10-volume *Encyclopedia of Language and Education* (3rd ed., 2017) and founding coeditor of the journal *Ethnicities*. He is a fellow of the American Educational Research Association (AERA) and of Te Apārangi, the Royal Society of New Zealand (FRSNZ). His homepage is http://www.education.auckland.ac.nz/uoa/stephen-may

1

REIMAGINING CRITICAL ETHNOGRAPHY

In this book, we make the case for a reimagined approach to critical ethnography in, of, and for education. In so doing, we pull through the threads of traditional ethnographic practice from the past, focus them strongly on the political, and reconceptualize them in the contemporary moment. We argue that the theoretical, social, and political issues currently facing education can be explored via a methodology that is personal, embodied, located, and lived, as well as unapologetically concentrated on relations of power. And we insist that ethnography – with its attention to people *and* environments, experience *and* histories, voices *and* the unspoken, discourse *and* materiality – offers a methodological way forward in the current moment.

This moment includes the contestation of qualitative methods; ongoing tensions between poststructuralism(s) and postcolonialism(s); the challenges of decolonizing; and the urgency of the posthuman. While these current theoretical and methodological debates have the potential to shift thinking in education, the field is also facing unprecedented privatizations of learning (and schooling) and the related neoliberalizing of educational systems globally, as well as the continued marginalizing of working class, poor, and precariat communities. Increased moves to digital schooling and health surveillance, a result of the Covid-19 pandemic, are creating different kinds of educational divides in relation to access and opportunity and are redefining cultures of teaching and learning as well as notions of safety, risk, and the body in education.

At the same time, social and political protest movements have (arguably) never been so strong. The *Black Lives Matter* and *#MeToo* movements – contesting endemic racism, and rape culture, sexual abuse, and harassment, respectively – now have a global audience. LGBTQI+ rights are also increasingly on the global agenda, alongside the need to address climate change, xenophobia, and the often-related

DOI: 10.4324/9781315208510-1

discriminatory treatment of minoritized groups, including both Indigenous and migrant/refugee populations. While nationalistic politics have swung decidedly to the right in some nation-states, social medias are both reproducing political positions across the spectrum, while also enabling cultures of resistance to thrive, especially among young people. Such social and political challenges can create productive methodological questions for education research and cause us to question both how we produce knowledge and the ontological bases of that production.

In a recent discussion about post-qualitative methodologies, Tesar (2021) argues that we should be slow to wholly reject or set ourselves against certain (old) methodologies in favor of new ones. He notes that we are all caught up in disciplinary ways of thinking and being, even as we question those ways so that "[t]he millions of marvelous, wonderful, and very 'useful' achievements of our scholarly practice that work so well for us on one hand, if singular, quick, and rigid, can equally impoverish, diminish, and destroy our scholarly activities" (p. 4). Advocating plurality instead, Tesar (2021) encourages us to engage the "ideas lying dormant in the deepest roots of our scholarly work" (p. 3–4). We take this challenge to think anew with established methodologies without discarding the methodological history of critical ethnography. In part, this not only requires remaining skeptical of academic cultures of fast research and mercenary approaches to method aligned to the more mechanistic tendencies of the university but also requires us to question the theories and methods we hold dear. We suggest that critical ethnography can attend to these tensions by glancing away from neoliberal approaches to research and slowing down the narrative of research productivity. Critical ethnography is located in a politics of asking uncomfortable questions about in/equity and privilege, and it is immersed in social theory. It is thus a located, messy, political, and versatile methodological approach; it is also embodied and relational, a methodology that assumes the researcher is also deeply implicated and cannot stand apart from their inquiry.

We describe critical ethnography here as a methodology, rather than a method. This is an important distinction. A methodology is an overarching philosophical framework that sets the broad direction for research. It is concerned with ontology, epistemology, and ethics and their interrelationships. Critical ethnography thus attends to what Barad (2007) has described as an underpinning ethico-onto-epistemology. This approach acknowledges that we are, as researchers, inextricably entangled in the contexts we inhabit and in the processes of knowledge production. In this sense, "[e]thics, knowing, and being . . . [are] productively entwined" (Geerts & Carstens, 2019, p. 920) in any project. The particular methods that emanate from ethnographic research, that are used in fieldwork, or that contribute to the research materials,[1] are less important than the theory-methodology nexus (which articulates with the context, field, or research site). Indeed, ethnography (or perhaps, ethnographers) neither dictate which methods to choose, nor precisely what to do (see Chapter 5). And method is not the starting point. Theories and contexts are, rather, the openings to research methodology, and the dialectic between theory and context is central to any critical ethnographic project (more about this in Chapter 3).

There are a myriad of possibilities that emerge in the intersection between ethico-onto-epistemology, research questions and contexts, the challenges of logistics, practicalities and materials, and the relationships (and relationalities) within and between settings. A researcher's interests, desires, and curiosities are important considerations, along with the kind of research materials we want to generate and how we want to re-present and communicate them (and with whom). The remaining chapters outline many examples, and a wide range of different methods, but these are certainly not exhaustive. Almost any method can be used with critical ethnography (including quantitative ones), as long as the general tenets are consistent with those that we will highlight in Chapter 2 (also see Madison, 2019).

In this book, we explore the potential for critical ethnography to work with and in contemporary inquiries in education, after (and with) the challenges of the *posts* – including poststructuralism, postcolonialism, and posthumanism. We argue that many researchers are already doing the kinds of critical ethnographies we imagine, whether they call their ethnographic projects critical or not. Such studies employ the tenets of ethnography and are engaged deeply in work that attends to, reimagines, troubles and questions notions of power, in/justice, in/equity, and marginalization. In this, different approaches to and definitions of "critical" are used (see Chapter 2 for a fuller discussion). While some critical educators insist that critical scholarship needs to work toward particular kinds of change, we accept Rasmussen's (2015) caution against seeing critical scholarship as a pathway toward alternative education utopias. Rasmussen (2015) draws on Berlant's (2011) notion of "cruel optimism" to "interrogate people's desires for things they think may improve their lot, but actually act as obstacles to flourishing" (Rasmussen, 2015, p. 192). Berlant argues that optimism is cruel when "the scene of fantasy . . . enables you to expect that *this* time, nearness to *this* thing will help you or a world to become different in just the right way" (2011, p. 2, emphasis in original). Rasmussen (2015) notes that critical work in education falls into such a trap when it engages in imagining educational utopias that are freed from various injustices; a belief in the hope (or expectation) of change then diverts our "attention from important ethical, social and political questions" (Rasmussen, 2015, p. 193). This is not to suggest that critical work can't disrupt or trouble existing practices, but working toward change can be approached with caution, especially if the imagined change is unaligned with wider sociopolitical transformation. We engage a more direct discussion of the "critical" in critical ethnography and with notions of change in Chapter 2.

Working with an expansive notion of critical, we argue that there are many studies that can be described as critically ethnographic and which, in their framing and orientation, draw on a wide array of critical theories. While neo-Marxist accounts of schooling have an important place historically in the critical ethnographic tradition, critical ethnography has moved and engaged with ongoing theoretical developments. We believe that many critically oriented theoretical approaches can be allied within and to ethnography in productive ways. Critical ethnography can be an expansive, eclectic, and inclusive methodology. We thus draw on a wide range of studies throughout this book and argue that such work can be seen as critically ethnographic, even if not specifically named or identified as such. This allows us to bring critical ethnography in education into the current moment – linking recent research across a wide range of topic areas to the critical ethnographic tradition.

Critical ethnography here then also highlights the importance of interdisciplinarity. Ethnographic fieldwork, with its origins in anthropology and sociology, and its wide application, has a strong interdisciplinary history (May & Fitzpatrick, 2019). Examining complex conditions, entrenched inequities, and their intersectionality – the confluence of dis/advantage across a range of indices, such as, class, ethnicity, gender/sexuality, and/or language – necessarily requires this kind of theoretical and disciplinary openness and engagement. This is what makes critical ethnography such exciting, rewarding, as well as, at times, challenging work.

But what about the *posts*? How can critical ethnography – located as it is historically in anthropological inquiry – possibly be flexible enough as a methodology to respond to the ontological questions raised by poststructuralism, new materialisms, and the methodological challenges of post-qualitative inquiry? We address these concerns in detail in Chapter 3 but, in short, we argue that the key tenets of critical ethnography in no way exclude the more-than-human – indeed, they are actually strengthened and extended by new materialist and posthuman questions. Many researchers already work productively between ethnographic approaches and poststructuralist theory, and critical ethnographers have always attended to how cultures, politics, environments, and histories intersect in complex ways in a research site. New theoretical emphases thus have the potential to extend the field of critical ethnography rather than dispense with it as a methodology. New forms of critical ethnography can (and do) engage with diverse ontological traditions and many have utilized the ideas of Foucault, Derrida, Butler, Bhabha, Deleuze, and others to engage across methodology and theory.

As we argue in Chapter 2, we are also methodologically inspired by the arguments of post-qualitative[2] researchers and we borrow some of the thinking of these scholars to question whether ethnography has become too rigid. As a result, we suggest a loosening of the methodological bounds of ethnography and a (re) turn to a new version of the old ethnography: the kind that required researchers to seek deep, engaged, and located experience without necessarily having a clear plan or exactly knowing the way. Ethnography has always allowed, even required, researchers to "get lost", both spatiotemporally and onto-epistemologically (Geertz, 1973; Lather, 2007). Earlier ethnographies – the kind that insisted that one couldn't understand a context unless (until) one lived a culture – have a lot to teach us still about how to give ourselves over to the research, how to attend to embodiment, and how to immerse the self in search of new insights. However, in drawing through threads from the old, we rework them and, also, reject the singularly anthropocentric narrative, the imperialistic and often colonizing voice of (masculinist and) White authority, and the conceited myth of the objective observer that so often attended earlier ethnographic work. We also reject the old dichotomies – insider/outsider, self/other, structure/agency, human/non-human – which tend to be upheld in such earlier studies (see Chapter 3).

Reclaiming and Reimagining Critical Ethnography in Education

We argue that critical ethnography is well placed to engage with issues of social justice, as well as other forms of justice (e.g., environmental, animal) in educational research. Its diachronic approach provides the basis for strong, intersectional analyses of education sites. In pursuing this, we also need to embrace the potential for critical ethnographic work to be controversial, as well as uncertain and exploratory. Biesta (2015) encourages educators to eschew certainty and predictability and embrace the risk of education. The risk of failure, the risk that things will go wrong, and the risk that we can't control the outcomes. Ethnographic work embraces these same risks. It is a form of inquiry that doesn't know the direction before setting out and doesn't attempt to answer the kinds of questions that are driven by logics of accountability and regulation.

In the last 20 years, there have been several "turns" in sociological work, including the turn to the body (Shilling, 2005), the spatial turn (Gulson & Symes, 2007; Harvey, 2006), and the rise of new materialist and posthuman perspectives (Barad, 2007; Braidotti, 2013; Haraway, 1989). In qualitative research, there are many new (and not-so-new, but still underused) modes of representation and research practice. These include visual methods (Pink, 2021), digital methods (Pink et al., 2016), narrative inquiry (Clandinin & Connelly, 2000), poetic inquiry (Richardson, 1992, 2004), and arts-based research methods (Barone & Eisner, 2012). In education, key social and political concerns continue to include problems as messy and complex as neoliberalism, globalization, digital learning, in/equity and achievement, big data and accountability regimes, gender and sexuality, student voice, exclusion and racialization, Indigenous education, superdiversity, language and culture, access, and pedagogical justice.

In this book, we offer an approach to research that weaves together these methodological concerns, making it possible to engage with current theoretical developments and contemporary social, political, and environmental issues in education. We draw together three different strands – social/political/environmental, theoretical, and methodological and suggest that these can be applied to different questions. The range of theoretical frameworks we draw on in the book is mostly a reflection of current inquiries but critical ethnography is not limited to these. The social/political/environmental, theoretical, and methodological might be considered then alongside the key tenets of critical ethnography, which we outline in Chapter 2. We argue that these tenets link pivotal critical ethnographic contributions to each other, as well as to a much wider range of critical ethnographic work in education. We will return throughout the book to key individual examples of critical ethnography in light of these tenets, highlighting them as illustrations of both their thematic concerns and the methodological approaches they employ. Meanwhile, we conclude this introductory chapter with a critique of the increasing prevalence of fast research and/or mercenary research in education – presenting critical ethnography as, potentially, a methodology that might grapple with some of these pressures at the same time as slowing down the research narrative.

Engaging Critical Ethnography to Counter Fast Research and Mercenary Methods

The growing predilection for fast research in education – a term popularized by Stephen Ball (2012) – is a consequence of the ascendancy of neoliberalism and the ongoing effects of neoliberal ideologies on the production of educational research in the academy. At its broadest, neoliberalism is a political approach to governing that values individual accountability and responsibility, the right/might of the market (as opposed to regulation or state-driven control), and profit and output over people. As a result, neoliberal discourse assumes that all individuals are "equal" in the system. In the case of access to education, for example, a neoliberal system disregards the socioeconomic status and social class positioning of students, along with their ethnic and language backgrounds, and instead upholds a meritocratic view of schooling that emphasizes individual responsibility and accountability as the keys to subsequent academic success (Apple, 2006). Harvey (2007) explains that, in neoliberal terms:

> While personal and individual freedom in the marketplace is guaranteed, each individual is held responsible and accountable for his or her own actions and well-being. This principle extends into . . . education. . . . Individual success or failure are [consequently] interpreted in terms of entrepreneurial virtues or personal failings.
>
> *(p. 65)*

Achieving success in education is thus often measured with no consideration of the differential resources available to communities on entry and/or related issues of power and dis/advantage faced within the educational system, once there. Fine has referred to this as the "ideological fetish . . . [of] universal access" (1991, p. 181), by which young people and communities come to believe that access to schooling automatically aligns with access to qualifications and success. Of course, we know that it doesn't, and that some communities often remain systemically dis/advantaged in relation to their (different) backgrounds and their related variable positioning and treatment within education.

Critical ethnography troubles the naïve valorization of meritocracy that still permeates so much educational research, policy, and practice. It also questions the types of research increasingly favored by neoliberal funding regimes within higher education. These regimes emphasize individual research productivity and privilege the application of "gold standard", overtly scientistic, approaches to research over all other methodological approaches. A scientistic approach to research is one that, as Hutchinson (2011) observes, views the natural sciences (and related positivist methodologies) as the only source of real knowledge. Consequently, in recent years, we have seen the entrenchment in educational and wider social sciences research of a hard science positivist model as the benchmark of quality research (hence, the term gold standard). The combined result, as Ball notes, has been the proliferation of research in education that is "calculable rather than memorable" (2012, p. 17).

The immediate flow-on effects for postgraduate research and supervision within the field of education are also apparent. New neoliberal research funding regimes internationally, such as the Research Excellence Framework (REF) in Britain, the Research Assessment Exercise (RAE) in Australia, and the Performance Based Research Fund (PBRF) in Aotearoa New Zealand, along with increased pressure for more and faster higher degree completions, are seeing fast research consistently chosen as the default position for students as well. As Green and Usher (2003) observe:

> The term "fast" is appropriate here in that students need to be positioned so as to formulate their research questions from the outset, satisfy demands for research proposal hurdles on time, collect data in ways free of unexpected impediments, and write (or produce a given artefact) without hesitation.
>
> *(p. 44)*

This creates an academic environment charged with the language and practice of neoliberalism and scientism. It is one in which both faculty and students are measured according to the rules of manipulability, interchangeable potential, linear ranking, and monetary value (Ball, 2012). A range of research approaches – notably those that emanate from and forward Indigenous research, for example – are marginalized in such a regime (Baice et al., 2021; Barber & Naepi, 2020). The measurement of research outputs and impact, underpinning the international research audit culture, thus drives the methodological choices of the research undertaken, while these methodological choices are more and more narrowly prescribed (and prescriptive). As Elizabeth St. Pierre (2015) observes:

> The stubborn persistence of positivism is evident, for example, when researchers cling to an objectivist epistemology by using terms like "bias"

and "triangulation", believe that knowledge accumulates and has gaps that findings can fill, believe in the clarity and transparency of language, and treat data (words in interview transcripts and field notes) as brute data and then code them out of context.

(p. 105)

A reductionist approach to educational research can be compounded by the closely related growth of what we term mercenary research. Driven by the neoliberal research agenda, mercenary research involves the regular "outsourcing" of research activity to research assistants and postgraduate students. Mercenary approaches are a response to pressures of time facing faculty and the related drive for research to be purchasable, outsourced, and efficient in the wider neoliberal university research regime. Such approaches can reinforce academic hierarchies, while also working against deep relationality, reciprocity, and connection with people and environments. Mercenary approaches can distance us as researchers from the lived, difficult, and messy realities of research sites and obscure the ethico-onto-epistemological (Barad, 2007) bases of research. Mercenary research risks reduction of the sensory elements of research that are lived, felt, evoked, experienced, and resisted by those directly involved – research that is embodied, moves the heart, evokes anger or tears, sadness, or rage. Mercenary research thus resists the challenges of deep, contextualized, emotional, lived experience, suggesting that the production of research materials can be undertaken by anyone, or, rather, that the personal, emotional, and embodied are not relevant. There is risk here that research materials, and their generation and analyses, can be decontextualized, disembodied, and disembedded; such an approach can move us back to positivistic approaches which assume the separation of researcher and the generation of research materials.

Critical ethnographic research, rather, takes time. It connects with the messy realities of people's lives, and it engages directly, and in depth, with complex and often-contested educational contexts, communities, and challenges. This kind of slow research (Becher & Trowler, 2001) is hugely valuable because it enables insights that take time and attend deeply to context. It begins by asking socially and politically inconvenient questions, including about our own entanglements in the research and the academy. Critical ethnography attempts to connect with the complex realities of people's lives and engages with individuals and communities both reflexively and reciprocally. It foregrounds and explores challenges and problems that are neither politically expedient nor easily solved through neat or easy recommendations or policy changes. These are challenges of in/ equity, achievement, social justice, and in/exclusion for which there are not easily formed or purchasable "solutions". Rather, the challenges are contextual, often intractable, and deeply located in existing historical, social, cultural, political, and environmental contexts. Such challenges require a sophisticated interdisciplinary theoretical engagement with, and interweaving of, theory and methodology, to address them effectively – both in relation to the research context itself and any changes that may result from it. This is what slow research, like critical ethnography, does best.

Of course, critical ethnography is not the only research approach by which this can be accomplished. However, it is, demonstrably, one that, as we noted earlier, begins with an ethical responsibility to attend to, highlight, disrupt, and trouble the status quo (Madison, 2019). Understanding and interrogating what counts as un/fairness or in/justice – when, under what conditions, and for whom – is also a precondition for any meaningful change that might ensue.

Outline of the Book

With all of this in mind, we offer this book on critical ethnography in education to highlight a methodology that engages theory and is personal, embodied, located, and lived, as well as unapologetically concentrated on relations of power. The book offers a critical and expansive commentary on contemporary approaches to critical ethnography as a research methodology. It is furnished with a wide range of examples, excerpts, and discussion from our own experiences, along with many others who have used these approaches in their research within education and related fields. It includes research we broadly define as critically ethnographic based on the tenets we outline in the next chapter. This allows us to (re)conceptualize critical ethnography, as we have already argued, as an expansive methodology, linking the genealogy of critical ethnography in education with more recent critically oriented developments in social theory. In so doing, we weave in a wide range of theoretical materials, and make links with a range of methods, which may be utilized within the broader framework of critical ethnography and education that we both propose and outline.

In this chapter, we have highlighted the methodological expansiveness and related possibilities that a (re)engagement with critical ethnography provides for work in education concerned with issues of power, as well as social and environmental justice. We concluded the chapter with a brief discussion of critical ethnography as an exemplar of slow research and as a counter to the growing pressures for fast and/or mercenary research within education and the social sciences. Chapter 2 outlines what we loosely suggest are the key tenets of critical ethnography when reconceived as a broad and inclusive methodology. Engaging with these tenets allows us to identify a much wider range of studies as critically ethnographic. Chapter 3 explores the central role of theory in critical ethnography over time and its crucial interweaving with research context(s). In so doing, we chart the history of critical ethnography in education and highlight the importance of exploring ethico-onto-epistemologies within any given critical ethnographic study. We also explore how critical ethnographic studies can engage with poststructuralist, postcolonial, posthumanist, and new materialist theoretical ideas. Chapter 4 details issues of ethics and representation in critical ethnographic work. It highlights the importance of positionality and critical reflexivity, as well as the ethical implications of establishing meaningful reciprocity and relationalities within research contexts. Chapter 5 considers the significance of writing as a key leaping-off point for the production of critical texts. It also explores how ethnographic fieldwork might be open and responsive, rather than intentional and/ or predetermined. Chapters 6 and 7 look at two different fields of critical ethnographic practice in education – language, race/ism, and education (Chapter 6) and gender and sexuality education (Chapter 7). In each of these, we consider how the intersection of these disciplines with critical ethnography has enabled important insights to emerge. We conclude in Chapter 8 by reflecting on the ends of ethnographic inquiry, including the boundaries of this work, ending projects, and the difficulties (and pleasures) of getting lost along the way.

Notes

1. We use the term "materials" instead of "data" for reasons that we outline more fully in Chapter 2.
2. As we discuss in Chapter 2, critical ethnography is not a post-qualitative approach to research but we find the work in this area productive for rethinking methodological constraints.

References

Apple, M. (2006). *Educating the right way: Markets, standards, God and inequality*. Routledge.

Baice, T., Lealaiauloto, B., Meiklejohn-Whiu, S., Fonua, S. M., Allen, J. M., Matapo, J., . . . Fa'avae, D. (2021). Responding to the call: talanoa, va-vā, early career network and enabling academic pathways at a university in New Zealand. *Higher Education Research & Development, 40*(1), 75–89.

Ball, S. J. (2012). *Global education inc.: New policy networks and the neo-liberal imaginary*. Routledge.

Barad, K. (2007). *Meeting the universe halfway: Quantum physics and the entanglement of matter and meaning*. Duke University Press.

Barber, S., & Naepi, S. (2020). Sociology in a crisis: Covid-19 and the colonial politics of knowledge production in Aotearoa New Zealand. *Journal of Sociology, 56*(4), 693–703.

Barone, T., & Eisner, E. W. (2012). *Arts based research*. Sage.

Becher, T., & Trowler, P. (2001). *Academic tribes and territories: Intellectual enquiry and the cultures of disciplines* (2nd ed.). Open University Press.

Berlant, L. (2011). *Cruel optimism*. Duke University Press.

Biesta, G. J. (2015). *Beautiful risk of education*. Routledge.

Braidotti, R. (2013). *The posthuman*. Polity Press.

Clandinin, D. J., & Connelly, F. M. (2000). *Narrative inquiry: Experience and story in qualitative research*. Jossey-Bass.

Fine, M. (1991). *Framing dropouts: Notes on the politics of an urban public high school*. State University of New York (SUNY) Press.

Geerts, E., & Carstens, D. (2019). Ethico-onto-epistemology. *Philosophy Today, 63*(4), 915–925

Geertz, C. (1973). Thick description: Toward an interpretive theory of culture. In *The interpretation of cultures* (pp. 3–30). Basic Books.

Green, P., & Usher, R. (2003). Fast supervision: Changing supervisory practice in changing times. *Studies in Continuing Education, 25*(1), 37–50. https://doi.org/10.1080/01580370309281

Gulson, K. N., & Symes, C. (2007). Knowing one's place: Educational theory, policy, and the spatial turn. In K. N. Gulson & C. Symes (Eds.), *Spatial theories of education: Policy and geography matters* (pp. 1–16). Routledge.

Haraway, D. J. (1989). *Primate visions: Gender, race, and nature in the world of modern science.* Psychology Press.

Harvey, D. (2006). *Spaces of global capitalism: Towards a theory of uneven geographical development.* Verso.

Harvey, D. (2007). *A brief history of neoliberalism.* Oxford University Press.

Hutchinson, I. (2011). *Monopolizing knowledge: A scientist refutes religion-denying, reason-destroying scientism.* Fias Publishing.

Lather, P. (2007). *Getting lost: Feminist efforts toward a double(d) science.* State University of New York (SUNY) Press.

Madison, D. S. (2019). *Critical ethnography: Method, ethics, and performance* (3rd ed.). Sage.

May, S., & Fitzpatrick, K. (2019). Critical ethnography. In P. Atkinson, S. Delamont, A. Cernat, J. Sakshaug, & R. Williams (Eds.), *Sage research methods foundations.* Sage Publications. http://dx.doi.org/10.4135/9781526421036831954

Pink, S. (2021). *Doing visual ethnography* (4th ed.). Sage.

Pink, S., Horst, H., Postill, J., Hjorth, L., Lewis, T., & Tacchi, J. (2016). *Digital ethnography: Principles and practice.* Sage.

Rasmussen, M. L. (2015). 'Cruel optimism' and contemporary Australian critical theory in educational research. *Educational Philosophy and Theory, 47*(2), 192–206.

Richardson, L. (1992). The consequences of poetic representation: Writing the other, rewriting the self. In C. Ellis & M. G. Flaherty (Eds.), *Investigating subjectivity: Research on lived experience* (pp. 125–137). Sage.

Richardson, L. (2004). Poetic representation. In J. Flood, S. Brice-Heath, & D. Lapp (Eds.), *Handbook of research on teaching literacy through the communicative and visual arts* (pp. 232–238). Routledge.

Shilling, C. (2005). *The body in culture, technology and society.* Sage.

St. Pierre, E. (2015). Refusing human being in humanist qualitative inquiry. In N. Denzin & M. Giardina (Eds.), *Qualitative inquiry: Past, present and future* (pp. 103–119). Routledge.

Tesar, M. (2021). Some thoughts concerning post-qualitative methodologies. *Qualitative Inquiry, 27*(2), 223–227. https://doi.org/10.1177/1077800420931141

2

CRITICAL ETHNOGRAPHY AS METHODOLOGICAL GUIDE

Some Key Tenets

As stated in Chapter 1, we are reimagining critical ethnography here (after and with the posts) in a looser way, as an expansive methodological approach. Recent methodological moves toward post-qualitative forms of research have "shaken the tree" regarding formulaic approaches to qualitative inquiry (e.g., see St. Pierre, 2018, 2021; Tesar, 2021). Coupled with the increasing theoretical salience of posthumanism and new materialisms, these challenges are (arguably) requiring qualitative researchers to (re)examine the ontological bases of their projects.

While critical ethnography is not a post-qualitative approach to research, we are inspired by the arguments of post-qualitative researchers, such as Elizabeth St. Pierre, to think about how we might conceive critical ethnography differently in light of the critiques these authors bring to the field. At the same time, we are cognizant of the important history of ethnographic approaches to research, and commitments in the field to balancing theory with context, deep relationalities, and empirical reflexivities. Central to St. Pierre's (2018) arguments is an insistence that theory cannot remain apart from method in a research project. She argues that:

> Conventional humanist qualitative methodology provides a handy pre-existing research process to follow, a container with well-identified categories into which researchers are expected to slot all aspects of their research projects so they are recognizable, clear, and accessible. And even though qualitative methodology still claims to be "emergent", its concepts and categories, which have been tightened up over the years, tend to control the study.
>
> *(p. 603)*

DOI: 10.4324/9781315208510-2

The first problem with this, she asserts, is that qualitative inquiry has become too prescriptive, too rigid; indeed, so rulebound that it looks more like positivism than it does qualitative inquiry, which rather has its roots in "understanding people's lived experiences . . . and, when those experiences seemed unjust, to transformation and liberation (critical research)" (p. 603). The second problem for St. Pierre is the incommensurability of humanistic qualitative inquiry – rooted in phenomenology – and approaches to power in poststructuralist theories. She suggests, instead, a methodology that begins with the theory, rejects set method, and instead "follow[s] the provocations that come from everywhere in the inquiry that is living and writing" (St. Pierre, 2018, p. 603).

Ethnography actually speaks to some of St. Pierre's critiques of qualitative inquiry. Ethnographers don't tend to follow set rules or specific methods necessarily (see Chapter 5). Ethnography begins with the experience(s) of the ethnographer. While conversations and experiences with others in the field are an important methodological tool, these are not necessarily used to seek any phenomenological "essence", nor to make truth claims, but rather to understand how people are living and representing what Willis (1977) calls, "the social creativity of a culture" (p. 121). We might add to this that (critical) ethnography is an inquiry into the social, political, and located creativities of culture/s. In this, ethnography is not necessarily (or singularly) interested in the individual but in the wider cultural contexts; this can include the spaces between people – and the more-than-human – which are only understandable sociohistorically, politically, and environmentally. Critical ethnography is fundamentally concerned with critique.

Ethnographers live and write their experiences, feeling their way as they go, inquiring "on the hop", responding to what happens. Such inquiring does not need to be bound by specific methods, and usually the methods emerge in relation to the questions, inquiries, and experiences of the ethnographer in the course of the research. Critical ethnography, however, begins not only with theory but also with context. In this, the theory needs to drive the questions, but the context also drives the inquiry so that the experiences of communities in lived and located ways are not overwritten by, or constructed through, the theory. This is important if we hope to challenge the Western-centric and masculinist (European-centric) dominance of many social theories, and to honor the emergent theories that come from place, relationalities, and experience. The imposition of Western social theories, for example, on non-Western and Indigenous communities should be actively questioned (Smith, 2012).

Critical ethnography is not a post-qualitative approach to research – its ontological roots are different – it is not limited to poststructuralist theories, it is not philosophy as method, and it is a planned and intentional methodological approach to research. However, we are inspired by St. Pierre's work to think about (or perhaps, remember) ethnography in less rigid and rulebound ways.

Ethnography is a process of discovery – not of a pre-existing reality or culture – but of the possibilities of theory-method when researchers are responsive, open, embodied, and curious. This also means that we need to be willing to let go of a recipe approach to method, and instead embrace "getting lost" (Lather, 2007), both ontologically and methodologically (and even spatially).

With this in mind, we seek to describe critical ethnography here as an expansive and inclusive methodological approach of openness and responsivity. We name a range of key tenets but suggest that these can be applied loosely, taken as inspiration and stimulus. While all these tenets will be present in some form (for it to be a critically ethnographic project), they can be taken lightly, as methodological guidance and inspiration, rather than as recipe. As we detail in Chapter 3, however, we do insist that this cannot be undertaken without attention to (critical) social theory, and thus to politics, power, and relationality. Critical social theory can be poststructuralist, but it can also draw from a potentially wide range of theoretical traditions.

What Is the "Critical" in Critical Ethnography?

To attempt then a kind of overview of the tenets of critical ethnography, without locking them (it) into a formula, we first consider what is meant by "critical" in relation to critical ethnography. All critical ethnography attends to power and relationalities, but researchers tend to take differing positions in terms of how they approach these. Critical work in education draws on a wide range of traditions, including work that is concerned with interrogating and critiquing social and political contexts and examining the related articulations of power. Some of this work aims not only to critique but also to insist on urgent social change. The latter tends toward more activist approaches, while the former may refuse arguments for particular kinds of change in favor of critique.

Lave (2011), for example, argues that the critical in critical ethnography has many meanings, including a critique of taken for granted practices and a commitment to making the usual and every day the subject of study, to make it novel. Critical ethnography is concerned with social justice (and other forms of justice) and issues of in/equity, as well as with ethics, positionality, and power. Lave (2011) notes, however, that critical ethnography also:

> [I]nvolves a relational, historical worldview and metaphysics that question a number of commonsense understandings. It envisions ethnographic research as a long struggle to illuminate social life, challenge commonplace theories and their political implications, and change theoretical practice in the process.
>
> *(p. 10)*

While social justice has been a particular focus of much critical ethnographic work, planetary justice, animal justice, and environmental justice are being increasingly attended to (see the following). For Lave (2011) "critical ethnography is not only an objection *to* something. The term 'critical ethnographic practice' here refers to the raft of ethnographic inquiry integral to a historical-materialist theoretical stance" (p. 2; emphasis in original).

Employing critical ethnography means that researchers cannot separate themselves from the contexts, places, histories, and people among whom they research. In this, of first and foremost importance, are the relationships we have with people, communities, and environments (see Chapter 4). It is impossible to do critical ethnography and not be present as a person (a flawed, uncertain, complex, and multiple person). Critical ethnography cannot be outsourced. It begins with the self, but it does not linger there. The self is embedded and entangled in the project from beginning to end, but the self is neither the focus of research questions nor the dominating narrative. Critical ethnography is a methodology that looks outward and engages with issues of importance to people, environments, and communities, and at the same time critiques and troubles understandings, practices, and processes of knowledge production.

Soyini Madison argues that "critical ethnography begins with an ethical responsibility to address processes of unfairness or injustice within a particular *lived* domain" (2019, p. 4; emphasis in original). She defines ethical responsibility as "a compelling sense of duty and commitment based on moral principles of human freedom and wellbeing, and, hence, a compassion for the suffering of living beings" (p. 4). Jim Thomas has argued that critical ethnography is "conventional ethnography with a political purpose" (1993, p. 4). While this statement might be a useful form of shorthand, it is important to note that there is nothing conventional about ethnographic research of any kind. It is difficult, messy, and resistant to methodological formula. Critical ethnography is a form of ethnography with an orientation to the political and to justice. Thomas' next statement is thus perhaps more helpful:

> Critical ethnography is a way of applying a subversive worldview to the conventional logic of cultural inquiry. It does not stand in opposition to conventional ethnography. Rather, it offers a more direct style of thinking about the relationships among knowledge, society and political action.
>
> *(1993, p. vii)*

Critical ethnography then can be seen to extend (or focus) ethnography specifically by attending directly to wider sociohistorical and sociopolitical contexts, and associated power relations, both external and internal to the research (Carspecken, 1996; Fine, 1991; Madison, 2019). But even this is a little misleading as many ethnographies attend to power relations (whether they call themselves critical or not). And so, defining the boundaries of the field is tricky; albeit a challenge we see as a strength rather than a drawback. For us, a critical ethnography can be identified as such if the researchers are interested in, and responsive to, theoretical and sociological questions of power and relationalities. This opens up the possibilities for inclusion of a much wider range of ethnographic work in education, not just those specifically termed critical ethnography.

Key Tenets of Critical Ethnography

In what follows, we outline briefly what we see as nine key tenets of critical ethnography as a methodological approach, drawing on a range of examples in the field to show how these tenets can be put to work in different ways. We suggest that the key tenets might include the following, but we also question these as we go and understand them as being able to be interpreted and applied in very different ways in different contexts:

- Orienting to power, in/justice, and in/equity
- (Social) theory and ontology
- Troubling the questions, being curious
- Relationalities, relationships, and reciprocity
- Positionality, reflection, reflexivity
- Time, "deep hanging out"
- An attempt to understand and communicate cultures, happenings, and their ethico-onto-epistemologies
- Writing, fieldwork, and other modes of production
- Change: wondering about change, creating change, troubling change, challenging inequities

The remainder of this chapter touches on each of these tenets and provides examples of how these might be used as inspiration for undertaking critical ethnographic work in education. We return throughout the book to these tenets, focusing more directly on each in different chapters and providing examples from a wide range of studies.

Orienting to Power, In/Justice, and In/Equity

Critical projects have in common an attention to issues of power, justice, and equity. These concerns are diverse and somewhat diffuse, woven through the tenets of critical ethnography (and through this book) via a myriad of examples, conceptual discussions and empirical concerns. Such concerns arrive in different forms. They might begin with a feeling in the body, a feeling that something is not right, that something hurts. Take this recent experience of Katie's:

> I'm reading Harris and Holman Jones' (2019) chapter on queer grief and I'm crying. I'm really weeping, openly and fully, sitting at my desk at home. Tears are dripping onto my keyboard and I'm starting to get worried about the moisture affecting my laptop. The screen blurs and unblurs as I read,

and my chest aches as I suck in my next breath. Why am I sitting here crying? I'm trying to write this book (and read work for the book). What is this chapter doing to me, evoking in me? What questions might I ask about my own experiences, about my own grief. What is my body telling me? What is happening? I decide to write. Writing and crying; the keyboard is blurred and I keep making mistakes. Unlike Harris, who says he has touch typed since he was young, I have to keep looking up and down between the screen and the keyboard, and deleting, rewriting, deleting, correcting as I go.

So, why is their chapter so evocative for me? I am not a queer woman: I am straight, white, middle class and cis. I live in a wealthy and very privileged country. My ancestors emigrated here from Europe and the UK in the second half of the 19th Century. They came here for a better life and, in so doing, lived on and farmed land that had been taken – in complex ways and over time – from the Indigenous Māori population of New Zealand. My privilege was and is secured by the uneven relationship between Māori and Pākehā [European New Zealanders] in the intervening 150 years, and by ongoing racism and classism. I am privileged, yes, but I am not (of course) immune to grief. Like everyone else, the last year has been defined by the global a/effects of Covid-19, and the subsequent lock downs, various forms of isolation, worry, change and forced digital communications. My year has also involved a range of personal griefs and the emotional landscapes that result from major life changes. I – like many around the world – have had a year of grieving. A year of trying to reimagine my life. A year of other people not necessarily understanding or recognizing the edges of my pain, or how my subjectivity and relationships intersect with my grief.

So, why is embodied experience relevant for thinking about issues of equity and justice in critical ethnography? Katie's bodily response to Harris and Holman Jones' (2019) chapter signals something about power and its relationalities. Often our bodies are the first to know when something isn't "right", when something is "off", when we need to inquire. Thomas suggests that we might begin by accepting that "power relations and knowledge are interconnected" (2003, p. 46). He goes on to argue that:

> [C]ritical ethnography challenges the conventional ideological images inherent in all research by investigating the possibility of alternative meanings. This does not necessarily require a rejection of conventional or "common sense" meanings. But it does demand that the researcher locate the meaning of events within the context of asymmetrical power relations.

(p. 46)

These power relations are complex, and they often evoke deeply emotional and affective responses. Relations of power are not limited to those between people, or only to the social. Relationalities exist between all things, including ideas, objects, the natural world, discourses, animals, and people. Relationalities are complex and context-specific, and they exist within as well as traverse temporalities and spaces.

Historically, critical ethnographers have undertaken social critiques that focus on both privilege and disadvantage – and, crucially, their dialectic – in the hope of promoting a more open, egalitarian, and inclusive society – or, at the very least, exploring and drawing attention to in/justice. Critical researchers have been primarily concerned with in/equities, actively interrogating relations of power in research settings (Carspecken, 1996). Underpinning this approach is what Michelle Fine calls "the political urgency of critical research" (2006, p. 86). In more recent work, critical ethnographic accounts have included a focus on issues of space, place, and materialities. Indeed, contemporary critical ethnographies – drawing on, for example, new materialism – are increasingly mapping spatial, materialist, and social concerns (e.g., Ball, 2016; Youdell & Armstrong, 2011, see also Chapter 7). Some critical ethnographers adopt an overtly activist stance – advocating for social and political change in certain circumstances. Carspecken, for example, asserts that "criticalists find contemporary society to be unfair, unequal, and both subtly and overtly oppressive to many people. We do not like it, and want to change it" (1996, p. 7). We could add to Carspecken's concerns here a focus on the mistreatment of the environment, including the effects of capitalism, globalization, and Western imperialisms. Researchers in this tradition have tended to move from an ostensibly disinterested and distanced account of phenomena to focus on understanding the damaging effects of troubling and complex power relations.

Again, it is important to note here that different ontological approaches to power necessarily affect the approach taken. Many of the early examples of critical educational ethnographies, for example, were inspired by neo-Marxist concerns with exposing social structures of oppression, particularly social class (Fine, 1991; Thomson, 2002; Willis, 1977). Later analyses have drawn more on poststructuralist ideas to provide insights into how power flows between people in more complex, unexpected, and nuanced ways, and to question forms of representation (e.g., Fields, 2008; Yon, 2000). Patti Lather's (2007) work has likewise challenged researchers to move beyond a position of "knowing" and seeking emancipation, toward one of greater uncertainty, questioning and, what she calls, "getting lost". She acknowledges that it is difficult to accept the challenges of poststructuralist theory – especially the contention that language, at best, allows for only partial and always power-laden representations, and that subjectivities are made within contexts. However, she challenges researchers to work at and expose injustice, while remaining simultaneously uncertain and continuing to trouble their own notions of what actually constitutes in/justice.

Such reflexive questioning highlights the complexities, double meanings, and possibilities of alternative readings. So, doing critical ethnography requires the researcher to attend to power and relationalities, as well as to question and trouble these categories, even while we are living (in and through) them. The first work to do in this regard is to interrogate and inquire into ontology and attempt to define how different theories understand power and its workings and a/effects. Critical research projects often begin with a sense that something is wrong, something is unjust, something must be done. Many critical researchers are driven and motivated by their own experiences of injustice, their observations of harm, and a commitment to making a difference. But we are also bound by our own assumptions, limited by our experiences of the world. That's why we need to begin with theory. We feel something and want to inquire into it. Seeking to understand that inquiry, and how power is working in and through us, in relation to theory, is thus a fundamental starting point.

Social Theory and Ontology

Denzin and Giardina (2019) observe that:

> In the humanities and social sciences today, there is no longer a God's-eye view that guarantees absolute methodological certainty. . . . All inquiry reflects the standpoint of the inquirer. All observation is theory-laden. There is no possibility of theory- or value-free knowledge. The days of naïve realism and naïve positivism are over. The criteria for evaluating research are now relative. A critical social science seeks its external grounding not in science, in any of its revisionist, postpositivist forms, but rather in a commitment to critical pedagogy and communitarian feminism with hope but no guarantees. It seeks to understand how power and ideology operate through and across systems of discourse, cultural commodities, and cultural texts.
>
> *(p. 6)*

To engage with what Lather (2007) calls a deep and doubled reflexivity, the researcher will also need to interrogate the gaps between theory and practice, and thus the limitations of the research. As noted earlier, there are many possibilities for how social theory might be productive with and in ethnographic research. In our own ethnographic studies, we have drawn on a range of theorists, including Bourdieu, Freire, Hall, Foucault, Butler, Bhabha, Gramsci, Giroux, Deleuze, and Guattari. The work of Bourdieu has been popular in critical educational ethnographies that have sought to understand the workings of social class and other identity positions (e.g., Fitzpatrick, 2013; Grenfell et al., 2012; Jones, 1991; May, 1994; Thomson, 2002; Willis, 1977). Foucault's highly influential work, along with that of Judith Butler, has been employed in multiple critical ethnographic studies addressing gender, sexuality, health, and the body (e.g., King, 1999; Leahy, 2014; Pascoe, 2007; Powell, 2020; Rasmussen et al., 2004; Russell & Thomson, 2011; Youdell, 2005, see also Chapter 7), while postcolonial theories have also been employed to understand ethnicity and culture (e.g., Fitzpatrick, 2013; Yon, 2000). More recently, the work of Deleuze and Guattari (1987, 2004a, 2004b) have informed new materialist ethnographic inquiries (e.g., Blaise et al., 2017; Dyke, 2013; Ringrose, 2011; Youdell & Armstrong, 2011). Others have employed Derrida (e.g., Lather, 2007) or posthumanism to displace the anthropocentric ethnographic imaginary (e.g., Pacini-Ketchabaw et al., 2016; Taylor & Pacini-Ketchabaw, 2015; Hamilton & Taylor, 2017; Pedersen, 2013).

It is important to note that not all these authors refer to their work as critical ethnography. For some, the term "critical" is perhaps too reminiscent of the Frankfurt School, neo-Marxism, and the work of Bourdieu and Gramsci, most often associated with early critical ethnographies. It is clear though that critical work has shifted over time, in line with emergent critiques and new theoretical insights, so that the term critical can incorporate the posts, including the post-critical (Lather, 2007; Noblit et al., 2004) and posthumanist. We discuss this more fully in Chapter 3, showing how different scholars draw on a range of social theorists, and how these various theoretical frameworks reflect on and impact the critical ethnographic research undertaken.

Whatever social theory one engages with, the theory underscores the research framing, analyses, and arguments, in articulation with context. Lather reflects, for example, that: "My central argument has been that the turn that matters in this moment of the post is away from abstract philosophizing and toward concrete efforts to put the theory to work" (2007, p. 157). Taking this further, St. Pierre (2018) argues that theory cannot be "put to work" as such (after the fact) but must be the starting point, that then works its way into the study, into the researcher's body, and into the project. She conceptualizes theory as an agent that makes itself known in the writing, because "[i]f one has read and read, one cannot not put theory to work – it will happen" (p. 605). However, some ethnographers also insist that the theory cannot (should not) blind us to context (Atkinson, 2019). We cannot ignore context, however, when we are immersed in it, in the theory and the context, and in the knowledge production. This is where Barad's (2007) ethico-onto-epistemology is useful for overcoming the divide between theory and field. The theory is already in the context and in the knowledge production as we engage ethnographically; it is in the body and the research ethics. Theory and context thus work dynamically and relationally in and through the ethnographer, in and through and in between the researcher, people, places, and non-human objects and animals. These relationalities are not static but are responsive. The intersection of theory and experience and context will give rise to questions which are in turn dynamic and evolving.

Troubling the Questions, Being Curious

Question setting is both key and consequential to the direction of any ethnographic work, as this vignette from Katie highlights:

> A few years ago, I (Katie) organized a symposium at my university on issues of youth health and schools. I invited scholars from different places, and from different research traditions (sociology, critical studies, pedagogy, psychology, indigenous education) to join a panel focused around the question: "What is the role of schools in addressing the health and wellbeing of children and youth?" A fairly broad question – I thought – and one that would invite a diversity of perspectives and engage the audience and panelists in debate and discussion.
>
> The first panelist – my colleague and a researcher in Indigenous and Māori health, Mera Penehira, was the opening speaker. She began the discussion by dismantling the question. She stated up front that the question was not one that Māori (Indigenous) communities would ask. She explained that, for Māori, health and wellbeing are so embedded in environments, families, and communities, and so woven through every part of a young person's life, including schooling, that it doesn't make ontological sense to separate them out in the way my question suggested. She spoke instead about the impact of historical trauma and colonization on young people's experiences, knowledge of themselves within communities, and ultimately, on their education in a broad sense. In her work, Penehira explains that wellbeing for Māori needs to be understood across at least seven different layers of conceptual and applied understandings. These are wairua (spirituality), mauri-ora (life force), hau-ora (holistic health), hau-aio (breath of life), hau-whenua (breath of land), hau-moana (breath of sea), and hau-tangata (human) (see *Penehira et al., 2011).*

This panel discussion highlighted the cultural narrowness and Eurocentricity of the question Katie was asking. In relation to Indigenous Māori students, school, and wellbeing, this was the wrong question; it is a question that fundamentally misunderstands a Māori worldview. Sometimes we learn a great deal from asking the wrong questions, but only if we are open and allow debate to address the very basis of the questions we ask. Curiosity and openness are important.

Managing these tensions effectively involves attention to individual stories but always in dynamic relation to social, historical, and political contexts, as well as locality and space. It requires acknowledgment of the power of the ethnographer's gaze (May, 1997), or what Bourdieu (1990, p. 14) described as "the epistemological privilege of the observer". Critical ethnographers thus need to interrogate the bases of their questions and inquiries, and ask, first and foremost, whether the topic of investigation connects with, and is important or useful to, the people and places with and among whom they are engaging. In this, ethnographers must move from being observers to participants to seeing ourselves as inextricably embedded in research contexts. Not as participant-observer but beyond that hyphen. Ethnographers are more than observers since we are immersed in complex contexts that we feel, live, see, hear, and experience. Mere observation is an impossible construct.

Researchers are inevitably emotionally invested in research and (typically) both personally and politically committed to their questions. This makes initial reflection on the inquiry even more important. Many researchers enter a site with a clear and certain framework and particular research foci that they think are important (some of these are their own and some are inherited from the field or colleagues). And yet, because of this, it is too easy for presumptive research foci to misunderstand the issues of the context, and/or to be irrelevant (or even at cross purposes) to those at the center of the research and the site/s of research. If this is to be avoided, Palmer and Caldas (2017) argue that knowledge must be "constructed and interpreted from the vantage point of the people whose voices are marginalized" (p. 384). In a critique of self-referential forms of autoethnography,[1] Madison (2006) similarly warns that:

> Although I find the term [autoethnography] politically problematic, it is not just the term that is a problem but the content of any work, particularly ethnographic work, where the rootedness and embellishments of the self diminish the thickness and complexities of the encompassing terrain. When the gaze is on one's own navel one cannot see the ground upon which one stands or significant others standing nearby.
>
> *(p. 321)*

The key questions to begin any inquiry, however, are: "do I have a right to do this research? Are these my stories to tell?" (Fine, 2006, p. 90). The researcher can, from the start, ask deep questions about their motivations for being involved in the research. They should leave space to reflect whether the project should be done at all, and if so, to interrogate whether they are really the best placed to do it. They need to be prepared to answer "no". In effect, then, critical ethnographers must continually ask "who-am-I-to do-this-work?" (Fine, 2006, p. 90) and to be ready to change the questions we are asking in response to the places and people we encounter and the contexts with(in) which we interact. This requires a dialogical performance with people and space that engages with reflexive knowledge (Madison, 2006), and with underpinning theory(ies). As Talburt (1999) argues:

> If ethnography's task is not merely to describe the selves, experiences, and voices it bears witness to but to question what it sees and hears as it does,

ethnography must always ask itself, "why these representations of these voices and experiences in these ways and not others?"

(p. 527)

This critically reflective theoretical process can be disconcerting, painful, and challenging (see Chapter 4). It keeps open the possibility, however, that the research undertaken ends up connecting – most importantly, not only to the research participants, their communities, and the challenges they face, but also to the fields into which the researcher hopes to write. Drawing on Butler (1993), Lather (2001a) encourages us not only to name the limits of our reflexive knowledge in research but also to "meet the limit, to open to it as the very vitality and force that propels the change to come" (p. 202). Asking uncomfortable questions at the start of the project is not enough. Continuing to explore how one's positionality impacts the research is also an important ongoing engagement.

Relationalities, Relationships, and Reciprocity

Grappling with research questions is a necessary initial step in critical ethnography. However, it is not a sufficient one. As Indigenous scholars have consistently highlighted over recent years, ethnographic fieldwork in Indigenous contexts – a historical staple of conventional ethnography – has most often provided very little, if any, benefit for Indigenous research participants in either the short or longer term. Instead, the research has most often contributed to the further re/colonizing of Indigenous peoples and the reinforcement of longstanding deficit conceptions of the Indigenous participants, their languages and cultures (Smith, 2012). Linda Tuhiwai Smith (2012; see also Smith et al., 2016), for one, has questioned whether White academics should be allowed to continue researching in Indigenous communities at all. Similar arguments have been made by BlackCrit and LatCrit scholars (see e.g., Coles, 2022; Dumas & ross, 2016; Villenas & Foley, 2011) with respect to their own communities.

Others working from critical Indigenous perspectives do not necessarily advocate the exclusion of White researchers but do, nonetheless, emphasize the importance of partnership, trust, accountability, and reciprocity in the research process as a necessary foundation for working equitably and constructively in Indigenous (and other minoritized) contexts (Bishop, 2005; Faircloth et al., 2020). We discuss in more detail the importance of partnership, accountability, and reciprocity in relation to ethics and social justice in Chapter 4. Here we simply emphasize that one important response to the unavoidable asymmetry of research relationships is to approach the field with humility and to explore these through dialogue, partnership, and with an open curiosity. Rethinking research relationships means attending closely to the research context and viewing research as a collaborative endeavor – researching with and for people (or places), rather than "on" them. This in turn requires the researcher to be connected with, accepted, and trusted by the research participants; the researcher orientation should thus be one of learner not expert.

Two critical ethnographies that focus on the bi/multilingual language practices of ethnic minority students in US schools (see also Chapter 6) provide examples of such a collaborative and dialogic research process. H. Samy Alim's (2004) study of the linguistic practices of African American students at an alternative US high school – particularly, their use of style shifting – explores the students' varied uses of African American English and how it is influenced by hip hop. Alim highlights how this varied and evolving language use is reflective of the students' sociocultural and sociopolitical identity formation in a context where American Standard English and racialized views of Black students and performance artists still clearly predominate. This analysis is further informed by Alim's own personal knowledge, command, and use of these language registers, which allow him to interact with the students in these registers throughout the course of the study. Django Paris (2011), in his critical ethnographic account of Black, Latino/a, and Pacific Island high school students, also shared directly in both the language practices and cultural performances of the students in his study.

Such a dialogic and relational research stance necessarily brings into question the still widely accepted notions in ethnographic fieldwork of the researcher as "insider" and/or "outsider". The insider/outsider dichotomy is ethically problematic because it requires the ethnographer to become a kind of undercover agent – a double agent who is, at once, seen as a trusted insider, while also doing the "dirty" business of collecting research evidence. Critical ethnography thus rejects such a dichotomy, rather assuming that we are all, at times, included and excluded in different social contexts, and that our engagement and relationships are thus also inevitably fluid (Naples, 1996). Issues of exclusion and inclusion occur at the intersection of social norms and power relations, which both researchers and participants are implicated in and engaged in reproducing. As critical ethnographers then, we need to be less concerned with insider/outsider designations and more concerned with the quality and reciprocity of our ongoing and dynamic research (inter)relationships.

Positionality, Reflection, and Reflexivity

Attending directly to the power relations between the researcher and the research participants necessarily requires the critical ethnographer to acknowledge and address their own subjectivity and positionality. Researcher subjectivity fundamentally impacts the project from beginning to end. As Madison observes, as ethnographers, we need "to understand that we bring our belongings into the field with us" (2019, p. 8). Positionality takes this one step further by requiring "that we direct our attention beyond our individual or subjective selves. Instead, we attend to how our subjectivity *in relation to others* informs and is informed by our engagement and representation of others" (p. 9; emphasis in original).

This is a process of critical reflection that takes specific account of the researcher's own positionality – their background, their experiences, their theoretical influences – as well as how this positionality frames the ethnographic research and related interpretative schema employed within it. It is also a dialogic process – requiring researchers to attend simultaneously to the wider spatial, social, and political contexts that shape both who they are and those with whom they interact.

Bourdieu has argued that researchers must remain reflexive, not only with regard to gender, social class, ethnicity, and the like (particularly as this relates to the study context and participants therein), but also in relation to the field of academia: their academic habitus which enables them to "see" certain things and not others (Bourdieu & Wacquant, 1992; May, 2014). As researchers then, we are all implicated in our studies in ways that require reflexivity and an orientation to the wider contexts of the research, as well as the relations between our own and other contexts. For example, researchers in a school might consider relations of power between them and teachers, students, and community members. However, they are also simultaneously immersed in academic hierarchies, subject disciplines, and the interrelationship between those and the school community. Returning to Madison's observation that we bring our belongings into the field with us, these include "not only the many others that constitute our being but how we belong to what we know, how our epistemologies are yet another site of our belonging with and for others" (Madison, 2019, p. 8). By fully contextualizing our positionality in these ways, we make "it accessible, transparent, and vulnerable to judgment and evaluation" (p. 8).

Within such a framework, then, we come to be accountable for our own research paradigms, our own positions of authority, and our own moral responsibility relative to representation and interpretation. Such a focus also extends to the research methods we use, and how positionality makes possible certain analytical directions or may privilege some arguments over others. In her study of students dropping out of school in New York city, Fine (1991) examined her privilege, as a White, middle-class academic, in counterpoint to the lives of the African American student "drop outs" in her study. Powell (2020) reflects on the issue of "voice" in his research with children. He explored discourses of the body and obesity, and how children engaged with both physical activity programs in their school, and the targeted interventions brought by various corporate players in child health:

> Voice, like an observation or piece of documentary evidence, must not be conflated with pure, clear, "concrete" evidence; voices are socially constructed, fluid, discursively formed, and constantly negotiated. The participants I chose (or was able to choose) to listen to, the questions I asked (or did not ask), the lines of conversations I chose to explore or ignore, how I listened to and interpreted participants' voices, and the voices I accepted

as "true", all shaped the representation of voices in my research. Throughout my research and analysis, I reflected on how conversations could act to "gag" certain voices and I became more critical of how I conducted my conversations. I attempted to elicit and listen to voices other than those that were easy to categorise and respond to, such as those voices that obviously related to my research questions or which agreed with my own view of the corporate "part of the solution" to obesity.

(p. 181)

Situating oneself contextually, biographically, and relationally in ethnographic work isn't easy. It can be disconcerting, and it is always partial and messy. It requires decisions about what to share and what to withhold, and it can feel vulnerable and exposing. We have tried to maintain a messy reflexivity in our own work, while resisting making the self the focus of the inquiry. This is an imperfect process. For example, Stephen revisits the origins of his critical ethnography of a progressive multicultural elementary school, Richmond Road School (May, 1994; see also Chapter 6), via a reflective exploration of his own professional experiences up until that point (May, 1998):

> The first day that I was there proved a revelation. As an erstwhile high school teacher, I had little experience of primary [elementary] schools and even less experience of the link between educational theory and practice. Like most New Zealand trained high school teachers, my only previous experience of the latter had been a cursory one-year graduate course at a teachers' training institution. . . . I say cursory because my teaching subject (and my undergraduate degree) was in English and we spent most of that all too brief year addressing English curriculum content and delivery. Precious little time was spent on the educational theories of teaching and learning and even less on the wider structural factors that impinge on these. (As an aside, this helps to explain why I found my first years of teaching so difficult!) I was thus wholly unprepared for the depth of educational engagement that I experienced on that first visit to Richmond Road. Having only just begun to experience and address these issues for myself, and having left teaching [to return to postgraduate study] to do so, it came as a shock to find teachers in situ who had been grappling with educational theory and practice, and their interconnections, for some considerable time. Coupled with the rather imperious view we had as secondary teachers of our primary [elementary] colleagues, this came as a double shock. As I was soon to find out, there was far more yet to learn about education than I had ever expected.

(p. 160)

Katie, likewise, begins her critical ethnographic account of a school in a low socioeconomic, culturally diverse community in South Auckland, New Zealand

(Fitzpatrick, 2013) with the juxtaposition of a very different cultural and class milieu to her own early life, and the journey that led to her teaching in the school in question. She reflects on her teaching experiences at two different schools, and how issues of social class and ethnicity underscored social patterns (see also Chapter 8):

> By the time I left [my teaching position at] Kikorangi High School at the end of 2003, I had personally taught over 400 students. Only two of those 400 went on to university, and a few others attended local tertiary institutions. This was in spite of relevant and progressive school programs, good attendance rates, and many students passing courses and external exams. The national norm-referenced assessment system of the time ensured grades were scaled, and prevented many students from acquiring the necessary qualifications to gain access to university (this assessment system has since changed). But many capable students dropped out of school before the final year, and some much earlier. A few students I taught were later convicted of crimes, and one young woman, to whom this book is dedicated, killed herself. I could not help but notice the vast differences between my two (geographically close) teaching positions, and the divide between these students and my own upbringing. I had witnessed many Pākehā/European students from my first South Auckland school go casually off to university, to travel, to other tertiary courses, or some such "successful" future, while the students from Kikorangi dawdled into low-paying jobs pumping gas or packing boxes, onto the unemployment benefit, or into gangs and crime. I felt as frustrated as they did that their local community was routinely traduced in the media, and that other schools in the area dismissed us. I also felt helpless when students left school early so they could earn money to support their families. Many students struggled with ongoing illnesses, or would fall asleep in class after working the night shift. The idea of higher education interested students, but many came from families who had never studied beyond year 11 (15 years of age), and they found it hard to even imagine what a university was like. When they did, it seemed like an expensive, scary, faraway, and White place; a place where they did not belong.

The key challenge here is how to engage in a reflection of the self, without making the discussion about ourselves (see also Chapter 4). What we see and say is only possible to see and to say because of our own positionality. But the focus is on the space between ourselves and others, and how this space enables particular explorations. We can also see, however, how our critical approaches to these studies also frame these narratives in certain ways. Katie "sees" and feels the impacts of how social class and ethnicity intersect in different ways in her life compared to the young people she teaches and studies, but this is only one kind of telling, framed as much by her theoretical lens at the time (postcolonial theory with Bourdieu) as by her positionality as a White woman. Other tellings were, of course, possible, but not available to her at the time. Stephen also juxtaposes his professional and research experiences in particular ways, although – at the time – he did not go beyond these to explore their intersections with his Whiteness, social class, and cisgender identities, for example (see Chapter 6).

In both our studies, we engaged a reflexive awareness about how our own habitus affected the way we "saw" the research site and our own experiences of the field. We each employed a range of strategies to "unpick" and expose our assumptions and, crucially, sought to understand the research site in its relations with other sites socially, politically, and historically. This not only exposes limitations but also creates new ones. Such reflexivity does not absolve the subject researcher (Pillow, 2003). It is simply a beginning, opening dialogues of difference, and providing an invitation to a rigorous engagement with one's own blind spots, assumptions, and bases for thinking. Lather suggests that "such a shift asks how we come to think of things this way and what would be made possible if we were to think ethnography otherwise, as a space surprised by difference into the performance of practices of not-knowing" (2007, p. 7).

In her book, *Risky Lessons* – a feminist ethnography of sexuality education and gender in schools – Fields (2008) notes that stories about gender and sexuality are at the heart of her investigation and the aim of her study is "fourfold: to shed light on those stories, to explore their volatility, to interrupt their construction, and to introduce new possibilities" (p. 179). These aims encapsulate the openness that is required of a critical ethnographer. We all "live" stories – our own stories and research/knowledge stories. Interrogating those stories – and, as Fields (2008) suggests, their related volatility – is thus an important, but difficult, starting point. In so doing, Fields does not assume a particular approach to gender and sexuality. Rather, she begins with an interest in stories and in understanding the incoherence, contradiction, nuance, and uncertainty of those stories, both in and of themselves, and in relation to each other.

Atkinson and Coffey (2001) note that reflexivity is important because it allows us to "acknowledge that the methods we use to describe the world are . . . constitutive of the realities they describe" (p. 807). Critical ethnographic approaches aim to unearth and name depoliticizing processes and our place within them, but the researcher is also deeply and inextricably implicated in relations of power, which is why reflexivity is such a key ongoing methodological component of critical ethnographic fieldwork. Positionality and reflexivity also specifically highlight, and make transparent, the links between the local context of the study and wider historical, social, and political forces. Weis et al. (2009) argue that while we have an ethical responsibility to understand the local in deep and nuanced ways, we must consider how highly connected, and at times seemingly disparate, locations also are. This requires an ethnographer to commit to a theory of method, weaving the local with the global in a dedicated and theorized fashion. However, it is also important to note that reflexive moves need to stop short of being "the answer" to what is missing or missed toward an assumption of truth (see Chapter 5). Lather (2001b) cautions here that "[r]eflexive ethnography authorizes itself by confronting its own processes of interpretation as some sort of cure toward better knowing". She instead suggests a deconstructive approach that seeks "knowing through not knowing":

> We often do not know what we are seeing, how much we are missing, what we are not understanding or even how to locate those lacks. This is an effort to trouble the sort of reflexive confession that becomes a narcissistic wound that will not heal and that eats up the world by monumentalizing loss.
>
> *(Lather, 2001b, p. 486)*

One way that ethnography addresses issues of lack is through temporality. The time that ethnographers spend in the field cannot guard against the limits that Lather (2001b) highlights earlier. But it does make it more difficult for researchers to ignore their ongoing and persistent effects. As we argued in Chapter 1, while fast and/or mercenary forms of research can easily "sample" research contexts, ethnographers instead seek more immersive, involved, and nuanced understandings over time.

Time, "Deep Hanging Out"

The next key tenet of critical ethnography relates to time. Time is, of course, uncertain, changeable, and context-specific, but it is not possible to do ethnographic work without attention to temporalities. This clearly sets ethnographic approaches apart from other kinds of research, such as interview studies. Historically, ethnographers were required to spend years in the field before beginning any research. Contemporary ethnographers have a more flexible approach but agree that significant time is still required to understand cultures and relationalities, form relationships with participants, and gain deep understandings of contexts (see also Chapter 5).

Time for research is, of course, highly contested in the modern academy wherein the drive for fast research outputs, impact, and clear recommendations is ubiquitous (see Chapter 1). Spending a year or more in the field may be a fantasy for tenured or untenured academic faculty, who are simultaneously teaching, advising/supervising, and involved in various academic and community-based service and engagement roles. Jeffrey and Troman (2004) note that it's important to remember that, regardless of the total time period of a study, ethnographers don't typically spend all their time on a singular project. In the case of our own school-based ethnographies, time in the field has varied from three to four days a week for an entire school year (42 weeks), to one day a week for 18 months, to three days a week for three school terms (31 weeks). There are, of course, a range of possibilities for ethnographic temporalities. Jeffrey and Troman (2004), for example, identified three different time modes for ethnography.

Compressed Time Mode

This is when an ethnographer lives in a research setting (usually day and night) for a compressed period of time, ranging from a few days to a few weeks. During this time, the researcher will attempt to live and breathe as much of life in the field as possible by literally immersing themselves in the setting. Jeffery and Troman note that this approach requires "a proliferation of observations and perspectives, which need organising in situ" (2004, p. 539).

Selective Intermittent Time Mode

Jeffery and Troman describe an intermittent and selective time mode as "one where the length of time spent doing the research is longer, for example, from three months to two years, but with a very flexible approach to the frequency of site visits" (p. 540). This approach allows the researcher to respond flexibly to possible areas of investigation, and revisit the site to gain experience of, and observe particular events or moments. It requires the researcher to follow areas of interest and remain open to exploring compelling themes.

A Recurrent Time Mode

A recurrent time mode is where visits to the site coincide with particular events (the end or beginning of certain phases or time periods), or at regular intervals regardless of what is happening. The purpose of this approach is to ascertain the significance of certain time periods and to gain a view of what happens over those time periods. Researchers might, for example, investigate and compare how things change over time. For Jeffrey and Troman, the recurrent time mode "enables the researcher to compare the different phases of a cycle, to identify change and to develop authentic narratives through respondent reflection and researcher challenge, the researcher taking the role of a narrative film maker" (p. 544).

Digital ethnographies (Varis, 2016; Pink et al., 2016) have allowed for expanded notions of time (and space) as researchers navigate across time zones and the liminalities of online spaces. Ethnographers are increasingly thinking of time in the setting in more expansive ways, attending to how research crosses into and out of digital contexts, and how relationships with participants and understandings of context are both mediated and enhanced by the digital. Digital environments engage temporalities in layered ways, allowing researchers to, for example, access conversations that have happened over a number of years. This exposes time in the setting as a varied and fluid notion. Sak (2016) notes that:

> [t]he digital realm establishes a new kind of movement through time and space that implies the flow of data and is dependent on flows rather than pauses. This flow reflects on human experience through which the human consciousness moves to witness close and distant spaces and times.
>
> *(p. 60)*

Time and temporalities are also increasingly becoming a feature of analysis, as ethnographers revisit previous studies with new thinking (e.g., Youdell, 2010; see Chapter 8) or explore temporalities as disciplining techniques across different sites (e.g., Benton et al., 2017). There is no one way to view or enact ethnographic temporalities. Geertz's (1998) notion of "deep hanging out" – a term he borrowed and reimagined from anthropologist James Clifford – is useful for many. It is a name for a method of "immersing oneself in a cultural, group or social experience on an informal level" (Walmsley, 2018, p. 277). The important consideration, for us, is that time attends to relationalities and researchers engage deeply and personally in contexts. What is enough time is a question for each project, along with how temporalities impact research possibilities (Pink et al., 2016).

An Attempt to Understand and Communicate Cultures, Happenings, and Their Ethico-Onto- Epistemologies

While time spent in research settings is one of the key things that sets ethnography apart from other methodologies, what is done with the time is also important. It is not possible to undertake ethnography successfully without seeking to understand cultural contexts in depth (and over time). Ethnography (and critical ethnography) began with anthropology which, as Geertz reminds us, carved out "a special place for itself as the study of culture" (2000, p. x). This is worth remembering in relation to choosing a methodological approach; to do critical ethnography, the researcher must be fundamentally interested in understanding, exploring, interrogating, and challenging cultures within context.

To achieve this, the critical ethnographer must simultaneously acknowledge, attend to, and evaluate critically and contextually, what Barad (2007) refers to as our "ethico-onto-epistemologies". This combination of ethics, knowing, and being situates us in relation to the study and wider flows of power, knowledge, and relationalities – highlighting how our worldviews, knowledge, ethics, and understandings inform, and are informed by our research experiences and interactions (see Chapter 3). This is a process that Barad describes as "intra-action" – highlighting that we are not only of/in the world, but also co-constituted by it. As she argues: " 'We' are not outside observers of the world. Nor are we simply located at places in the world; rather, we are part of the world in its ongoing intra-activity" (p. 828).

When seen in this light, ethnography clearly requires a lot from us as researchers – perhaps more than most other methodologies. It also highlights what ethnographic research is not. For example, there have recently been a plethora of educational research studies claiming to be ethnographic. Many of these involve participant observation of a series of lessons along with teacher and/or student interviews (see also Chapter 5). This approach is not ethnographic because the time spent doesn't allow researchers to become part of and fully immersed in the context, relationally. Crucially, these researchers cannot form deep reciprocal relationships with participants, nor can they understand the nuances of cultural expression or the varied interactions and contradictions that emerge over time. More than that though, ethnographers are not only interested in the views of participants but also in how actors (people, objects, ideas, spaces) interact and intersect in the research site, and how these are located historically and politically.

The only way to achieve this level of engagement, relationality, and reciprocity is to spend time becoming familiar with and getting "inside" the spaces of the research setting. If a researcher is not interested in culture, then the project is not ethnographic. If a researcher is not interested in power, then the study is not critical. A study design of observations and/or interviews does not attend to the more subtle goings-on, the spaces in between the formal research moments, and the material and political happenings of the research setting. These might include the researcher's own sensual engagement with how it feels to be in a room at a particular moment, how power flows between people and objects in a space, or how things feel, look, smell. These sensory elements recognize "the emplaced ethnographer as . . . part of a social, sensory and material environment and acknowledges the political and ideological agendas and power relations integral to the contexts and circumstances of ethnographic processes" (Pink, 2009, p. 23). Attending to cultures does not mean limiting ethnographic inquiry to people. It should also be expansive in terms of attending to materialities, place, and historicities, including the more-than-human and the digital.

Writing, Fieldwork, and Other Modes of Production

Every time we write about these tenets of critical ethnography, they shift slightly, emerge differently, morph and change shape, and/or take on a different order. We have, up until now, avoided explaining what we mean by the modes of production (which might be called "qualitative research tools"), because it seems obvious what we mean and, simultaneously, too difficult and vast to discuss. We could advise picking up any qualitative research handbook. But which one? At which point in time? And on which continent? The field of qualitative research is huge and includes work calling itself: mixed methods, autoethnography, interviews, arts-based methods, family history, narrative inquiry, case study, life history, and so many other things. So, employing particular methods is not straightforward at all.

Traditionally, ethnographers engaged in something called "fieldwork" and there are excellent texts providing discussion of what this is, what it might be, and how it might be undertaken (e.g., Delamont, 2016). But fieldwork itself is quite a loose term (perhaps helpfully so); it returns us to Geertz's notion of deep hanging out, to the idea of a wandering anthropologist seeking new experiences and writing about them. Like all ethnography, critical ethnography requires the researcher to develop deep, lived understandings of a context and to reflect on the meanings of cultures within that context. This requires significant time in the field, but it can also engage with materiality in the form of places, spaces, objects, landscapes, and architectures.

Ethnographic methods can be diverse and responsive depending on the focus of the site (see also Chapter 5). They can include field notes on one's own experiences, visual artifacts (such as photos and artwork), interviews, observations, participation, and a range of visual and arts-based methods. Documents such as official policies and email conversations, historical artifacts, statutes, newsletters, websites, and the like, can also be drawn upon. Contemporary ethnographers are increasingly using participant-generated research methods and engaging participants as co-researchers, videographers, diarists, and interviewers (Cammarota & Fine, 2008; Delamont & Atkinson, 2018; Pink, 2021; Pink et al., 2016). As Delamont (2016) observes, ethnographic methods can thus also extend to:

> [R]esearch on documents such as Tweets or blogs, interviewing with open-ended questions, oral history, life history, collecting informants' drawings, photographs or "films", exploring personal constructions and mental maps as well as observation, whether the observer is participating or trying to be unobtrusive.
>
> *(p. 8)*

As we consistently argue throughout this book, ethnographic work is not bound by any rigid methodological rules. Rather, it draws on a range of methods and is flexible, dependent on practicality, the research foci, and relationships between participants and researchers. This is possible in ethnography as a range of methodological tools can be used within a broad framework and, crucially, wider social and political contexts can be analyzed alongside, and in relation to, specific contextual incidences. Writing is central to the process of critical ethnography, and we dedicate significant attention to writing and fieldwork in Chapter 5. Here, however, we want to make a note about the term (ethnographic) "data", which we resist using in the book (unless it appears in a quotation). We agree with Denzin when he insists that "Data Are Dead" and argues that "[p]oststructuralism took away positivism's claim to a God's eye view of the world, that view which said objective observers could turn the world and its happenings into things that could be turned into data" (2015, p. 187). Denzin notes that the term has, nevertheless, continued in common use, even in poststructuralist research accounts, and he argues that we should reject it. In critical ethnography, there are at least two good reasons to avoid using the word data. The first is Denzin's (2015) insistence that it turns research into a commodity that can be bought or sold – much like the neoliberal forms of fast and mercenary research approaches we discussed in Chapter 1. The second is that it reinforces the idea that research contexts can be objectively captured and understood via research methods. As he points out:

> The politics and political economy of evidence, also known as data, is not a question of evidence or no evidence. It is rather a question of who has the power to control the definition of evidence, who defines the kinds of materials that count as evidence, who determines what methods best produce the best forms of evidence, whose criteria and standards are used to evaluate quality evidence. The politics of data, the politics of evidence, cannot be separated from the ethics of evidence.
>
> *(p. 200)*

Research materials then, and how they are used, are unavoidably political considerations. Ethnographers can choose to reject the term data and instead talk about empirical materials, research materials, notes, writings, musings, qualitative materials, ethnographic evidence, poetry, art, stories, or many other terms that narrate our research performances and how we created them. It might still be useful to critique "data" and how it is also produced, especially in relation to big data, audit cultures, and digital surveillance, but critical ethnographers might resist producing "data" as part of a research project.

Change: Wondering About Change, Creating Change, Troubling Change, Challenging Inequities

Should critical ethnographers seek to create change and challenge inequities in research sites, in themselves, in the academy, in the communities in which we live? This question continues to trouble us. One obvious answer – given the issues of in/equity and in/justice we are concerned about – is yes. And many researchers advocating for such forms of justice do demand change. Critical approaches to education, however, have a problematic history with notions of emancipation that assume external intervention and tend toward paternalistic relationships that reinscribe power relations even while attempting to work against them (Biesta, 2015). As we noted in Chapter 1, Rasmussen (2015) argues that some critical projects are driven by a desire for change such they imagine a utopian vision of education. The expectation for critical analysis to lead to such change is a form of cruel optimism (Berlant, 2011), a fantasy about an ideal state that is impossible to achieve. Rasmussen (2015) observes that this kind of "appeal to such a utopian logic" can actually prevent in-depth and nuanced political analyses.

Seeking change can so often be an act of blind arrogance. Who gets to choose what change is needed? Whose ethico-onto-epistemological position is privileged and how do we know the change(s) we propose or try to enact won't create other kinds of inequity? Returning to Fine's question "who-am-I-to do-this-work?" (Fine, 2006, p. 90), we must also then ask "who am I to make this change?" And what of the stories we tell; the voices we highlight? We noted earlier Palmer and Caldas's observation that knowledge must be "constructed and interpreted from the vantage point of the people whose voices are marginalized" (2017, p. 384) but as Fine (1994) cautions, giving voice to participants is also a power move that can all too easily slip into ventriloquy (see also Biesta, 2015). We explore these challenges in our focus on ethnographic writing in Chapter 5.

Understanding context, people, relationalities, and positionalities must precede making change, and meaningful change needs to engage social, historical, and political contexts. Lather (2007) suggests we should embrace getting lost rather than trying to find some (often elusive) "solution". We suggest that this is also necessary if we want change to be meaningful, located, and culturally connected. We might need to entirely lose our ontological way to come to a notion of what might change and how that isn't predetermined and ultimately self-interested. We explore these questions more fully in our chapter on ethics. We feel, however, that change must be sought with caution and with continual reflection. The only change one can perhaps be confident about is changing the self. Change might not be the ultimate purpose of critical ethnographic projects. If it is desired then it might be approached slowly, seriously, selectively, and collaboratively.

Note

1. There are, in fact, a number of critical autoethnographic publications that do attend to reflexivity and theory (see e.g., Harris & Holman Jones, 2019; Moriarty, 2019).

References

Alim, H. S. (2004). *You know my steez: An ethnographic and sociolinguistic study of styleshifting in a black American speech community*. Duke University Press.

Atkinson, P. (2019). *Writing ethnographically*. Sage.

Atkinson, P., & Coffey, A. (2001). Revisiting the relationship between participant observation and interviewing. In J. F. Gubrium & J. Holstein (Eds.), *Handbook of interview research* (pp. 801–814). Sage.

Ball, S. J. (2016). Following policy: Networks, network ethnography and education policy mobilities. *Journal of Education Policy, 31*(5), 549–566. https://doi.org/10.1080/02680 939.2015.1122232

Barad, K. (2007). *Meeting the universe halfway: Quantum physics and the entanglement of matter and meaning*. Duke University Press.

Benton, A., Sangaramoorthy, T., & Kalofonos, I. (2017). Temporality and positive living in the age of HIV/AIDS: A Multisited ethnography. *Current Anthropology, 58*(4), 454–476.

Berlant, L. (2011). *Cruel optimism.* Duke University Press.

Biesta, G. J. (2015). *Beautiful risk of education.* Routledge.

Bishop, R. (2005). Freeing ourselves from neo-colonial domination in research: A Kaupapa Maori approach to creating knowledge. In N. Denzin & Y. Lincoln (Eds.), *Sage handbook of qualitative research* (pp. 109–138). Sage.

Blaise, M., Hamm, C., & Iorio, J. M. (2017). Modest witness (ing) and lively stories: Paying attention to matters of concern in early childhood. Pedagogy, *Culture & Society, 25*(1), 31–42.

Bourdieu, P. (1990). *The logic of practice.* Polity Press.

Bourdieu, P., & Wacquant, L. (1992). *An invitation to reflexive sociology.* Polity Press

Butler, J. (1993). *Bodies that matter: On the discursive limits of sex.* Routledge.

Cammarota, J., & Fine, M. (Eds.). (2008). *Revolutionizing education: Youth participatory action research in motion.* Routledge.

Carspecken, P. (1996). *Critical ethnography in educational research: A theoretical and practical guide.* Routledge.

Coles, J. (2022). Beyond silence: Disrupting antiblackness through BlackCrit ethnography and black youth voice. In S. May & B. Caldas (Eds.), *Critical ethnography, language, race/ism and education.* Multilingual Matters.

Delamont, S. (2016). *Fieldwork in educational settings: Methods, pitfalls and perspectives* (3rd ed.). Routledge. https://doi.org/10.4324/9781315758831

Delamont, S., & Atkinson, P. (2018). The ethics of ethnography. In *The Sage handbook of qualitative research ethics* (pp. 119–132). Sage.

Deleuze, G., & Guattari, F. (1987). *A thousand plateaus: Capitalism and schizophrenia* (B. Massumi, Trans.). University of Minnesota Press.

Deleuze, G., & Guattari, F. (2004a). *Anti-oedipus.* Continuum.

Deleuze, G., & Guattari, F. (2004b). *A thousand plateaus: Volume 2 of capitalism and schizophrenia.* Continuum.

Denzin, N. (2015). Coda: The death of data? In N. K. Denzin & M. D. Giardina (Eds.), *Qualitative inquiry and the politics of research* (pp. 197–206). Left Coast Press.

Denzin, N. K., & Giardina, M. D. (Eds.). (2019). *Qualitative inquiry at a crossroads: Political, performative, and methodological reflections.* Routledge.

Dumas, M. J., & ross, k. m. (2016). 'Be real black for me": Imaging BlackCrit in education. *Urban Education, 51*(4), 415–442.

Dyke, S. (2013). Disrupting anorexia nervosa: An ethnography of the Deleuzian event. In R. Coleman & J. Ringrose (Eds.), *Deleuze and research methodologies* (pp. 145–163). Edinburgh University Press.

Faircloth, S. C., Hynds, A., & Webber, M. (2020). Exploring methodological and ethical opportunities and challenges when researching with Indigenous youth on issues of identity and culture. *International Journal of Qualitative Studies in Education, 33*(9), 971–986.

Fields, J. (2008). *Risky lessons: Sex education and social inequality.* Rutgers University Press.

Fine, M. (1991). *Framing dropouts: Notes on the politics of an urban public high school.* State University of New York Press.

Fine, M. (1994). Dis-tance and other stances: Negotiations of power inside feminist research. In A. Gitlin (Ed.), *Power and methods* (pp. 13–55). Routledge.

Fine, M. (2006). Bearing witness: Methods for researching oppression and resistance – A textbook for critical research. *Social Justice Research, 19*(2), 83–108. https://doi. org/10.1007/s11211-006-0001-0

Fitzpatrick, K. (2013). *Critical pedagogy, physical education and urban schooling*. Peter Lang.

Geertz, C. (1998). Deep hanging out. *The New York Review of Books, 45*(16), 69.

Geertz, C. (2000). *Available light: Anthropological reflections on philosophical topics*. Princeton University Press.

Grenfell, M., Bloom, D., Hardy, C., Pahl, K., Rosswell, J., & Street, B. (2012). *Language, ethnography and education: Bridging new literacy studies and Bourdieu*. Routledge.

Hamilton, L., & Taylor, N. (2017). *Ethnography after humanism: Power, politics and method in multi-species research*. Springer.

Harris, A., & Holman Jones, S. (2019). Between bodies: Queer grief in the Anthropocene. In N. K. Denzin & M. D. Giardina (Eds.), *Qualitative inquiry at a crossroads: Political, performative, and methodological reflections* (pp 19–31). Routledge.

Jeffrey, B., & Troman, G. (2004). Time for ethnography. *British Educational Research Journal, 30*(4), 535–548. https://doi.org/10.1080/0141192042000237220

Jones, A. (1991). *'At school I've got a chance': Culture/privilege: Pacific islands and pakeha girls at school*. Dunmore Press.

King, J. R. (1999). Am not! Are too! Using queer standpoint in postmodern critical ethnography. *International Journal of Qualitative Studies in Education, 12*(5), 473–490. https://doi.org/10.1080/095183999235908

Lather, P. (2001a). Postbook: Working the ruins of feminist ethnography. *Journal of Women in Culture and Society, 27*(1), 199–227.

Lather, P. (2001b). Postmodernism, post-structuralism and post(critical) ethnography: Of ruins, aporias and angels. In *Handbook of ethnography* (pp. 477–506). Sage.

Lather, P. (2007). *Getting lost: Feminist efforts toward a double(d) science*. SUNY Press.

Lave, J. (2011). *Apprenticeship in critical ethnographic practice*. University of Chicago Press.

Leahy, D. (2014). Assembling a health [y] subject: Risky and shameful pedagogies in health education. *Critical Public Health, 24*(2), 171–181.

Madison, D. S. (2006). The dialogic performative in critical ethnography. *Text and Performance Quarterly, 26*(4), 320–324. https://doi.org/10.1080/10462930600828675

Madison, D. S. (2019). *Critical ethnography: Method, ethics, and performance* (3rd ed.). Sage.

May, S. (1994). *Making multicultural education work*. Multilingual Matters.

May, S. (1997). Critical ethnography. In N. Hornberger (Ed.), *Research methods and education. Encyclopedia of language and education* (1st ed., Vol. 8, pp. 197–206). Kluwer.

May, S. (1998). On what might have been: Some reflections on critical multiculturalism. In G. Shacklock & J. Smyth (Eds.), *Being reflexive in critical educational and social research* (pp. 159–170). Falmer Press.

May, S. (2014). *The multilingual turn: Implications for SLA, TESOL and bilingual education*. Routledge.

Moriarty, J. (Ed.). (2019). *Autoethnographies from the neoliberal academy: Rewilding, writing and resistance in higher education*. Routledge.

Naples, N. A. (1996). A feminist revisiting of the insider/outsider debate: The "outsider phenomenon" in rural Iowa. *Qualitative Sociology, 19*(1), 83–106. https://doi. org/10.1007/BF02393249

Noblit, G. W., Flores, S. Y., & Murillo, E., Jr (Eds.). (2004). *Postcritical ethnography: Rein-scribing critique*. Hampton Press.

Pacini-Ketchabaw, V., Taylor, A., & Blaise, M. (2016). Decentring the human in multi-species ethnographies. In C. Taylor & C. Hughes (Eds.), *Posthuman research practices in education* (pp. 149–167). Palgrave Macmillan.

Palmer, D., & Caldas, B. (2017). Critical ethnography. In K. King, Y. Lai & S. May (Eds.), Research methods in language and education. *Encyclopedia of language and education* (3rd ed., pp. 381–392). Springer.

Paris, D. (2011). *Language across difference: Ethnicity, communication, and youth identities in changing urban schools.* Cambridge University Press.

Pascoe, C. J. (2007). *Dude, you're a fag: Masculinity and sexuality in high school.* University of California Press.

Pedersen, H. (2013). Follow the Judas sheep: Materializing post-qualitative methodology in zooethnographic space. *International Journal of Qualitative Studies in Education, 26*(6), 717–731. https://doi.org/10.1080/09518398.2013.788760

Penehira, M., Smith, L. T., Green, A., & Aspin, C. (2011). Mouri matters: Contextualising mouri in Māori health discourse. *AlterNative: An International Journal of Indigenous Peoples, 7*(2), 177–187.

Pillow, W. S. (2003). Confession, catharsis or cure? Rethinking the uses of reflexivity as methodological power in qualitative research. *International Journal of Qualitative Studies in Education 16*(2), 175–196.

Pink, S. (2009). *Doing sensory ethnography.* Sage.

Pink, S. (2021). *Doing visual ethnography* (4th ed.). Sage.

Pink, S., Horst, H., Postill, J., Hjorth, L., Lewis, T., & Tacchi, J. (2016). *Digital ethnography: Principles and practice.* Sage.

Powell, D. (2020). *Schools, corporations, and the war on childhood obesity.* Routledge.

Rasmussen, M. L. (2015). 'Cruel optimism' and contemporary Australian critical theory in educational research. *Educational Philosophy and Theory, 47*(2), 192–206.

Rasmussen, M. L., Rofes, E., & Talburt, S. (Eds.). (2004). *Youth and sexualities: Pleasure, subversion, and insubordination in and out of schools.* Palgrave Macmillan.

Ringrose, J. (2011). Beyond discourse? Using Deleuze and Guattari's schizoanalysis to explore affective assemblages, heterosexually striated space, and lines of flight online and at school. *Educational Philosophy and Theory, 43*(6), 598–618. https://doi.org/10.1111/j.1469-5812.2009.00601.x

Russell, L., & Thomson, P. (2011). Girls and gender in alternative education provision. *Ethnography and Education, 6*(3), 293–308. https://doi.org/10.1080/17457823.2011.610581

Sak, S. (2016). Socio-spatial approaches for media and communication research. In S. Kubitschko & A Kaun (Eds.), *Innovative methods in media and communication research* (pp. 59–74). Palgrave Macmillan.

Smith, L. T. (2012). *Decolonising methodologies: Research and indigenous peoples* (2nd ed.). Zed Books.

Smith, L. T., Maxwell, T. K., Puke, H., & Temara, P. (2016). Indigenous knowledge, methodology and mayhem. What is the role of methodology in producing Indigenous insights? A discussion from mātauranga Māori. *Knowledge Cultures, 4*(3), 131–156

St. Pierre, E. A. (2018). Writing post qualitative inquiry. *Qualitative Inquiry, 24*(9), 603–608.

St. Pierre, E. A. (2021). Post qualitative inquiry, the refusal of method, and the risk of the new. *Qualitative Inquiry, 27*(1), 3–9.

Talburt, S. (1999). Open secrets and problems of queer ethnography: Readings from a religious studies classroom. *International Journal of Qualitative Studies in Education, 12*(5), 525–539. https://doi.org/10.1080/095183999235935

Taylor, A., & Pacini-Ketchabaw, V. (2015). Learning with children, ants, and worms in the Anthropocene: Towards a common world pedagogy of multispecies vulnerability. *Pedagogy, Culture, Society, 23*(4), 507–529. https://doi.org/10.1080/14681366.2015.1039050 b

Tesar, M. (2021). Some thoughts concerning post-qualitative methodologies. *Qualitative Inquiry, 27*(2), 223–227.

Thomas, J. (1993). *Doing critical ethnography*. Sage.

Thomas, J. (2003). Musings on critical ethnography, meanings and symbolic violence. In R. Clair (Ed.), *Expressions of ethnography: Novel approaches to qualitative methods* (pp. 45–54). State University of New York (SUNY) Press.

Thomson, P. (2002). *Schooling the rustbelt kids: Making the difference in changing times*. Allen & Unwin.

Varis, P. (2016). Digital ethnography. In A. Georgakopoulou & T Spilioti (Eds.), *Routledge handbook of language and digital communication* (pp. 55–68). Routledge.

Villenas, S., & Foley, D. (2011). Critical ethnographies of education in the Latino/a diaspora. In R. R. Valencia (Ed.), *Chicano school failure and success: Past, present and future* (3rd ed., pp. 175–196). Routledge.

Walmsley, B. (2018). Deep hanging out in the arts: An anthropological approach to capturing cultural value. *International Journal of Cultural Policy, 24*(2), 272–291. https://doi.org/10.1080/10286632.2016.1153081

Weis, L., Fine, M., & Dimitriadis, G. (2009). Towards a critical theory of method in shifting times. In M. W. Apple, W. Au, & L. Armando Gandin (Eds.), *Routledge international handbook of critical education* (pp. 437–448). Routledge.

Willis, P. (1977). *Learning to labor: How working class kids get working class jobs*. Saxon House.

Yon, D. (2000). *Elusive culture: Schooling, race, and identity in global times*. State University of New York Press.

Youdell, D. (2005). Sex-gender-sexuality: How sex, gender and sexuality constellations are constituted in secondary schools. *Gender and Education, 17*(3), 249–270. https://doi.org/10.1080/09540250500145148

Youdell, D. (2010). Queer outings: Uncomfortable stories about the subjects of poststructural school ethnography. *International Journal of Qualitative Studies in Education, 23*(1), 87–100. http://doi.org/10.1080/09518390903447168

Youdell, D., & Armstrong, F. (2011). A politics beyond subjects: The affective choreographies and smooth spaces of schooling. *Emotion, Space and Society, 4*(3), 144–150. https://doi.org/10.1016/j.emospa.2011.01.002

3

WORKING THE THEORY (AND CONTEXT) IN CRITICAL ETHNOGRAPHY

In this chapter, we explore the interrelationship of theory and methodology in critical ethnography. The significance of theory, of theorizing, lies not just in its orientation, but in its dynamic articulation with research contexts. We take an open approach to the use of theory in ethnographic research and argue that critical ethnography is an interdisciplinary, inclusive approach that can engage a wide range of critically oriented social theories. Delanty argues that one of the original aims of critical social theory was to link philosophy with social research because "social phenomena . . . cannot be discerned only through empirical knowledge; critique requires knowledge of core constitutive forces, which are the grounds of the possibility of society" (2020, p. 1).

Throughout the chapter, we connect with and name a range of broad theoretical fields, none of these is bounded and there is, intentionally, slippage and overlap between and among them. We draw on work that could be labeled as aligned with neo-Marxism, poststructuralism, feminist poststructuralism, cultural studies, postcolonialism, and posthumanism, as well as work that might be broadly thought of (or which is named by authors) as related to new materialisms; some of these writers employ affect theory, agential realism, or name their work as postfoundational. While we do group some of these together to consider how they have shifted the field, we don't attempt clear definitions of these different ontologies or the specific theories or theorists they engage with in this chapter. We do try to give enough context to make each position clear but primarily aim to show how different theories can be productive in different ways in critical ethnographic studies. A wide range of examples of critical ethnographic work is used throughout to show how different educational researchers create possibilities at the intersection of social theories and methodology. We do this to insist that ontologies matter in knowledge production. Pascale notes that "[o]ntological

DOI: 10.4324/9781315208510-3

questions are fundamental to social research" so that the "neglect of philosophical foundations in social research results in ontological assumptions that function as untheorized truths" (2011, p. 3).

In critical ethnography, theory and methodology work together and actively co-constitute each other. As Grenfell and James suggest, "practice and theorizing are not regarded as separate activities, displaced in time and place during the research process, but mutually generative" (1998, p. 155). Theoretical understandings necessarily inform and form us as researchers before we enter the field, but are then challenged, extended, rethought, reinforced, and sometimes displaced, in the actual experience of doing the research. This kind of theorizing is dynamic because it is developed as an active process in and through research relationships and interactions. The boundaries of the theory-methodology-researcher are brought actively into tension as we engage with theory. This, in turn, requires us to work reflexively with our own ethico-onto-epistemological positionings (Barad, 2007) – our worldviews, knowledge, ethics, and understandings, along with, for example, social, cultural, and gendered experiences and commitments – as these inform, and are informed by research experiences and interactions. This is necessarily messy and is neither easy nor easily mapped. We explore the ethical importance of these dynamic, reciprocal, and reflexive processes of engagement in more detail in Chapter 4.

The sociohistorical and sociopolitical *situatedness* of the research context, or field, is also central to theorizing critical ethnography. As Weis and Fine (2012) argue:

> Social theory and analyses cannot afford to separate lives or . . . even conditions tagged as social "problems" from global and local structures. We cannot reproduce the conceptual firewalls separating present from past; resilience from oppression; achievement from opportunity; progress from decline.
>
> *(p. 175)*

In response, Weis and Fine suggest employing a

> critical bifocality [as] a dedicated theoretical and methodological commitment to . . . documenting at once the linkages and capillaries of structural arrangements and the discursive and lived-out practices by which [people] . . . make sense of their circumstances.
>
> *(p. 176)*

Lave argues that "part of critical ethnographic practice is an ongoing commitment to re-thinking and redoing one's work as an ethnographer and activist" (2011, p. 2). She notes that fieldwork transforms the researcher and argues that it is not only "deeply empirical" but also "just as deeply a matter of theoretical formation" (p. 2). For Lather (2007), the empirical and the theoretical are likewise both deeply implicated in questions of epistemology and she argues that all too often questions of method obscure the production of knowledge in research. Lather advocates, instead, a disruptive theoretical practice, so that researchers can simultaneously apply and critique their ontological approach. Such a dynamic articulation helps us to recognize and interrogate how wider power relations operate to frame knowledge, create contexts and subjectivities, as well as particular spaces and conditions in any research context. Theory is, in part, "inevitably, about developing an understanding of how we have come to know and to better understand our prejudices, attachments and affiliations to particular ways of seeing" (Rasmussen, 2020, p. 9). It also requires us to attend to both the local and the global – making transparent the links between the focus of the study and wider historical, social, and political contexts. As critical ethnographers, we thus need to commit to a theory of method, weaving the local with the global and the theoretical, as lived in a dedicated and theorized fashion (May & Fitzpatrick, 2019; Weis et al., 2009).

In this chapter, we consider how critical ethnographers in education contexts have actively engaged theory-methodology in their studies in order to create different kinds of educational inquiries. We are interested in how some are working playfully between theory and methodology, experimenting with new approaches, and how the theories they employ construct the possibilities for their ethnographic inquiries. We begin with a brief consideration of how critical ethnography has got to this point with respect to the interweaving of theory, methodology, and context, with the local and the global. We first reflect on the origins of critical ethnography and early examples of its application in education. We then map how various broad theoretical fields have shifted ethnographic practice through neo-Marxist and social class analyses, intersectional approaches, feminist and poststructuralist, and postcritical work, as well as considering new materialist and posthuman analyses. Throughout the chapter, we illustrate the productive potential of theory by interspersing five different examples of specific theoretical engagements with critical ethnography. Example 1 details a Bourdieusian study undertaken by Jane Kenway and Aaron Koh (2013). Example 2 employs postcolonialism in the work of Daniel Yon (2000). Example 3 looks at poststructuralist feminism via Foucault and Butler in the work of Deborah Youdell (2005; Youdell & Armstrong, 2011). Example 4 focuses on BlackCrit and critical race theory in the work of Justin Coles (2019, 2020, 2022), while Example 5 looks at Helena Pedersen's (2013) posthumanist zooethnography. In each, we consider how the theoretical framework creates possibilities for the critical ethnographic research undertaken.

We end the chapter with some thoughts about what critical ethnography might learn from recent work in post-qualitative methodologies and assert that these arguments (along with the aforementioned social theories) can enable critical ethnography to become both more expansive and more epistemologically open.

Origins of Critical Ethnography

Critical ethnography is situated within the wider tradition of ethnographic field-work. Ethnography first emerged as a research methodology within anthropology in the early part of the 20th century and was, perhaps, most prominently associated with the work of Bronislav Malinowski in Britain and Franz Boas in the United States. Its anthropological origins were also complemented by parallel developments within sociology, most notably the advent of urban studies associated with Robert Park and the Chicago School of Urban Sociology.

The aims of ethnography, in this classic sense, are interpretive; one's goal as an ethnographer is to focus on a setting and discover what is going on there. This can be achieved by describing the norms, rules, and expectations that identify participants with(in) the particular culture, setting, or institution being studied. However, if the ethnographer wants to ascribe meaning to behavior in a fuller sense, they need also to *share* in the meanings that participants take for granted in informing their behavior, and to *describe* and *explain* these meanings for the benefit of the reader.

Geertz (1973, 2000) describes this process as one of "thick description", which seeks to narrate the important and recurring variables in a setting – as they relate to one another, and as they affect or produce certain results and outcomes within it. In traditional ethnographic accounts, this process of thick description is usually situated within a "realist narrative" account, with ethnographers cast as disinterested/distantiated observers (for more on different kinds of accounts, see Chapter 5). Realist writing tends to *recount* the story of the research setting and the multiple stories of the participants within it, allowing meaning to *emerge* from the data – an approach consonant with grounded theory.

This broadly interpretive approach to ethnographic fieldwork – exemplified in Malinowski's anthropology and the Chicago School's urban sociology – reinforced an emphasis on the micro exploration and explication of local sites and communities. Wider historical and social forces, and their interconnections with and impact on local sites, went largely unexamined in these early accounts. Burawoy describes this kind of early ethnographic fieldwork as one of "solitary confinement" (2000, p. 4), bound to a particular space and time, hermetically sealed and resolutely ahistorical. As Blommaert similarly observes, this early approach to ethnography "is a reduction of ethnography to *fieldwork*" which, in turn, "is perceived as *description*: an account of acts and experiences captured under the label of 'context', but in itself often un- or undercontextualized" (2018, p. 2 emphasis in original).

There were, however, some notable exceptions to this descriptivist, atheoretical approach, which were to provide a touchstone for the later development of more critical ethnographic work. Perhaps, the most notable of these was the Manchester School of anthropology established by Max Gluckman in the late 1940s. Gluckman and his associates at Manchester in England explored the intersection of class relations and colonial capitalism in Africa from predominantly Marxist perspectives, specifically combining micro and macro analyses (see Kapferer, 2006). In the 1960s, Alvin Gouldner mounted a robust critique of the Chicago School of urban sociology, which by then had shifted its initial focus on the study of urban localities to urban institutions, such as prisons, asylums, and factories. Gouldner argued that this approach, in focusing solely on participant experiences within these institutions, failed to "interrogate" the wider historical, social, and economic forces within which such institutions were inevitably situated. For Gouldner, this resulted in an unacceptable lack of reflexivity, with ethnographers unaware of how their research contributed to the reinforcement of discriminatory institutional practices and the related pathologizing of participants (see Burawoy, 2000; see also Chapter 4).

These critiques were expanded upon by the US anthropologist Sol Tax (1963), who also specifically repudiated the traditionally disinterested, interpretivist, ethnographic stance in early anthropological work, focusing instead on the importance of intervention in the research setting. In his early work on the Indigenous Mesquaki settlement in Iowa, for example, Tax advocated for "action anthropologists", who would be both more collaborative with, and politically engaged in, the communities they researched – producing research that might resolve, and be seen to resolve by the participants, significant community problems. This more openly engaged, critical, and activist approach to ethnography was illustrated elsewhere in the United States by the likes of Charles Valentine's (1968) work with African American action groups contesting police brutality (still a highly topical issue today), and Peggy Sanday's (1976) advocacy of approaches to anthropological research that more directly served wider public interests.

There were also allied developments in the 1960s toward a more theorized approach to ethnography in the emergent field of linguistic ethnography. Linguistic ethnography combines linguistic and ethnographic approaches to explore the interaction of language practices and social life in a wide range of settings (Copland et al., 2015; see also Chapter 6). This includes, crucially, how those language practices impact differentially on participants, privileging some and disadvantaging others. One of the early proponents of linguistic ethnography, the sociolinguist Dell Hymes (2002 [1969]), saw this approach as a "descriptive theory", arguing for the importance of grounding all ethnographic description ontologically, methodologically, and epistemologically. Hymes also prominently advocated for the importance of "voice" – focusing on how participants produce meaning, often in ways that differ from dominant or hegemonic norms. Indeed, for Hymes, a critical approach to linguistic ethnography was both an inherently academic and political program. This combination was essential for challenging "established" views of the value of particular language practices – privileging national languages over Indigenous or other minoritized languages being one obvious example. As Hymes concludes of this approach: "I would hope to see the consensual ethos of anthropology move from a liberal humanism, defending the powerless, to a socialist humanism, confronting the powerful and seeking to transform the structures of power" (p. 52).

Neo-Marxism, Cultural Studies, and the Work of Pierre Bourdieu

So, the potential for a more critical and critically engaged ethnography has clear precedents in these interdisciplinary developments in the mid-20th century. But it was in Britain, and within the field of education, that critical ethnography first came to be identified as a specific ethnographic approach – most notably, through Paul Willis's *Learning to labor* (1977), Angela McRobbie's (1978) "Working class girls and the culture of femininity", and Paul Corrigan's *Schooling the Smash Street kids* (1979). These ethnographic accounts were heavily influenced by neo-Marxism and cultural studies, and the work of Pierre Bourdieu, and they explored the alienating experiences of working-class young people in England.

Willis's account was to be particularly influential. He explored how a group of White working-class "lads" deliberately resisted and subverted their schooling experiences, ridiculing academic work via a highly masculinist class-based counterculture. Their aim in so doing was to leave school as soon as possible to work on the "factory floor". But, as Willis points out, their acts of resistance ironically ended up entrenching their class and occupational trajectories rather than subverting them.

Willis's account has since been heavily criticized for its tacit endorsement of the lads' outright misogynistic cultural practices, along with its privileging of a neo-Marxist/class-based analysis. Feminists lament the silences of gender in the study, arguing that girls are represented by Willis in narrow ways, primarily via the lads' views of their girlfriends (McRobbie, 2003). Angela McRobbie's (1978) work with teenage girls interrogated issues of gender and social class more directly, and other research about the lives of young women followed (e.g., Lees, 1986; Scraton, 1985; Skeggs, 2004; see also McRobbie, 1990).

Subsequent critical ethnographic accounts in education continued to be dominated by neo-Marxist analyses of social class – at least, initially. Peter McLaren, for example, undertook two significant critical ethnographic accounts: *Schooling as ritual performance* (1999), first published in 1986, and *Life in schools* (2015), first published in 1989. In both accounts, he drew on his experiences teaching in poor urban schools in Toronto, Canada and employed a Freirean critical pedagogy framework to analyze the often-oppressive rituals of schooling and the various forms of resistance to them. McLaren's use of Freire is something of an outlier here as the many other ethnographic accounts that drew on cultural studies, and the work of Pierre Bourdieu, in particular, began to have major traction. Bourdieu has been used consistently in critical ethnographic work in education ever since and has been integral to a wide range of analyses in education, especially in the United Kingdom, Australia, and New Zealand.

Bourdieu's theory of cultural reproduction directly engages theory-methodology together and lends itself to ethnographic inquiry, in part, because of Bourdieu's own anthropological research; he insisted that method should not be devoid of theory, and he argued that failing to theorize methodology was problematic (Bourdieu et al., 1991; see also Chapter 5). Bourdieu's key concepts of field, capital, and habitus, as well as symbolic violence and doxa, have been used extensively, and many critical ethnographic studies have applied these concepts to explore social class, achievement, academic success, social mobility, and the intersections between class and other subject positions such as gender and ethnicity (e.g., Dillabough, 2004; Grenfell et al., 2012; May, 1994, 1998; Ong, 1999; Teese & Polesel, 2003; see also Fitzpatrick & May, 2015; Reay, 2004).

The notion of field – a cultural and social space – is central to any Bourdieusian analysis. The field is infused with forms of capital and culturally embedded in the bodies of individuals via habitus. Social histories can, therefore, be read through embodiment:

> Because practice is the product of a habitus that is itself a product of the embodiment of the immanent regularities and tendencies of the world, it contains within itself an anticipation of these tendencies and regularities. . . . Time is engendered in the actualisation of the act, or the thought . . . habitus, adjusted to the immanent tendencies of the field, is an act of temporalisation through which the agent transcends the immediate present via practical mobilisation of the past and practical anticipation of the future.
> *(Bourdieu and Wacquant, 1992, p. 138)*

Pat Thomson's *Schooling the rustbelt kids* (2002) is a clear example of a rich Bourdieusian critical ethnographic account of schooling in Australia. She uses the theory to undertake a sophisticated analysis of how young people's experiences of schooling are a function of access to various forms of capital, including curriculum, and how the changing landscape of the job market and other social and political shifts intersect with schooling. Alison Jones' (1991) *At school I've got a chance* is another powerful example that uses Bourdieu to explore the intersection of social class and ethnicity in a school in New Zealand, demonstrating how these structure academic success for Pacific Island girls in very different ways to their White peers. Jones' (1991) study also exemplifies how a Bourdieusian theoretical framework can be broadened beyond social class to include, for example, ethnicity, language, gender, and sexuality as key variables in the ongoing entrenchment of educational and wider economic and social dis/advantage, along with any associated resistance to these forces.

Lois Weis (1985) captures these interests and tensions in the United States when she describes the student cultures in her critical ethnographic study of Black and other minority students in a local US community college as "semiautonomous", arguing that they "arise in relation to structural conditions mediated by both the experience of schooling and the lived experiences of youth in their own communities" (p. 219). In another important contribution, Michelle Fine (1991) examined the racism directed at African American students as a key contributing factor to their disproportionate dropout rates from school. Subsequently, Weis and Fine have both been influential in critically examining the links between educational disadvantage, poverty, and the related impact of neoliberalism and deindustrialization (see e.g., Fine & Weis, 1998).

Bourdieu's theory continues to be used productively in a range of education critical ethnographies (e.g., Fahey et al., 2015a, 2015b; Fitzpatrick, 2013; Forbes & Lingard, 2015; Grenfell & Pahl, 2018; Stahl, 2017; Weis et al., 2014; Windle & Nogueira, 2015). One of the reasons it continues to have such salience is because the theory is deeply relational and critical ethnographers, like those listed earlier, necessarily interrogate any particular research site in terms of how it is interconnected with and to other sites and spaces (Bourdieu & Wacquant, 1992). A prominent recent example is the *Elite schools project* undertaken by Jane Kenway and colleagues. This project was a five-year (2010–2014) multi-sited global ethnography exploring how elite schools in a range of different places engage in the reproduction of privilege and access to educational capital (see Fahey et al., 2015a; Kenway & Koh, 2015; Kenway & McCarthy, 2017). The project included one school each in England, Australia, Barbados, Hong Kong, India, Singapore, South Africa, Cyprus, and Argentina. The researchers note that:

> Studying multiple schools in multiple countries that share a common status as elite schools means that we are able to consider a complex of "small societies" across the globe and the ways in which they sustain each other, but also contemplate the ways in which these small societies are interdependent with a world beyond the school gates: with their localities, their regions and with contemporary globalization.
>
> *(Fahey et al., 2015b, p. 8)*

Example 1: Jane Kenway and Aaron Koh (Pierre Bourdieu; Transnationalism)

As part of their wider research project on elite schooling and globalization, Kenway and Koh (2013) report on ethnographic fieldwork they conducted in an elite high school in Singapore, known by the pseudonym "Clarence High". They do so by drawing on Bourdieu's (1996) analysis of how institutionalized state and educational support mechanisms – in particular, elite schools and academies – shape and reinforce individual class and educational privilege, providing the students who attend these elite institutions with easy access subsequently to influential positions in the civil service and wider society. Bourdieu (1996) terms this almost symbiotic process one of "state nobility" although he also insists that it is not a causal relationship. Rather, it is a game, a field of power, albeit one in which the already advantaged are most likely to succeed. As he observes, a field of power is

> a gaming space in which those agents and institutions possessing enough specific capital to be able to occupy the dominant positions within their respective fields confront each other using strategies aimed at preserving or transforming their relations of power.
>
> *(p. 264)*

While Bourdieu's study is specific to France, he did suggest that its principles of elite replication could be portable to other contexts. Kenway and Koh (2013) do precisely this in their analysis – applying Bourdieu's analysis of state nobility and fields of power to Singapore. They highlight how elite schools like Clarence High are situated within and responsive to the imperatives set in the wider social and political context – particularly, the emphasis placed by Singapore's longstanding ruling political party on technical and scientific knowledge as the basis for Singapore's expanding economy and international/transnational influence. As Wacquant observes in his Foreword in Bourdieu (1996), Bourdieu sees the school as "the state's most potent conduit and servant" (p. 7). This is certainly so in Singapore's schooling system, which is characterized by hyper-competition and rigid tracking/streaming, both underpinned by extensive testing from elementary school onward. This leads to the clear stratification of schools by prestige/academic success/curriculum focus, with schools like Clarence High at its apogee, since only the top 5% of students academically are admitted to it from elementary schools.

Kenway and Koh explore the role Clarence High has then in the consecration of wider social hierarchies in Singapore via Bourdieu's notion of "social alchemy". For Bourdieu, such schools are involved in acts of consecration that are aimed at producing a "separate sacred group". In so doing, they act as both producers of "distinction" and agents of "ritual exclusion" (of others) (1996, p. 74). In their ethnographic work, Kenway and Koh also highlight how both teachers and students at Clarence High see the school as an "incubator of excellence" and the students as especially "gifted" – gaining entry via (individual) merit. Much like Bourdieu's analysis of the French system, however, Kenway and Koh note that this sense of giftedness is self-confirming. As Bourdieu (1996) observes of this:

> The tag of gifted tends to produce a consecrated elite, one that is not only distinctive and separate but also recognized by others and by itself as worthy of being so. Students are distinguished from the commonplace and come to know and feel that they are destined for greatness.
>
> *(p. 103)*

Consequently, there is considerable emphasis on high level, intense competition within Clarence High, albeit in a broad-based, engaging curriculum. As Kenway and Koh (2013) note:

> Throughout the students' school career the focus is on winning; winning awards within the school, within the elite schools sector and in any national- or international-based competition, for example, maths, science and chemistry Olympiads. The school instils a will to win and this is accompanied by a sense of intensity and urgency. Like Bourdieu's elite schools, Clarence "turns students" life into a competition placed under the sign of urgency.
>
> *(p. 283)*

There are clear and obvious parallels drawn by Kenway and Koh throughout their ethnography with respect to Bourdieu's (1996) earlier analysis. However, they also extend his analysis by focusing on the significance of transnationalism in/to the Singaporean context. This is evident in Clarence High's curriculum, which includes students' involvement in education programs provided for them outside of Singapore. As Kenway and Koh observe, "[t]hese study trips provide extended opportunities to learn, and also to develop transnational social and cultural capital" (2013, pp. 282–283). Here they specifically differentiate their own study from Bourdieu's – noting that while "Bourdieu's elite schools were national to their core", Clarence High "has national roots but a very global outlook" (p. 287). As they conclude: "[Clarence High] knows that the capitals with the greatest exchange rate in Singapore's field of power are not to be found in Singapore alone. . . . Clarence [thus] seeks to develop transnational capitals *for* the national field of power" (p. 287).

Kenway and Koh (2013) are not the only Bourdieusian analysis in this wider research project on elite schools internationally – see, for example, Forbes and Lingard's (2015) study of an elite Scottish girls' school and Windle and Nogueira's (2015) study of schooling for Brazilian elites. But it is a very clear example of the application of Bourdieusian theory to (critical) ethnography, along with its expansion and rearticulation in a postcolonial Asian context, quite different from Bourdieu's own original French national context – highlighting the portability (and limits) of Bourdieu's theoretical reach and application.

While those undertaking Bourdieusian studies have continued to look beyond social class, other critical ethnographers have taken up theories that employ intersectionality more directly, along with critical race theory, in conversation with gender.

Interdisciplinary and Intersectional Ethnographies of Education

The close involvement of critical ethnographers and their active collaboration with their research communities is another important feature of critical ethnographies in education. As Palmer and Caldas (2017) observe, Carspecken (1991, 1996) and May (1994) – Stephen's critical ethnography of Richmond Road School (see Chapter 6) – provide examples of critical, collaborative, and engaged school and community accounts. Stephen – and later Monica Heller (2006) and Django Paris (2011) – also provide overtly interdisciplinary critical ethnographies, bridging education, critical multiculturalism, critical race theory, and sociolinguistics in their examinations of minoritized language practices among students in both liberatory and oppressive spaces in schools in New Zealand, Canada, and the United States, respectively. Gender and sexuality have also been a key focus of critical ethnographies in education, including Mac an Ghaill's (1994) powerful exploration of the construction of masculinities and sexualities in schooling in Britain (another critical counterpoint to Willis), Debbie Epstein's ethnographic work on masculinities and femininities in schools (Epstein et al., 2001; Epstein & Johnson, 1998), and C. J. Pascoe's (2007) examination of these issues from a US perspective. Deborah Youdell's (2005) work on the performance of gender and sexuality at school in the United Kingdom, and Jessica Fields's (2008) account of sexuality education in the United States are other important examples (see further discussion of these in Chapter 7).

More recent critical ethnographic work in education has extended its methodological engagement even further by providing intersectional analyses that foreground the complexities and interrelationships among a wide range of variables, including class, ethnicity, gender and sexuality, and youth culture, rather than privileging one over the other. Daniel Yon (2000; see Example 2) draws on cultural studies and postcolonialism to explore students' hybrid identities. Katie's critical ethnography, *Critical pedagogy, physical education, and urban schooling* (Fitzpatrick, 2013), examines how young people in New Zealand experience schooling at the intersection of ethnicity and place, gender, and social class, and how each of these identity positions cohere to create particular life trajectories. Kustatscher (2017) explores the role of emotion in the social identities of children at the intersection of ethnicity, race, nationality, class, gender, and culture in a Scottish primary school. Qin and Li (2020) provide a further example from the United States, through the intersection of race, gender, and language in the racialized masculinities of high school migrants. This more expansive emphasis on intersectionality has been allied with an increasing focus on the role and influence of the researcher in critical ethnographic accounts of education, a move that is also apparent in feminist and poststructuralist informed ethnographies.

Example 2: Daniel Yon: Elusive Culture (Homi Bhabha, Hybridity, Postcolonialism)

In his critical ethnographic study, *Elusive Culture: Schooling, race and identity in global times*, Daniel Yon (2000) adopts a postcolonial reading as his primary theoretical frame. The study is located in a diverse Toronto school where Yon attended English classes and set up group discussions with students. He draws predominantly on the work of Homi Bhabha (1994), particularly the notion of hybridity, and applies this frame to explore the multiple identity positions of youth in the school. Bhabha argues that hybrid identities are a form of resistance to colonial power. Hybridity provides a way to explain how individuals do not have a unified singular self but rather a multiplicity, a plurality of subjectivities in constant fluid articulation. Hybridity is, at once, a result of power structures and the basis for multiple creative and contested responses to them. From this, Bhabha argues that moments of oppression can actually be productive.

Following Bhabha, Yon thus challenges essentialist notions of culture and provides examples of the diverse and creative ways the young people in his critical ethnographic study actively assert their identities:

> The youths' identity claims . . . go in multiple directions. These youth are aware of the representations and the stereotypes through which their various cultural identities are made, and nearly always refuse to be seen as the passive objects of imagined racial and cultural identities . . . the making of racial identities is a two directional process: In the process of claiming who one is, one is also announcing who one is not.
>
> *(p. 102)*

Yon emphasizes the contested and fluid nature of identity and the contradictions the youth in his study embraced. He argues that the student relationships and their visible cultural enunciations are not necessarily aligned with their claimed identity/s. Rather than becoming "identity confused", he contends that these youth actively embrace contradiction and reject fixed categories of culture, race, ethnicity, and gender. Indeed, his students employ identity positions strategically in social situations. Yon concludes that culture is elusive, "an ongoing process attuned to the ambivalent and contradictory processes of everyday life" (p. 123). Yon's use of hybridity theory here privileges agency and multiple identities. The social theory of Bhabha thus allows Yon to move beyond explanations of structural racism to highlight the complex articulations of power evident in the school.

Parallel Developments in Feminist (and) Poststructuralist Ethnography

The way we have described the history of critical ethnography in education is inevitably only one reading of it (see also, e.g., Foley & Valenzuela, 2005; Noblit et al., 2004; Quantz, 1992). And these developments didn't occur in isolation. At the same time, other theoretical and methodological moves were afoot in line with poststructuralist theory, and especially the work of Foucault, Butler, Derrida, and Deleuze, among others. This work intersected strongly with critical ethnographies of schooling. But it also took its own pathway, as some critical researchers moved strongly toward gender analyses via feminist ethnography and poststructuralist ethnography. Some continuing in the neo-Marxist traditions of critical ethnography tended to ignore the significant methodological challenges of feminist work and its attention to gender; meanwhile those engaging with poststructuralism found themselves in an uneasy relationship with the term "critical". Lather (2001a), for example, explained that what she called the "new ethnography" emerged from a literary turn in the 1980s, along with related concerns with issues of reflexivity, textuality, and dissatisfaction with realist forms of writing. This was a move toward "partial and fluid epistemological and cultural assumptions, fragmented writing styles, and troubled notions of ethnographic legitimacy" (2001a, p. 201). For Lather,

> [f]eminist work both challenged and built on this move, particularly in terms of a sense of failed promises, charged anxieties, and a "self-abjection" at the limit, as a way to live on in the face of the loss of legitimating metanarratives.
>
> *(p. 201)*

Youdell likewise notes that "[p]ost-structural ethnography has also troubled ethnography, moving from concerns with authenticity and reciprocity to processes of subjectivation in research and representation" (2010, p. 92).

Example 3: Deborah Youdell (Michel Foucault, Judith Butler, Gilles Deleuze, and Felix Guattari)

Youdell's (2005) critical ethnographic study of gender at a high school in South London, England, is an excellent example of how the social theory of Butler and Foucault can be applied to empirical materials and analyses. Building at the time on a tradition of ethnographic inquiry into gender and schooling in the United

Kingdom, Youdell explores embodied and complex gendered performances. She explains the theoretical framework as:

> [U]nderpinned by Foucault's understanding of power, discourse and subjectivation. . . . [It] engages extensively with Judith Butler's work with these ideas [and] takes up Butler's understanding of the subjectivated subject who is simultaneously rendered a subject and opened up to relations of power. . . . [The approach also] takes up Butler's assertion that with subjection comes discursive agency and, therefore, the possibility of a politics of performative resignification.
>
> *(p. 252)*

The theory highlights the double-bind of performing gender at school, the way that discourses shape gendered subjectivities, and the limits of possibility for the young people in the school. Youdell (2005) notes that the students draw on different resources to *perform* gender and sexuality, while they are also subject to:

> [D]iscursive demands . . . that open up different possibilities and impose different constraints for sex – gender – sexualities. For instance, the analysis shows how working class girls deploy significant discursive resources to navigate a virgin/whore dichotomy even as their discursive practices are implicated in its inscription. It shows how this discourse takes on new forms as girls struggle to tease out third space . . . that allows heterosexual feminine desire within the context of a mainstream working class youth subculture, even as such a subjectivity is rendered unintelligible by the terms of this dichotomy.
>
> *(p. 267)*

The Foucauldian and Butlerian analyses provide a poststructuralist reading of the ethnographic fieldwork that, in turn, leads Youdell to a nuanced analysis of performance. Butler's heterosexual matrix is reimagined as a sex-gender-sexuality constellation whereby each category signifies the other.

In more recent work (Youdell & Armstrong, 2011), Youdell moves with Foucault and Butler to a new materialist analysis of the emotional geographies of schooling by adding Deleuzian theory and focusing on space. This shifts the locus of analysis away from the individual subject and body "to a concern with bodies as amalgam and an analysis that foregrounds collectivities and the event – an 'anti-subjectivation' stance, in effect" (Youdell & Armstrong, 2011, p. 144).

Youdell and Armstrong reflect on two "events" from their earlier work, one is an autobiographical description of a confrontation on a school trip and the other a "tussle" over seats at a special school in 2008. They revisit these moments using Deleuze's notion of assemblage which highlights how "apparently 'whole' entities, such as societies or institutions, might be understood as assemblages of heterogeneous components that crosscut state, social, representational, discursive, subjective and affective orders" (p. 144). This Deleuzian theory then places greater emphasis on the flow of power (desire) between bodies (which can be animate or inanimate) and leads them to focus on the affective flows (rather than a subject's feelings). Youdell and Armstrong explain that: "Thinking about affectivity in this way invites us to think beyond the subject's rational (or irrational) ideas, actions or feelings. Instead, it is the affective flows of the event that are fore-grounded" (p. 145).

Youdell and Armstrong's use of theory clearly drives the analysis and allows the researchers to engage with ethnography in different ways. In terms of the kind of critical questions being asked – in this example in relation to gender, sexuality, and spaces of schooling – the advancement of theory also allows the researchers to see and notice particular methodological implications, linking theory inextricably to practice as well as research positionalities. In particular, they argue that the theoretical approach allows them to show how lines of flight and affective flows "scatter" and disrupt the educational assemblage.

The critical ethnographic project of "giving voice to the voiceless" was also challenged by poststructuralism's repositioning of representation and subjectivity. Commenting on cultural studies ethnography, Van Loon argued that "[t]he feminist intervention in cultural studies could thus be seen as, on the one hand, engendering a generic interest in 'lived experiences', and on the other hand, a politicization of researching these experiences" (2001, p. 277). Van Loon further noted that poststructuralism drew attention to the connections between "subjectivity and identity as profoundly (con)textual and historiographical" so that:

> [N]o identity is ever simply "present" or "given"; all identities are temporal and symbolic constructions that engage in determining boundaries and establish relationships (between selves and others). These boundaries may be discursively presented as "fixed"; however the complexity of everyday life processes of "identification" inevitably reveals their deeply permeable and unstable character.
>
> *(p. 278)*

Deborah Britzman's (2003) critical ethnography of learning to be a high school teacher in the United States asks important questions about the intersection of critical ethnography and poststructuralist thinking. She notes that "while educational ethnography promises the narrative cohesiveness of experience and identity and the researcher's skill of representing the subject, poststructuralist theories disrupt any desire for a seamless narrative, a cohesive identity, or a mimetic representation" (2003, p. 247). Her focus on uncertainty and vulnerability assists this and she notes that underlying her project "are the assumptions that meaning is historically contingent, contextually bound, socially constructed, and always problematic" (p. 34). Poststructuralist accounts then "define ethnography as both a set of practices and a set of discourses" so that the "ground upon which ethnography is built turns out to be a contested and fictive geography" (p. 244). For Britzman, poststructuralist ethnographers "read the absent against the present" so that the

> promise of a holistic account is betrayed by the slippage born from the partiality of language – of what cannot be said precisely because of what is said, and of the impossible difference within what is said, what is intended, what is signified, what is repressed, what is taken, and what remains.
>
> *(p. 244)*

In another example, Youdell (2010) reflects on the place of queer (theory, subjectivities, imaginings) in her own ethnographic practice. She calls this "post-structurally-informed ethnography" (p. 89) and she employs this to revisit an earlier ethnographic project, drawing on the psychoanalytic notion of the "uncanny". She also engages Pillow's (2003) "uncomfortable reflexivity" to contest the latent assumption that reflexivity can act to neutralize power relations (see Chapter 4). Youdell (2010) engages therein in a process of "re-encountering" her interactions with a research participant, "Molly" and, in so doing, she also re-encounters herself – as student, educator, researcher, and queer subject:

> A series of re-encounters is evident in my struggle to find ways to engage with telling these stories. I re-encounter Molly and myself in my encounters with her; I re-encounter the school and its discursive regulation; I re-encounter myself early in my academic career, convinced by queer theory and concerned to "get it right"; I encounter myself in the present, now an established academic, still committed to but more questioning of queer theory and struggling against the abiding struggle to "get it right"; and I encounter a spectre of myself at secondary school, among a cluster of girls in corners and corridors where some secrets were told keenly and others were as keenly silenced and where we struggled to get our punk/new-wave cool "right" without ever really giving up on the hetero-femininity that we claimed to despise.
>
> *(p. 93)*

This is an exemplar of Lather's (2001a) suggestion that researchers employ "the concept of doubled practices . . . that might be of use in negotiating the tensions between the political imperative of feminism to make women's experiences visible and poststructuralism's critiques of representation" (p. 199). Youdell (2010) engages such doubled practices at the intersection of critical ethnography and poststructuralism in a move that exemplifies these shifts and the related challenges that poststructuralist feminist work brought to (critical) ethnography. Lather suggests that feminist poststructuralism thus allowed a move from the realist writing that initially dominated such ethnographic work to a more "interrogative" text, reflecting "the epistemological paradox of knowing through not knowing" (2001a; p. 205). Britzman, Lather, and Youdell, all simultaneously disrupt their own textual and interpretive practices, even while engaging with them and continuing to write through and with them. Britzman (2003) encourages reading (and writing) "with suspicion" so that textual practices, contingent identities, and assumptions about representation are disrupted and held in messy tension. All three also engage messy and overlapping temporalities that disrupt any "stable" ethnographic narrative (see Chapter 5).

The ontological challenges foregrounded in feminist (and) poststructuralist work are further complexified in relation to postcolonial and Black feminist writings, critical race theory (see Chapter 6), and the challenges and extensions brought by writers in posthumanism and new materialism. We discuss the latter shortly but first consider what work labeled "postcritical ethnography" has to offer to these broader developments in, and articulations with, critical ethnographic work.

Postcritical Ethnography, Critical Race Theory (CRT), and Postcolonial Theory

Postcritical ethnographers focused on acknowledging the sometimes overly deterministic use of theory in earlier critical ethnographic work. They emphasized instead the contingencies of context, situatedness, and in particular, the construction of knowledge, along with the inevitably partial, positional, and personal representations of (and in) their own critical accounts (Anders, 2019; Clifford & Marcus, 1986; Lather, 2007; Noblit, 2003). As Anders usefully summarizes, "[t]here were no conclusions in post-critical work; understandings were always contingent on context, one's biography and community. . . . Power and history worked through ethnography . . . and always present was incommensurability between experience and representation" (2019, p. 7). Anders notes that, in postcritical ethnography, the "post" rejects stable positions and unified accounts. However, she also points out that this recognition of "the importance of reflexivity, positionality, or the contingencies of context, situatedness . . . and the particular . . . in knowledge production" (p. 6) has long been recognized by African American, Latinx, feminist, post/neocolonial, critical race, and critical race feminist scholars. The likes of Donna Haraway, W.E.B. Du Bois, Gloria Anzaldúa, Derrick Bell, Franz Fanon, and Kimberlé Crenshaw "had [all] understood their significance" and in so doing "confronted, resisted, and delegitimated white,

Anglo, settler-colonial and colonial, cis-heteronormative, patriarchal, positivist Western histories and discourses" (Anders, 2019, p. 6). The important legacy of this work, and its ongoing challenge to these power-laden normativities, can be seen, for example, in more recent developments in critical race theory and BlackCrit.

Example 4: Justin Coles (BlackCrit, Black Lit, Critical Race Ethnography)

Coles (2019, 2020, 2022) undertook what he refers to as an urban BlackCrit ethnography in a Philadelphia high school. The principal focus of his study was the dynamic use of student participants' Black language and literacy practices, exploring these as a means of contesting the organizing role of antiblackness in their educational and societal lives. Situated broadly within critical race theory (CRT), Coles, nonetheless, extends previous work in CRT in a number of key ways.

First, he argues that BlackCrit provides a more specific framework than CRT's more generalized concern with race and racism. For example, his use of Black-Crit ethnography, developed by Dumas and ross (2016), extends the notion of critical race ethnography that was first outlined by Duncan (2005) and described as "the analysis of the various ontological categories that inform the way race functions as a stratifying force in school and society, as one measure to build around and advance the rich corpus of CRT studies in education" (p. 95). For Coles, BlackCrit allows him to analyze education in the United States for Black youths, through a specific Black lens – highlighting "how antiblackness serves to reinforce the ideological and material 'infrastructure' of educational inequity – the misrecognition of students and communities of color, and the (racialized) maldistribution of educational resources" (Dumas and ross, 2016, p. 432).

Coles' focus on antiblackness via the Black language and literacy practices of his students also extends CRT in new interdisciplinary directions. As he observes:

> Given their unique social positioning and identities, Black urban youth experience antiblackness and thus it is not necessarily something that they find difficult to talk about or strive to imagine as out of sight. Through the uniqueness of their experiences, Black youth have the power to lead the charge in critically examining their conditions.
>
> *(Coles, 2019, pp. 5–6).*

In this, Coles draws on the work of Yamamoto's (1997) concept of "critical race praxis", the central organizing ideal of which "is that racial justice requires antisubordination practice . . . justice is something experienced through practice" (pp. 829–830). As Coles (2022) argues, critical race praxis focuses on how the youth actually *experience*, not just imagine, justice through the process of centering their lived realities in order to understand and resist antiblackness. In so doing, Coles also extends the use of counter-storying in CRT to one of Black storywork (see also Chapter 6):

> I define Black storywork as the individual or collective stories, which emerge from the lived experiences of Black people and communities that uses Black knowledge/s as a tool to extend and author oneself beyond the conditions of anti-Blackness. Here, Black storywork captures the youth's critical collective storying rooted in their own words to bridge the contradictions between their lived experiences and distorted anti-Black narratives.
> *(Coles, 2020, p. 4)*

Such storywork, he argues, is characterized by a combination of collective storying layered with dialogue, freestyle rapping, writing, reading, drawing images, sharing photos, clothing (e.g., #BlackLivesMatter shirts), social media posts, and dancing (Coles, 2022). As he concludes, his pairing of BlackCrit (a Black-specific Race Crit) aims to disrupt the silences of Black youth voice, via their languages and literacies, thus proving to be a theoretically and methodologically sound pairing for continuing the work of youth voice in critical race scholarship.

Lather (2007) describes postcritical ethnography as a process of not being sure, of remaining with ambiguity and uncertainty, of being slow to make claims, as "the performance of practices of not-knowing" (p. 7). Lather understands such an approach to knowledge in the "aftermath of poststructuralism" as a "less comfortable social science" (p. 4) and she argues for researchers to engage in a methodology of "getting lost" to both take seriously the epistemological demands of poststructuralism and its predecessors, and to re-engage with the messiness and uncertainty of research in contemporary times.

As is apparent here, much of this work overlaps with poststructuralist-informed ethnographic accounts but, crucially, some postcritical ethnographers moved to engage more directly with the silences of ethnicity, race, and racism apparent in the field. Lather (2007) notes that the postcritical opens a space between poststructuralism and postcolonialism that isn't easily reconciled. Indeed, she argues elsewhere for it not to be reconciled. Rather, "[t]he move is . . . to endorse complexity, partial truths and multiple subjectivities. Such tensions surface the uneasy interface between the post of post-colonialism and the post of post-structuralism" (2001b, 484). The tension then lies in the tendency for the postcolonial to "retain a referential purchase on oppositional truth-claims while simultaneously drawing on the poststructural suspicion of the referent in order to deconstruct colonial power", while the poststructuralist "wants to historicize all truth-claims, opposi-tional or not" (p. 484).

Postcritical ethnographers went about unearthing and working with these ten-sions in productive ways, while some explored more directly how the postcolo-nial theories of Bhabha (1994) and Young (2001), among others, might work in ethnographic studies (e.g., Yon, 2000; Urrieta & Martínez, 2011; Chimbutane, 2011; see also Gonzalez, 2003). Gonzalez argued that "postcolonial ethnography . . . is not merely an act of defiance, but one of great courage" because via such an inquiry "[o]ne's 'buy in' to the colonial systems of costs and rewards is tested" (2003, p. 81). Cruz Banks (2010), for example, undertook just such a postcolonial ethnography by exploring how a dance program in the United States drew on West African dance as part of a decolonizing, critical pedagogy project, observ-ing that: "West African dance puts forward an epistemology of dance with edu-cational purposes different from those associated with Western styles of dance. Study of West African dance is a case of dance education in a dialectical relation-ship with colonial power" (p. 19).

In their introduction to postcritical approaches to ethnography, Noblit et al. (2004) argue that one of the catalysts for the development of critical ethnography was the troubled relationship between critical social theory (which was accused of lacking a method) and ethnography (which was accused of being overly func-tional and insufficiently scientific). At that time, they noted that a group of US scholars were examining critical ethnography and its blind spots, in particular, its lack of attention to issues of race, marginality (in a postcolonial sense), and its reinforcement of Western imperialisms. Murillo (1999), for example, had already questioned the complicity of ethnographers in forwarding colonial agendas and failing to question their privilege and tendency to "othering". Murillo offered instead a postcritical (postcolonial) ethnographic approach to self as other, a conversation between postcolonialism and postmodernism, and an engagement with borderlands and marginalities, by repurposing the notion of *mojado* (wet-back) – a term for Mexicans crossing the US border. Given these developments, Noblit et al. (2004) propose a move toward postcritical ethnography, although they admit this is not coherent or easily defined, but rather an eclectic critical space. For them, "postcritical ethnography is neither a rejection of critique nor of ethnography. Rather the many different critical ethnographies are reinscrip-tions of critique in ethnography" (p. 3). They nonetheless assert that theory and method must be seen as inseparable so that issues of representation, subjectivity, and reflexivity are woven through a theory-method nexus in any postcritical eth-nography (see also Chapter 5).

Postcritical ethnographers, like feminist poststructuralists, reject the idea of stable identities, along with the idea of the all-knowing subject. For this reason, actions, statements, and wider social contexts are always interrogated by and in relation to each other. Temporalities can be engaged (see Youdell, 2010) so that interactions can be revisited, repeated, reimagined, and retheorized. These critical ethnographers also interrogate how their own constructions and fieldwork practices are an articulation of subjectivity, as well as how the sites they research are sociohistorically and sociopolitically constructed, contingent, and changing. As Anders observes, "[c]ritical ethnography required ethnographers to identify and reflect on their own value systems in relation to the design and production of their work and on their own authorial power in the practice of doing, interpreting, and representing research" (2019, p. 5). Lather (2007) notes that easily demarcated notions of power are disrupted in postcritical work. Notions of emancipation and liberation (which were mainstays of previous critical work), for example, are dismantled in favor of a more nuanced and complex engagement with multiple relations of power. She also notes, however, that such a move "may have more to do with the end of some speaking for others than the end of liberatory struggle" (pp. 6–7). Still, it remains clear that the sensibility required is "that which shakes any assured ontology of the 'real', of presence and absence, a postcritical logic of haunting and undecidables" (p. 6).

Postcritical work, along with feminist poststructuralism, usefully continues to inform and expand critical ethnographic research. That said, such approaches have also been challenged more recently by scholars working to bring materialities and the more-than-human into ethnographic research inquiries. Spaces have thus now opened for new materialist and posthuman (critical) ethnographic work as well.

New Materialisms, Posthuman Ethnography, and the Challenges of the Post-Qualitative

Scholars drawing on posthumanism and new materialisms have recently combined these theoretical moves with ethnography to explore education contexts. For Lather, the "new" in new materialism "is the ontological insistence on the weight of the material and a relational ontology that transverses binaries" (2016, p. 100). In relation to posthumanism, the work of Rosi Braidotti (2013) has been particularly influential. Braidotti explains that:

> The common denominator for the posthuman condition is an assumption about the vital, self-organizing and yet non-naturalistic structure of living matter itself. This nature – culture continuum is the shared starting point for my take on posthuman theory.
>
> (p. 2)

Thinking with Braidotti, Lather (2016) reflects on how new materialisms and posthumanist thinking impacts methodologies:

> [T]hese methodological perspectives range across what Braidotti lists as deconstructive, post-anthropocentric, post-constructionist, the new

empiricism, critical posthumanism, new feminist materialism, "after" actor-network theory . . . new science studies, neo-Foucauldian bio-politics, and the neo-humanism of global post-colonialism.

(p. 99)

New materialisms and posthumanism are shorthand for a wide range of work with varied theoretical commitments. Work from these fields, while diverse, does intervene in ethnography in two important ways. It questions human exceptionalism and anthropocentrism, while shifting the ontological gaze to the agency of things and more-than-human subjectivities. In so doing, ethnography's positioning as "a research endeavour which secures ontological and epistemological privilege for humans" and which "privileges certain forms of knowledge and some knowers over others" (Taylor & Fairchild, 2020, p. 512) is called into question. Geerts and Carstens (2019, p. 917) suggest that, in education, this requires us "to venture beyond the narrow confines of how the exclusivist ideality and materiality of our being-human has been thought and taught".

These theories have the potential to threaten the very basis of ethnographic research or, alternatively, to expand and change it. We argue, along with others, that a focus on the more-than-human and on materialities – exploring the "nature – culture continuum" (Braidotti, 2013, p. 2) – can be consonant with critical ethnography. Even more, it can enhance ethnography and open new modes of inquiry and new ethical questions. As discussed in Chapter 1, critical ethnographers have always looked beyond the (individual) speaking subject and, instead, have attended to how cultures, politics, environments, and histories intersect in complex ways in any given research site. Materialities and non-human actors can be foci of critical ethnography if and when the ontological positioning of the project is expansive enough. New materialist ethnographies in education are discussed further, by way of example, in Chapter 7; here we briefly consider examples of posthuman educational ethnography and how these are expanding critical ethnographic work in the field.

Posthuman Ethnography

Pedersen and Pini (2017) admit:

Many of us will not quite know how to let go of our familiar "humanist" concepts, approaches, ontologies, and thoughts, most of which carry the epistemological promise that the world is accessible for us as researchers and possible to understand and conceptualize as a source of endless scientific knowledge production and accumulation.

(p. 1051)

Posthuman ethnography requires such a shift. Hamilton and Taylor (2017) argue that "the reality is that the animals themselves tend to be written out of the story by humans, particularly if one uses traditional, human-centered methods to try and understand human – animal relations" (p. 2). For them, the ontological shift required of ethnographers is from "a tendency to consider what other species mean to humans" toward "considering or seeking to understand how humans and animals co-constitute the world" (p. 2). Many researchers draw on a common worlds approach – that combines the work of Latour (2005) with Donna Haraway's (2003, 2004, 2008) "queer kin" work on species and border crossings (Somerville, 2020). Such an approach "starts from the assumption of entanglement, disavowing 'pure' categories of human and animal, or social and natural, to recognize that we share common worlds that are collectively made, and that we impact one another intersubjectively" (Hamilton & Taylor, 2017, p. 182).

A number of posthuman approaches have since emerged, including posthuman ethnography, zooethnography, and multispecies ethnography. Multsipecies ethnography, for example, is defined by Kirksey and Helmreich (2010, p. 545; see also Locke, 2018) as ethnographies that center "on how a multitude of organisms' livelihoods shape and are shaped by political, economic, and cultural forces". Hamilton and Taylor (2017) argue against narrow definitions and use a range of terms to explore the interconnections between animals and humans in ethnographic research. However, they insist that such work must rearticulate away from human-centered storytelling and animal-human binaries, and, crucially, engage with the ethics of animal research, thus attending to asymmetrical power relations and actively working against routine animal abuse. They argue that researchers engaging posthuman ethnography can "engage physically, discursively and emotionally with those under investigation" and move from "seeing research 'objects' to seeing – and often working alongside – research 'subjects'" (p. 10).

Example 5: Helena Pedersen: Posthuman Ethnography, Zooethnography

Helena Pedersen (2013) explores veterinary education and asks, "what becomes of education when performed in a slaughterhouse?" (p. 717). She explores the "routine violence nonhumans are exposed to in a society where their bodies are viewed as raw material for capitalist expansion and economic growth" (p. 717). Pedersen's portrayal of the slaughterhouse for cows and pigs is evocative and atmospheric. She describes walking with students along a path in the same direction as the cows, close by in their journeys toward being killed, and she analyzes this experience along lines of power as species differentiation:

> Physically, the distance between us is only a few decimeters, but in all respects this distance equals the perimeter of Earth minus these decimeters.

We and the cows enter parallel universes. The radical species-coded separation, demarcating who of us will be killed at the end of the line and
who will not, makes the momentary intimacy between us and them appear
almost obscene.

(p. 723)

Pedersen offers an emotive and detailed account of animal production, of life and
death at the hands of consumerism and capitalism. Of the production of meat
in the momentary experiences of animal death, and the complicity of humans
(including herself) in such practices. This posthuman ethnography is deeply critical, challenging the role of educators in silencing critique, of de-emotionalizing
students, to the treatment of animals:

Violence does not become educationalized simply when education syn-
chronizes with and follows parallel routes and circuits of the animal production system. It also requires specific acts of intervention at crucial moments
and nodes of convergence. These are acts that can be performed when
the veterinarian teacher assumes the role of "professional neutralizer" by
affirming and accommodating student emotional responses to what is done
to the animals, and comforting them by being by their side as a reliable and
trusted authority.

(p. 726)

Pedersen imagines this study as an ethnography (or zooethnography) approaching a post-qualitative approach to research, which she also troubles as it articulates
in difficult ways with the post-qualitative arguments of St. Pierre and Lather (see
Chapter 2). For example, she notes that, in her own study, there is

[A] total mismatch between modes of analysis and subjective reality. Field
notes have been engaged in vital and open-ended ways, but there is no
coherence whatsoever between this vital open-endedness and the conditions researched. They are separate and incompatible realities. This is part
of what I have referred to as the impossibility of zooethnographic representation – our infinite ontological distance from the animals. There are no
Deleuzian lines of flight in a slaughterhouse.

(p. 728)

Drawing on Lather, she notes that her study was "not a space where 'data get
lived' rather, 'data die' with their bovine research subjects, or, more accurately, are
slaughtered, dismembered, and fragmented together with them" (p. 728). This
account seems to be the kind of uncertain social science that Lather argues for. It
is also an example of what critical ethnographic research looks like when brought

into a serious consideration with posthuman ontologies, the limitations of (human) social theory, and the ethical affective landscapes of (critical) ethnographic research.

A number of researchers are engaging productively with various forms of post-human ethnography in education, attending directly to power relations, issues of in/justice (including animal justice and planetary justice). As well as Pederson's (2010, 2013) work, Nxumalo and Pacini-Ketchabaw (2017) explore engagements between insects and children in a childcare center in the United States and argue for a relational ethics when educational institutions enact pet pedagogies. Like-wise, Taylor and Pacini-Ketchabaw's (2015) research encounters between young children and worms in British Columbia, and ants in Australia, to argue that such encounters can show how "paying close attention to our mortal entanglements and vulnerabilities with other species, no matter how small, can help us to learn with other species and rethink our place in the world" (p. 507, see also Taylor & Pacini-Ketchabaw, 2017; Taylor et al., 2013). Lloro-Bidart's (2018) study explores the agency of birds through feminist posthumanist notions of performativity and intersectionality. These few examples (for a discussion of others, see Harris & Holman Jones, 2022; Jokinen & Nordstrom, 2020; Somerville, 2020) show that there is significant potential for productive engagement and an expansion of criti-cal ethnography in education when researchers shift their ontological inquir-ies and question the human-centric nature of research. We end this chapter by considering what critical ethnography might learn from recent debates in post-qualitative inquiry.

What Can (Critical) Ethnography Learn From the Post-Qualitative?

Recent work in post-qualitative inquiry also has important implications for criti-cal ethnography. In this section, we briefly consider what critical ethnography can learn methodologically from the theoretical challenges that the post-qualitative is currently bringing to the field of qualitative inquiry. It is important to note that we are not arguing that critical ethnography is a post-qualitative methodology. But we do think that engaging with post-qualitative debates and thinking can be productive for rethinking and expanding critical ethnography along the lines that we are proposing in this book.

As noted in Chapter 2, recent developments in post-qualitative inquiry have disrupted thinking in qualitative research. There are several parts to this challenge but, in essence, post-qualitative researchers argue that poststructuralist theory and qualitative methods as they have developed are ontologically inconsistent (St. Pierre, 2018). While qualitative methods have stayed rooted in humanism, poststructuralism has shifted thinking away from phenomenological inquiries and toward the discursive. St. Pierre explains, "I realized those two structures could not be thought together, that their ontologies and epistemologies were incompatible because of their very different descriptions of human being, language, discourse, power, agency, resistance, freedom, and so on" (2018, p. 603).

At the same time, qualitative methods have become even more prescriptive, a move that leans back toward positivistic approaches to research and truth seeking, while poststructuralist theory questions the basis of all truth claims. So, a related concern is with theory-less qualitative methods that offer a recipe approach to methods as if they are:

> [A] stand-alone, instrumental set of research practices that can be organized in different ways (e.g., grounded theory, case study, narrative "research designs"); that describes what counts as data (that which can be textualized in interview transcripts and field notes); that employs two chief methods of data collection (interviewing and observation); that describes what counts as data analysis (usually the quasi-statistical practice of coding of data); that relies heavily on a positivist validity (triangulation, bias, accuracy); that requires representation and a certain kind of representation at that (rich, thick description that assumes the transparency of language); and so on.
>
> *(St. Pierre, 2016, p. 115)*

St. Pierre observes that "this is especially true in texts published after the recent installation of scientifically-based or evidence-based research, the phenomenon that restored positivism in social science research during the first decade of the twenty-first century" (2016, p. 115; see also Lather, 2007). This argumentation leads Lather and St. Pierre (2013) to ask:

> If we cease to privilege knowing over being; if we refuse positivist and phenomenological assumptions about the nature of lived experience and the world; if we give up representational and binary logics; if we see language, the human, and the material not as separate entities mixed together but as completely imbricated "on the surface" – if we do all that and the "more" it will open up – will qualitative inquiry as we know it be possible? Perhaps not.
>
> *(pp. 629–630)*

St. Pierre (2016), furthermore, argues that there is an important ethics to poststucturalist theory – the responsibility for researchers to dismantle the essentialist human subject within themselves and to work against discourse. She concedes that "we are always being subjected even as we resist that subjection, but, nonetheless, we can be different. For that reason, we can no longer get off the hook by saying, 'this is just the way I am'" (p 112). She argues (with Butler) that we might work against repeating ourselves endlessly and, instead, see the self as less singular and more connected to others, both human and non-human, and so the "I" in humanistic research is erased in contemporary theory and gives itself over to concepts that connect and show relationality (such as assemblage, network, rhizome, discourse). St. Pierre concludes that:

> Once the "I" fails, qualitative inquiry, dependent as it is on humanism's description of human being, fails as well. Its deeply phenomenological approach . . . no longer works. The observing subject is, of course, also the knowing, speaking, inquiring subject of qualitative inquiry.
>
> *(pp. 113–114)*

The central question of post-qualitative work is how one might inquire without method. This is not what we are considering here but we are interested in how critical ethnographers can learn from post-qualitative critique, particularly the way it highlights the challenges of poststructuralism, the importance of ontology, and the direct criticism of prescriptive methods. As demonstrated earlier, in discussions of poststructuralist feminist work, many critical ethnographers question any positioning of the knowing subject and disrupt or reject binaries. Post-qualitative work then might act as a reminder to critical ethnographers to continue interrogating actions, statements, and wider social contexts in relational ways and to explore how ethnographic temporalities allow researchers to see discursive repetitions, overlaps, echoes, and inconsistencies. While some ethnographers have certainly presented their narratives as truth, there are many poststructuralist ethnographers (see earlier) who do interrogate how their own constructions and fieldwork practices are an articulation of their subjectivity, as well as how the sites they research are sociohistorically and sociopolitically constructed, contingent, and relational (see also Chapter 5). This move does not erase the "I" of qualitative inquiry, but it does call it into question, disrupting it. Lather's (2007) work is an example of poststructuralist critical ethnography that eschews claims to truth and engages in:

> [E]pistemological wrestling with representation, blurred genres and the ethics of the gaze, such a shift asks how we come to think of things this way and what would be made possible if we were to think ethnography otherwise, as a space surprised by difference into the performance of practices of not-knowing.
>
> *(p. 7)*

Lather argues that one approach to this is to unlock concepts such as "[m]eaning, reference, subjectivity, objectivity, truth, tradition, ethics" (p. 7), and free them from regulation and normalizing. These are not easy challenges for ethnography but the post-qualitative critique offers some freedoms to ethnographers to loosen the reins of ethnographic practice, freeing it from the (rule) bounds of qualitative inquiry and methods recipes – a process we elaborate on in Chapter 5. Critical ethnography, broadly conceived, has long eschewed a prescriptivist approach and thus can "play" with poststructuralist and posthumanist developments, rather than being replaced by them (e.g. Jokinen & Nordstrom, 2020; Pedersen, 2013). Post-qualitative work might encourage us to continue disrupting methodological assumptions, to reject set and rulebound pre-planned methods, to engage in dislocated temporalities, and to take an organic and responsive, relational approach to our critical ethnographic studies.

References

Anders, A. (2019). *Post-critical ethnography*. Oxford Research Encyclopedia. Oxford University Press. https://doi.org/10.1093/acrefore/9780190264093.013.342

Barad, K. (2007). *Meeting the universe halfway: Quantum physics and the entanglement of matter and meaning*. Duke University Press.

Bhabha, H. (1994). *The location of culture*. Routledge.

Blommaert, J. (2018). *Dialogues with ethnography: Notes on classics and how I read them*. Multilingual Matters.

Bourdieu P. (1996). *The state nobility: Elite schools in the field of power*. Stanford University Press.

Bourdieu, P., Chamboredon, J., & Passeron, J. (1991). *The craft of sociology: Epistemological preliminaries*. Walter de Gruyter.

Bourdieu, P., & Wacquant, L. (1992). *An invitation to reflexive sociology*. University of Chicago Press.

Braidotti, R. (2013). *The posthuman*. Polity Press.

Britzman, D. P. (2003). *Practice makes practice: A critical study of learning to teach* (Rev. ed.). State University of New York Press.

Burawoy, M. (2000). Introduction: Reaching for the global. In M. Burawoy et al. (Eds.), *Global ethnography: Forces, connections and imaginations in a postmodern world* (pp. 1–40). University of California Press.

Carspecken, P. (1991). *Community schooling and the nature of power: The battle for Croxteth comprehensive*. Routledge.

Carspecken, P. (1996). *Critical ethnography in educational research: A theoretical and practical guide*. Routledge.

Chimbutane, F. (2011). *Rethinking bilingual education in postcolonial contexts*. Multilingual Matters.

Clifford, J., & Marcus, G. E. (Eds.). (1986). *Writing culture: The poetics and politics of ethnography*. University of California Press.

Coles, J. (2019). The Black literacies of urban high school youth countering antiblackness in the context of neoliberal multiculturalism. *Journal of Language & Literacy Education, 15*(2), 1–35.

Coles, J. (2020). A BlackCrit re/imagining of urban schooling social education through Black youth enactments of Black storywork. *Urban Education*, 1–30. https://doi.org/10.1177/0042085920908919

Coles, J. (2022). Beyond silence: Disrupting antiblackness through BlackCrit ethnography and Black youth voice. In S. May & B. Caldas (Eds.), *Critical ethnography, language, race/ism and education*. Multilingual Matters.

Copland, F., Shaw, F., & Snell, J. (Eds.). (2015). *Linguistic ethnography: Interdiscplinary explorations*. Palgrave.

Corrigan, P. (1979). *Schooling the Smash Street kids*. Macmillan Press.

Cruz Banks, O. (2010). Critical postcolonial dance pedagogy: The relevance of West African dance education in the United States. *Anthropology & Education Quarterly, 41*(1), 18–34.

Delanty, G. (2020). *Critical theory and social transformation: Crises of the present and future possibilities*. Routledge.

Dillabough, J. (2004). Class, culture and the 'predicaments of masculine domination': Encountering Pierre Bourdieu, *British Journal of Sociology of Education, 25*(4), 489–506.

Dumas, M., & ross, K. (2016). "Be real black for me": Imagining BlackCrit in education. *Urban Education, 51*(4), 415–442.

Duncan, G. (2005). Critical race ethnography in education: Narrative, inequality and the problem of epistemology. *Race Ethnicity and Education, 8*(1), 93–114.

Epstein, D., & Johnson, R. (1998). *Schooling sexualities*. McGraw-Hill Education.

Epstein, D., Kehily, M., Mac An Ghaill, M., & Redman, P. (2001). Boys and girls come out to play: Making masculinities and femininities in school playgrounds. *Men and Masculinities, 4*(2), 158–172.

Fahey, J., Prosser, H., & Shaw, M. (Eds.). (2015a). *In the realm of the senses: Social aesthetics and the sensory dynamics of privilege*. Springer.

Fahey, J., Prosser, H., & Shaw, M. (2015b). Introduction: Local classes, global influences – Considerations on the social aesthetics of elite schools. In J. Fahey, H Prosser & M. Shaw (Eds.), *In the realm of the senses: Social aesthetics and the sensory dynamics of privilege*. Springer.

Fields, J. (2008). *Risky lessons: Sex education and social inequality*. Rutgers University Press.

Fine, M. (1991). *Framing dropouts: Notes on the politics of an urban public high school*. State University of New York Press.

Fine, M., & Weis, L. (1998). *The unknown city: Lives of poor and working class young adults*. Beacon Press.

Fitzpatrick, K. (2013). *Critical pedagogy, physical education and urban schooling*. Peter Lang.

Fitzpatrick, K., & May, S. (2015). Doing critical educational ethnography with Bourdieu. In M. Murphy & C. Costa (Eds.), *Theory as method in research: On Bourdieu, education and society* (pp. 101–114). Routledge.

Foley, D., & Valenzuela, A. (2005). Critical ethnography: The politics of collaboration. In N. K. Denzin & Y. S. Lincoln (Eds.), *Handbook of qualitative research* (pp. 217–234). Sage.

Forbes, J., & Lingard, B. (2015). Assured optimism in a Scottish girls' school: Habitus and the (re)production of global privilege, *British Journal of Sociology of Education, 36*(1), 116–136. https://doi.org/10.1080/01425692.2014.967839

Geerts, E., & Carstens, D. (2019). Ethico-onto-epistemology. *Philosophy Today, 63*(4), 915–925.

Geertz, C. (1973). Thick description: Toward an interpretive theory of culture. In *The interpretation of cultures* (pp. 3–30). Basic Books.

Geertz, C. (2000). *Available light: Anthropological reflections on philosophical topics*. Princeton University Press.

Gonzalez, M. C. (2003). An ethics for postcolonial ethnography. *Expressions of Ethnography: Novel Approaches to Qualitative Methods*, 77–86.

Grenfell, M., Bloom, D., Hardy, C., Pahl, K., Rosswell, J., & Street, B. (2012). *Language, ethnography and education: Bridging new literacy studies and Bourdieu*. Routledge.

Grenfell, M., & James, D. (1998). *Bourdieu and education: Acts of practical theory*. Falmer Press.

Grenfell, M., & Pahl, K. (2018). *Bourdieu, language-based ethnographies and reflexivity: Putting theory into practice*. Routledge.

Hamilton, L., & Taylor, N. (2017). *Ethnography after humanism: Power, politics and method in multi-species research*. Springer.

Haraway, D. (2003). *The companion species manifesto*. Prickly Paradigm Press.

Haraway, D. (2004). Cyborgs to Companion Species: Reconfiguring kinship in technoscience. In D. Haraway (Ed.), *The Haraway reader* (pp. 295–320). Routledge.

Haraway, D. (2008). *When species meet*. University of Minnesota Press.

Harris, D., & Holman Jones, S. (2022). A manifesto for posthuman creativity studies. *Qualitative Inquiry*. doi: https://doi.org/10.1177/10778004211066632.

Heller, M. (2006). *Linguistic minorities and modernity* (2nd ed.). Longman.

Hymes, D. (Ed.). (2002). The use of anthropology: Critical, political, personal. In *Reinventing anthropology* (pp. 3–79). University of Michigan Press (original work published 1969).

Jokinen, P., & Nordstrom, S. (2020). A queer cyborg ethnographer in the performative friction of dissenting ontologies. *Qualitative Inquiry, 26*(6), 639–649.

Jones, A. (1991). *At school I've got a chance*. Dunmore Press.

Kapferer, B. (2006). Situations, crisis and the anthropology of the concrete: The contribution of Max Gluckman. In T. Evens & D. Handelman (Eds.), *The Manchester school: Practice and ethnographic praxis in anthropology*. Berghahn Books.

Kenway, J., & Koh, A. (Eds.). (2013). The elite school as 'cognitive machine' and 'social paradise': Developing transnational capitals for the national 'field of power'. *Journal of Sociology, 49*(2–3), 272–290.

Kenway, J., & Koh, A. (Eds.). (2015). Special Issue: New sociologies of elite schooling: Theoretical, methodological and empirical explorations. *British Journal of Sociology of Education, 36*(1), 1–192.

Kenway, J., & McCarthy, C. (Eds.). (2017). *Elite schools in globalising circumstances: New conceptual directions and connections*. Routledge.

Kirksey, S. E., & Helmreich, S. (2010). The emergence of multispecies ethnography. *Cultural Anthropology, 25*(4), 545–576. https://doi.org/10.1111/j.1548-1360.2010.01069.x

Kustatscher, M. (2017). The emotional geographies of belonging: Children's intersectional identities in primary school. *Children's Geographies, 15*(1), 65–79.

Lather, P. (2001a). Postbook: Working the ruins of feminist ethnography. *Signs: Journal of Women in Culture and Society, 27*(1), 199–227.

Lather, P. (2001b). Postmodernism, post-structuralism and post(critical) ethnography: Of ruins, aporias and angels. In P. Atkinson, A. Coffey, S. Delamont, J. Lofland & L. Lofland (Eds.), *Handbook of ethnography* (pp. 477–492). Sage.

Lather, P. (2007). *Getting lost: Feminist efforts toward a double(d) science*. SUNY Press.

Lather, P. (2016). The work of thought and the politics of research:(Post) qualitative research. In N. K. Denzin & M. D. Giardina (Eds.), *Qualitative inquiry and the politics of research* (pp. 97–118). Routledge.

Lather, P., & St. Pierre, E. A. (2013). Post-qualitative research. *International Journal of Qualitative Studies in Education, 26*(6), 629–633.

Latour, B. (2005). *Reassembling the Social: An introduction to actor-network-theory*. Oxford University Press

Lave, J. (2011). *Apprenticeship in critical ethnographic practice*. University of Chicago Press.

Lees, S. (1986). *Losing out: Sexuality and adolescent girls*. Taylor & Francis.

Lloro-Bidart, T. (2018). A feminist posthumanist multispecies ethnography for educational studies. *Educational Studies, 54*(3), 253–270.

Locke, P. (2018). Multispecies ethnography. *The International Encyclopedia of Anthropology*, 1–3. https://doi.org/10.1002/9781118924396.wbiea1491

Mac An Ghaill, M. (1994). *The making of men*. Open University Press.

May, S. (1994). *Making multicultural education work*. Multilingual Matters.

May, S. (1998). On what might have been: Some reflections on critical multiculturalism. In G. Shacklock & J. Smyth (Eds.), *Being reflexive in critical educational and social research* (pp. 159–170). Falmer Press.

May, S., & Fitzpatrick, K. (2019). Critical ethnography. In P. Atkinson, S. Delamont, A. Cernat, J. W. Sakshaug, & R. A. Williams (Eds.), *Sage research methods foundations*. https://doi.org/10.4135/9781526421036831954

McLaren, P. (1999). *Schooling as a ritual performance* (3rd ed.). Rowman & Littlefield.

McLaren, P. (2015). *Life in schools* (6th ed.). Routledge. https://doi.org/10.4324/9781315633640

McRobbie, A. (1978). Working class girls and the culture of femininity. In Women's Study Group (Ed.), *Women take issue: Aspects of women's subordination* (pp. 96–108). Routledge.

McRobbie, A. (1990). *Feminism and youth culture: From 'Jackie' to 'Just Seventeen'*. Macmillan International Higher Education.

McRobbie, A. (2003). Settling accounts with subcultures: A feminist critique. In C. Jenks (Ed.), *Culture: Critical concepts in sociology* (pp. 246–258). Routledge.

Murillo, E. G. (1999). Mojado crossings along neoliberal borderlands. *Educational Foundations, 13*, 7–30.

Noblit, G. (2003). Reinscribing critique in educational ethnography: Critical and post-critical ethnography. In K. B. deMarrais & S. D. Lapan (Eds.), *Foundations for research* (pp. 197–218). Routledge.

Noblit, G., Flores, S., & Murillo, E. (2004). Introduction. In G. Noblit, S. Flores, & E. Murillo (Eds.), *Postcritical ethnography: Reinscribing critique* (pp. 1–52): Hampton Press.

Nxumalo, F., & Pacini-Ketchabaw, V. (2017). 'Staying with the trouble' in child-insect-educator common worlds. *Environmental Education Research, 23*, 1–13. https://doi.org/10.1080/13504622.2017.1325447

Ong, A. 1999. *Flexible citizenship: The cultural logics of transnationality*. Duke University.

Palmer, D., & Caldas, B. (2017). Critical ethnography. In K. King, Y. Lai, & S. May (Eds.), *Research methods in language and education. Encyclopedia of language and education* (3rd ed., pp. 381–392). Springer.

Paris, D. (2011). *Language across difference: Ethnicity, communication, and youth identities in changing urban schools*. Cambridge University Press.

Pascale, C. M. (2011). *Cartographies of knowledge: Exploring qualitative epistemologies*. Sage Publications.

Pascoe, C. J. (2007). *Dude, you're a fag: Masculinity and sexuality in high school*. University of California Press.

Pedersen, H. (2010). *Animals in schools: Processes and strategies in human-animal education*. Purdue University Press.

Pedersen, H. (2013). Follow the Judas sheep: Materializing post-qualitative methodology in zooethnographic space. *International Journal of Qualitative Studies in Education, 26*(6), 717–731. https://doi.org/10.1080/09518398.2013.788760

Pedersen, H., & Pini, B. (2017). Educational epistemologies and methods in a more-than-human world. *Educational Philosophy and Theory, 49*(11), 1051–1054, https://doi.org/10.1080/00131857.2016.1199925

Pillow, W. S. (2003). Confession, catharsis or cure? Rethinking the uses of reflexivity as methodological power in qualitative research. *International Journal of Qualitative Studies in Education, 16*(2), 175–196.

Qin, K., & Li, G. (2020). Understanding immigrant youths' negotiation of racialized masculinities in one US high school: An intersectionality lens on race, gender, and language. *Sexuality & Culture, 24,* 1046–1063

Quantz, R. (1992). Interpretive method in historical research: Ethnohistory reconsidered. In R. Altenbaugh (Ed.), *The teacher's voice: A social history of teaching* (pp. 174–190). Falmer.

Rasmussen, M. L. (2020). Working with social theory in health education. In D. Leahy, K. Fitzpatrick & J. Wright (Eds.), *Social theory and health education* (pp. 7–18). Routledge.

Reay, D. (2004). 'It's all becoming a habitus': Beyond the habitual use of habitus in educational research, *British Journal of Sociology of Education, 25*(4), 431–444.

Sanday, P. (1976). *Anthropology and the public interest: Fieldwork and theory.* Academic Press.

Scraton, S. (1985). 'Boys muscle in where angels fear to tread' – girls' sub-cultures and physical activities. *The Sociological Review, 33*(1_suppl), 160–186.

Skeggs, B. (2004). *Class, self, culture.* London: Routledge.

Somerville, M. (2020). Posthuman theory and practice in early years learning. In A. Cutter-Mackenzie-Knowles, K. Malone, & E. Barratt Hacking (Eds.), *Research handbook on childhoodnature* (pp. 103–127). Springer. https://doi.org/10.1007/978-3-319-67286-1_6

Stahl, G. (2017). *Ethnography of a neoliberal school: Building cultures of success.* Routledge.

St. Pierre, E. A. (2016). Refusing human being in humanist qualitative inquiry. In *Qualitative inquiry – past, present, and future* (pp. 103–118). Routledge.

St. Pierre, E. A. (2018). Writing post qualitative inquiry. *Qualitative Inquiry, 24*(9), 603–608.

Tax, S. (1963). *Penny capitalism: A Guatemalan Indian history.* University of Chicago Press.

Taylor, A., Blaise, M., & Giugni, M. (2013). Haraway's 'bag lady story-telling': Relocating childhood and learning within a 'post-human landscape'. Discourse: *Studies in the Cultural Politics of Education, 34*(1), 48–62.

Taylor, A., & Pacini-Ketchabaw, V. (2015). Learning with children, ants, and worms in the Anthropocene: Towards a common world pedagogy of multispecies vulnerability. *Pedagogy, Culture, Society, 23*(4), 507–529. https://doi.org/10.1080/14681366.2015.1039050

Taylor, A., & Pacini-Ketchabaw, V. (2017). Kids, raccoons, and roos: Awkward encounters and mixed affects. *Children's Geographies, 15*(2), 131–145. https://doi.org/10.1080/14733285.2016.1199849

Taylor, C. A., & Fairchild, N. (2020). Towards a posthumanist institutional ethnography: Viscous matterings and gendered bodies. *Ethnography and Education, 15*(4), 509–527.

Teese, R., & Polesel, J. (2003). *Undemocratic schooling: Equity and quality in mass secondary education in Australia.* Melbourne University

Thomson, P. (2002). *Schooling the rustbelt kids: Making the difference in changing times.* Allen & Unwin.

Urrieta Jr, L., & Martínez, S. (2011). Diasporic community knowledge and school absenteeism: Mexican immigrant pueblo parents' and grandparents' Postcolonial ways of educating. *Interventions, 13*(2), 256–277.

Valentine, C. (1968). *Culture and poverty: Critique and counter-proposals.* University of Chicago Press.

Van Loon, J. (2001). Ethnography: A critical turn in cultural studies. In P. Atkinson, A. Coffey, S. Delamont, J. Lofland, & L. Lofland (Eds.), *Handbook of ethnography* (pp. 273–284). Sage. https://doi.org/10.4135/9781848608337.n19

Weis, L. (1985). *Between two worlds: Black students in an urban community college.* Routledge.

Weis, L., Cipollone, K., & Jenkins, H. (2014). *Class warfare: Class, race, and college admissions in top-tier secondary schools.* University of Chicago Press.

Weis, L., & Fine, M. (2012). Critical bifocality and circuit of privilege: Expanding critical ethnographic theory and design. *Harvard Educational Review, 82*(2), 173–201.

Weis, L., Fine, M., & Dimitriadis, G. (2009). Towards a critical theory of method in shifting times. In M. W. Apple, W. Au, & L. Armando Gandin (Eds.), *The Routledge international handbook of critical education.* Routledge.

Willis, P. (1977). *Learning to labor: How working class kids get working class jobs.* Columbia University Press.

Windle, J., & Nogueira, M. (2015). The role of internationalisation in the schooling of Brazilian elites: Distinctions between two class fractions. *British Journal of Sociology of Education, 36*(1), 174–192. https://doi.org/10.1080/01425692.2014.967841

Yamamoto, E. (1997). Critical race praxis: Race theory and political lawyering practice in post-civil rights America. *Michigan Law Review, 95*(4), 821–900.

Yon, D. (2000). *Elusive culture: Schooling, race and identity in global times.* State University of New York Press.

Youdell, D. (2005). Sex-gender-sexuality: How sex, gender and sexuality constellations are constituted in secondary schools. *Gender and Education, 17*(3), 249–270. https://doi.org/10.1080/09540250500145148

Youdell, D. (2010). Queer outings: Uncomfortable stories about the subjects of post-structural school ethnography. *International Journal of Qualitative Studies in Education, 23*(1), 87–100. http://doi.org/10.1080/09518390903447168

Youdell, D., & Armstrong, F. (2011). A politics beyond subjects: The affective choreographies and smooth spaces of schooling. *Emotion, Space and Society, 4*(3), 144–150. https://doi.org/10.1016/j.emospa.2011.01.002

Young, R. (2001). *Postcolonialism: A historical introduction.* Blackwell.

4

CONSIDERING ETHICAL PRACTICES IN CRITICAL ETHNOGRAPHIC RESEARCH

In his powerfully reflective and reflexive piece "One hundred dollars and a dead man", Steven Vanderstaay explores the ethical complexities he experienced in ethnographic fieldwork, noting that "case studies of ethical dilemmas concern emotion as well as logic and the interstices in which they meet" (2005, p. 374). With this in mind, we want to frame this chapter around a number of key vignettes, along with their implications for developing and maintaining ethical practices in critical ethnography. The first relates to an academic workshop on Indigenous language use that Stephen attended in Australia in 2019:

> It is the last academic presentation of the day. The presenter is a senior White academic, and co-convenor of the workshop, who has a long history of researching collaboratively in Australian Aboriginal contexts. Today, she is discussing the use of translanguaging – the fluid, dynamic combination of language varieties that bi/multilinguals use every day (see Chapter 6) – among Australian Aboriginal students. The context is a major ethnographic research study that she leads, involving non-Indigenous researchers and Indigenous "cultural advisors". Throughout her presentation, she strongly, passionately, advocates for both the social justice and academic merits of student translanguaging, arguing that its recognition and validation allow also for the wider valuing of different Australian Aboriginal language varieties (traditional Aboriginal languages, Kriol, Aboriginal English). However, as the presentation progresses, one of the research group's cultural advisors – an older Aboriginal woman – increasingly disputes the positive representation of translanguaging under discussion. For her, these language practices are clearly neither legitimate nor helpful – an example simply of the "poor" and inadequate language use of young people. The presenter initially tries

DOI: 10.4324/9781315208510-4

to incorporate time and space for the Aboriginal speaker's concerns but, as it escalates (and the audience becomes increasingly uncomfortable), the latter is closed down for reasons "of time". As a result, the Aboriginal speaker leaves the room before the presentation is finished. Her leaving, and the tensions inherent in the contested exchanges preceding it, go unremarked.

This vignette highlights a range of key ethical issues. The first is around the conventions, or rules of engagement, that shape this context. This is a (Western) academic lecture, where undermining the speaker, especially a senior scholar, is deemed inappropriate, or at least unusual. That the audience of predominantly White academics felt increasingly uncomfortable about the exchange reflects their (implicit) adherence to these conventions. Then there are related questions of power. Who has authority to speak, whose knowledge is valued, given preference, or legitimacy here? Clearly, in this context, it is the senior (White) academic presenter.

What of the contradictions and inequities exemplified in a presentation by a White researcher who argues passionately for the merits of Aboriginal language use while, at the same time, publicly contesting, and eventually dismissing, an Indigenous Aboriginal counter-perspective? This raises the additional ethical question of the appropriateness of White researchers speaking about, speaking for and, in this case, also speaking against the research participants they are discussing. Here, the White ethnographer's gaze, and their related interpretation, while ostensibly positive and collaborative, still results in both a silencing of and symbolic violence toward Indigenous peoples. And finally, there is the related tension between the missionary advocacy of a critical and progressive Western research position (the value of translanguaging, in this instance) and its active contestation by Indigenous research participants on whose behalf it has been ostensibly deployed – albeit for reasons primarily of generational difference.

In this chapter, we will explore the ethical implications, tensions, and conundrums exemplified by this vignette. We will also explore the broader related challenges attendant upon developing and maintaining a robust, socially just, ethics of engagement and collaboration – what Guillemin and Gillam (2004) usefully describe as "ethics in practice" – in critical ethnographic research. This necessarily involves dispensing with the idea that ethics are only something we address at the beginning of a research project. Institutional Review Board (IRB) processes, and their like, are an important dimension of any research. However, they are a starting not an end point, and they also have their own challenges and limitations, to which we will return. In short, ethical practices should permeate *all* aspects of the research process – beginning with the research questions we ask, and then proceeding to explore their ongoing implications as the research unfolds.

Question Setting

Any methodological or theoretical choice is, of course, political. The methods we employ compel us to ask certain kinds of questions and to focus on certain kinds of "problems". Indeed, how we view a problem or ask a question lead the research in a particular direction. So, critically examining our questions is an important place to start when considering the ethical implications of our research (see also Chapter 2). What interests us and why? How have these questions been informed by our own experiences, commitments, and associated presumptions? Are the questions appropriate? Are we the people who should be asking them (and, if not, who should)? What will exploring these research questions achieve and whom will they help – what for and for whom are we doing this research?

Take obesity research, for example, as an illustration of how different initial questions lead to radically different kinds of research, and related social, theoretical, and ethical outcomes. The media and many members of the health field have stated repeatedly in the last 20 years that obesity is a problem for Western nations. All kinds of evidence are brought to bear on this "problem", including evidence that body sizes across populations are increasing. There are, broadly, two different research approaches to this issue. The first approach assumes that body size is related to health outcomes, and so being fat is seen as a bad thing. Simplistically, research underpinned by this assumption focuses on various interventionist approaches to weight loss for individuals or populations. The second approach to obesity critically questions this underpinning assumption that being fat is a problem and, instead, looks at the power relations inherent in the construction of bodies, as well as how such assumptions affect people's experiences, levels of discrimination, and related social responses. A body size focus, for example, aims to promote particular approaches to diet and exercise among the *target population* (see later). A focus on the social construction of fatness (and its related pathologizing) might instead inquire about how people who are fat experience everyday stigma and social exclusion, and highlight how views of body size are sociologically framed as a result of testing regimes, body image imaginaries, and a wide range of moralisms. Obesity science might, for example, investigate the relationship between levels of physical activity and body weight, while a critical sociological approach might look at the relationship between body discrimination and mental health.

This example gets to the heart of what is "critical" in critical research. While there is no singular approach to critical scholarship, all critical research is interested in relations of power, social in/exclusion, in/equity issues, social justice, and the political and historical contexts of human, and more-than-human, relations. This may include relations between people – and between people, environments, and non-human objects – along with their ethical implications. So, as critical researchers researching obesity, for example, we are obviously far more likely to opt for the second of these two approaches. This might involve questioning the social construction of obesity, the related moral panic surrounding it, and the ethical implications of imposing the often unstated body norms of White middle-class societies on other social and ethnic groups, the latter of whom are an all too regular "target" of obesity "interventions".

But even this is not enough if we don't ask appropriate questions in the first place. To acknowledge and address the issue of question setting critically, we first need to understand the emotional investments we bring to the research, the social, cultural, and situational experiences that underpin these investments, and the ways that shape our interest in, concerns about, and commitments to the research study. This requires acknowledgment of the power of the "ethnographer's gaze" (May, 1997), or what Bourdieu has described as "the epistemological privilege of the observer" (1990, p. 14), as well as a commitment to constructing and interpreting knowledge "from the vantage point of the people whose voices are marginalized" (Palmer & Caldas, 2017, p. 384). Critical ethnographers thus need to interrogate the bases of questions and inquiries and ask whether the topic of investigation connects with, and is important or useful to, the people with whom they are engaging. Recentering the perspectives of, and potential consequences for, our research participants in these ways allows for the possibilities of rethinking, revising, and/or discarding the initial research questions, should these prove to be inappropriate and/or unhelpful. There is no certain or "right" way to approach this. Engaging in critical ethnography invites us to be curious, open, and to let go of set expectations about the way forward. Our projects are most likely to be limited by our own unquestioned assumptions about what counts as knowledge, what the "problem" is, and how we might go about understanding it better. Critical ethnography requires an orientation that is open to surprise.

We described an example of this in Chapter 2, where Katie convened an Indigenous Māori health workshop around the question: "What is the role of schools in addressing the health and wellbeing of children and youth?" While clearly focused on issues of in/exclusion and social justice, this question was nonetheless immediately deconstructed by one of her Indigenous colleagues, Mera Penehira, who stated, up front, that the question was not one that Māori (Indigenous) communities would ask. Rather, for Māori, health and wellbeing are so embedded in environments, families, and communities, and so woven through every part of a young person's life, including schooling, that it doesn't make ontological sense to separate them in the way this framing question suggested. Moreover, this question did little to highlight the impact of historical trauma and colonization on Indigenous young people's experiences, knowledge of themselves within communities, and ultimately, on their education in a broad sense (see Penehira et al., 2011). Its intrinsic cultural narrowness and Eurocentricity meant it was simply the wrong question to ask regarding Māori students' experiences of health and wellbeing in schools.

As this vignette highlights, coming to a research study with a set of intended or presumptive questions, however well-intentioned, may simply miss the mark and/or fail to meet the expectations, understandings, or needs of research communities. However, asking unhelpful questions initially is not a barrier in itself to conducting critical ethnographic fieldwork effectively. Sometimes we learn a great deal from asking the wrong questions initially, but only if we are open to being told that they are wrong, and if we allow any subsequent debate to address and reconstitute the very basis of the questions we ask. The key is to remain open and responsive to revising and/or dispensing with those questions accordingly as the research progresses – particularly in light of how research participants' respond to them.

However, this requires us, in turn, to examine continuously what constitutes the field of study, and how, as researchers, we enter and operate within it (Subedi, 2006) – that is, how we are *situated* in relation to, and within, the research context and process. To do this, we need to be able to examine reflexively the question of (our) positionality in relation to the research, including the epistemological and cultural assumptions we bring to it. Markham argues, for example, that in both online and face-to-face research, "drawing boundaries around the research context, or 'identifying the field' involves a series of decisions that both presuppose and reveal the researcher's underlying ontological and epistemological assumptions" (2005, p. 801). Revealing these assumptions also necessarily raises issues of and questions about, among others, Whiteness, power, gender, privilege, and how these impact on the relationalities we establish and maintain in the research.

Positionality/Reflexivity

Considering positionality is a complex and difficult ethical process. While some researchers tend to avoid questions of researcher subjectivity, others fetishize it. Alice Goffman's (2015) controversial six-year ethnographic study, *On the run* provides an interesting example of the former in this regard. Goffman's research foregrounded the experiences of young African American men in a poor neighborhood in West Philadelphia, focusing on a group of friends, some of them low-level drug dealers, who lived under constant threat of arrest and who thus found themselves regularly in and out of prison. Goffman's aim in examining these lived experiences in a still highly racialized and materially disadvantaged context was to both complexify and contest the de rigueur negative construction and positioning of Black American men vis-à-vis criminality, as well as highlighting the disproportionate incarceration rates that they faced.

The ethnography was widely celebrated, at least initially, for the power of its ethnographic representation and the social justice issues it foregrounded. However, the ethics of Goffman's own involvement in potentially illicit activities, along with her vivid ethnographic representation of these activities in her account, have since been brought into serious question. A key criticism that also subsequently emerged with respect to her ethnography focused on the relative invisibility of her own positionality as a young, wealthy, White, middle-class woman, and academic, chronicling the lives of marginalized Black men and their families (Flaherty, 2017; Lewis-Kraus, 2016). In a methodological postscript to her study, Goffman does acknowledge the tensions inherent in this juxtaposition when she notes:

> People have asked me how I "negotiated my privilege" while conducting fieldwork. Given that I am a white woman who comes from an educated and well-off family, this is a good question. In fact, I had more privilege than whiteness, education, and wealth, my father [Erving Goffman] was a prominent sociologist and field worker. . . . This background may have given me the confidence and resources to embark on this research as an undergraduate and consequently the years to get it established and take it in various directions.
>
> *(2015, pp. 230–231)*

This observation risks reinforcing, rather than critiquing, the social, economic, cultural, and academic capital that Goffman clearly brought to the research process. She does proceed to argue that this background actually highlighted her lack of knowledge in this context: "I often felt like an idiot, an outsider, and at times a powerless young woman. . . . In many situations, my lack of knowledge put me at the bottom of the social hierarchy" (p. 231). However, she does little more than assert that this relative lack of knowledge provided her with the incentive for more deeply exploring and better understanding her research context – a traditional ethnographic "outsider" perspective. Beyond this, any critical reflexivity with respect to her positionality went unremarked.

Much of the subsequent criticism leveled at Goffman's study could also be read as a reassertion of academic hierarchies and disciplinary gatekeeping by senior academics in the field, wanting to put her "in her place" (she undertook the study as an undergraduate and it was her first book; see Lewis-Kraus, 2016). Some attacks were sexist – much like those directed at Margaret Mead's groundbreaking ethnographic work on Samoan sexuality in the early 20th century by established, conservative, and predominantly male ethnographers (see Shankman, 2009). We do not wish to add to these problematic discourses here, and these debates need to be understood in the social, cultural, and political context within which they arose. In a now deleted internet post, a group of graduate students at New York University wrote an openly critical online letter to Goffman, which concluded by asking:

> [S]hould you have ever attempted this book in the first place? For us, the short answer is "no". The long answer – an affirmative answer – would require a deep and thorough consideration of whether it's possible to formulate an ethical, anti-colonial model of ethnography suitable for a project of this nature.
>
> *It would require much more of the ethnographer.* It would necessitate engagement with those who directly address the politics of knowledge production

in the academy from an anti-colonial standpoint. . . . *And it would require a much more explicit code of ethics and transparency, as well as lines of reciprocal accountability so that the study might benefit "researched" people and communities, not only the author* [emphasis added].

These are important, unresolved, questions. The notion of reciprocal accountability highlighted here – or what the critical scholar Mikhail Bakhtin (1990) has termed "answerability" – is a key means of directing analytical attention to the different kinds of privilege(s) that we as researchers may bring to the research project and process. We will discuss this more fully in the next section.

While Goffman perhaps didn't attend to her positionality enough, others risk fetishizing it. Geertz (1973, p. 345) once stated that "[a]ll ethnography is part philosophy, and a good deal of the rest is confession". If we view ethnography simply as some kind of individual confessional, we can end up recentering the researcher at the expense of the participants (Pillow, 2003). Self-disclosure, in and of itself, does not absolve the researcher. As Patai has noted, "we do not escape from the consequences of our positions by talking about them endlessly" (1994, p. 70). Likewise, Fabian has observed that there is no "guarantee that oppressors will be less oppressive just because they become self-conscious" (1990, p. 768). Focus on the ethnographer at the expense of context and relationalities can risk what Van Maanen (2011, p. 93) calls "vanity ethnography". Such a position, particularly when it is coupled with Whiteness, can also embed/entrench a White savior/missionary motif – either wittingly or unwittingly – within the research. It can also mean that ethnographers end up telling stories or inquiring into contexts which are not theirs to interrogate. Popkewitz (1998) argues that we need to avoid this kind of "redemptive" research at all costs, since it inevitably positions the researcher as the agent of change. More broadly, if we simply stay with the individual researcher confessional, we neither question the uneven power dynamics in our fieldwork nor the agency of marginalized participants, and the Western self as the creator and the bearer of knowledge remains front and center (Subedi, 2006).

Critical reflexivity is one tool we can employ to address these issues in order to consider how we are positioned in the research in ways that are complicit with, and reinforcing of, existing hierarchies of power. Reflexivity is different to reflection. Chiseri-Strater observes that "to be reflective does not demand an 'other', while to be reflexive demands both an other and some self-conscious awareness of the process of self-scrutiny" (1996, p. 130). Reflexivity then "is not to be misunderstood here as the mere self-reflection of the researcher. Rather, reflexivity involves a complex dialectic between the researcher, the research process, and the research outcome(s)" (May, 1997, p. 200). Emirbayer and Desmond, in their discussion of race reflexivity, similarly assert that scholars should not simply narrate their life-history, but rather engage in "rigorous institutional analyzes of the social and historical structures that condition one's thinking and inner experience" (2012, p. 591). Reflexivity is thus more than an engagement not only with positionality (see Chapter 2) but also concerns ontology and epistemology (see Chapter 3).

These observations are usefully reinforced by Jackson's (2004) distinction between "mechanical" and "rigorous" approaches to reflexivity. For Jackson, mechanical reflexivity can consist of "empty autobiographical gestures" (p. 37), which do nothing to address the workings of oppression. Rigorous reflexivity, on the other hand, actively explores "how we see – and how others see us seeing them" (p. 37) in the research process, the research project, and the wider fields within which we are all situated. Rigorous or critical reflexivity is thus more than a positionality statement because this kind of reflexivity requires a serious epistemological consideration of one's subjective privileges and solidarities within broader sociohistorical realms, as well as within particular research settings (Bell et al., 2022). As Noblit et al. observe, "[c]ritical ethnographers must explicitly consider how their own acts of studying and representing people and situations are acts of domination even as critical ethnographers reveal the same in what they study" (2004, p. 3). Such a critical examination should also necessarily include our positioning as researchers in the broader field of academia: that is, as Bourdieu (1990) has outlined, our academic habitus, which enables us to see certain things and not others. For example, researchers in a school are implicated not only in the relations of power they experience within the school but also with regard to their place in academic hierarchies, subject disciplines, and the interrelationship between those and the school and wider community (May & Fitzpatrick, 2019).

Given all this, Madison argues that "[w]hile critical ethnography must take up the charge of life-sustaining knowledges and restorative justice, it must also take up the charge of positionality" (2019, p. 6). For this to be achieved, she explains, a focus on justice must include both self-reflection and a rigorous critique of the implications of one's own positionality in the associated relations of power and social hierarchies. Within such a framework then "we are accountable for our own research paradigms, our own positions of authority, and our own moral responsibility relative to representation and interpretation" (pp. 6–7). Combining both positionality and critical reflexivity in this way also specifically highlights, and makes transparent, the links between the local context of the study and wider historical, social, and political forces. Weis et al. (2009) argue that this is precisely the kind of ethnography that is required for our contemporary times, one that contextualizes the local in relation to the global and seeks to understand how representations of culture shift and change both within and across contexts.

Critical reflexivity, Pillow asserts, then deliberately "pushes toward an unfamiliar, toward the uncomfortable, [it] cannot be a simple story of subjects, subjectivity, and transcendence or self-indulgent tellings" (2003, p. 192). It requires the researcher "to be critically conscious through personal accounting of how your self-location (across, for example, gender, race, class, sexuality, ethnicity, nationality), position, and interests influence all stages of the research process" (p. 178).

Pillow (2003) highlights here how critical reflexivity has been a key feature of feminist research from the 1980s onward. As she observes, questions that arise from this focus on critical reflexivity within feminist research include:

> How can one be a nonexploitative researcher? How does one produce research that is useful and empowering? How do we make research that is linked with political action? How would our research practices be different if we were reflective at each step of the research process?
>
> *(p. 178)*

Such questions are challenging, and they don't always, or perhaps even seldom, result in clear-cut answers. Critical reflexivity thus requires us, as researchers, to live with tension and uncertainty, with "not knowing" (Lather, 2001). Adopting a critically reflexive approach to ethnographic work can also be personally and professionally unsettling. Take Fields' (2008, see also Chapter 7) ethnography of sexuality education in three middle schools in the United States, for example, and how she attempted to negotiate her sexuality in what were predominantly conservative school environments:

> My status as an adult complicated my fieldwork; so too did my lesbian sexuality. . . . I interviewed conservative Christians who participated in school board debates and who during interviews explained to me that homosexuality was a sin and unnatural. I chose a passive response in those moments: I nodded, took notes, and left those interviews exhausted and scared. Some interactions were particularly trying. . . . I did not always pursue questions about sexuality and morality that left me feeling especially vulnerable. I also sat silently through lessons in which teachers explained to their students that homosexuality was illegal. I listened to students call one another "fag" and "lezzie". Sometimes even the silence – from students, adults, and myself – about lesbian, gay, bisexual, transgender, or queer (LGBTQ+) sexuality and gender was deafening. These classrooms, like the interviews with conservative Christians, often left me exhausted. I passed as straight in the public middle schools. At the private Quaker school, which was known for its liberal and tolerant attitudes, I disclosed my sexuality to the teacher whose classes I observed and to an out gay teacher whom I interviewed. Nonetheless, I expect that at each school some participants had their suspicions.
>
> *(p. 177)*

Fields (2008) goes on to note that she managed her sexuality:

> [N]ot only by not disclosing it verbally, but also by adopting a more conventionally feminine mode of self-presentation. I had been aware of dressing in

modest skirts and blouses when I interacted with Christian activists; now I understood that I had also made a concerted – if unconscious – effort to mask my lesbianism while visiting schools and interacting with teachers, students, and administrators. I understand these varying practices to reflect the different school settings themselves. Like many ethnographers and others who do not conform to normative gender and sexual expectations, I had assessed the three schools and decided whether I would be able to come out as a lesbian and still have access to the teachers and students.

(p. 178)

As Fields' (2008) commentary highlights, critical reflexivity involves both a depth of personal engagement and vulnerability that other forms of research may not require from us. Fields' experiences likewise foreground how adopting a critically reflexive approach necessitates us acknowledging and negotiating the relational dimensions of our research context. In this regard, if we are to avoid perpetuating the usual asymmetries of power between researcher and "researched", this in turn entails us engaging actively and meaningfully with *relationalities* and *reciprocity*.

Relationalities/Reciprocity

In her powerful and pivotal book, *Decolonizing methodologies*, the eminent Māori scholar and activist, Linda Tuhiwai Smith (2012), explores the ethical implications of working in Indigenous education contexts, and with (not on) Indigenous participants. As she argues, Indigenous peoples are perhaps the most "researched on" of any group in education, and yet the vast majority of this research has provided palpably few benefits for Indigenous peoples themselves. For the most part, the research has instead benefited researchers, many of whom were/are non-Indigenous, while at the same time reinforcing longstanding deficit conceptions of the Indigenous participants, their languages, and cultures (see also Bishop, 2005).

This all too familiar situation of the researcher benefiting from Indigenous participants illustrates a worldwide issue of how to conduct ethical research practices in communities in ways that safeguard Indigenous status and knowledge, and which do not contribute to yet another form of colonial mis/appropriation. Formal advisory structures that include Indigenous participants are a key means of mitigating such patterns of mis/appropriation and are becoming an increasingly common formal requirement for working in Indigenous research contexts. However, remembering the vignette with which we began this chapter, where the voice of an Indigenous advisor was effectively silenced in a public academic forum, clearly such consultative/advisory frameworks do not always mitigate ongoing ethical violations in such contexts.

Smith (2012) questions whether White academics should be allowed to continue researching in Indigenous communities at all. Similar arguments have been made by BlackCrit and LatCrit scholars (see e.g., Coles, 2022; Dumas & ross,

2016; Villenas & Foley, 2011) with respect to their own communities. Being a member of a particular community is not, however, the only consideration. The notion of preferential status that it necessarily accords *insider* versus *outsider*, or *insider/outsider*, ethnographic accounts is not straightforward. While there are considerable advantages to a mainly insider position – not least, the potential for richer, thicker descriptions that are more likely to reflect the actual community culture – there are also clearly risks and disadvantages. Delgado-Gaitan (1993) asserts that even researchers who share similar ethnic backgrounds or experiences with their participants cannot make claims about being more knowledgeable regarding the participants' experiences. Likewise, being part of the community that one is researching does not automatically result in the research being egalitarian (Pillow, 2003). Paechter (2012) further argues that communities can have particular expectations when they are researched by one of their members, especially around how that community comes to be represented. As she observes, an insider's account can come to be read in a certain way that may limit, rather than extend, their access, while insider research may also compromise, or be affected by, the social relationships within which they are enmeshed.

Problems of cultural mis/appropriation and the researcher benefiting at the specific expense of participants remain a key feature of much ethnographic work in education, particularly those conducted with Indigenous and/or other minoritized groups. To contest the asymmetry of this traditional ethnographic research/researched relationship, and the often-deleterious effects on research participants that ensues from it, recasting the research relationship as one of dialogue and partnership can be a useful way forward. Rethinking research relationships in this more equitable and dialogic way requires us as critical ethnographers to attend closely to the research context and to re/orient the research as a collaborative endeavor. This also brings into question the very usefulness of the distinctions between insider and/or outsider, discussed earlier. Critical ethnography assumes that we are all, at times, included and excluded in different social contexts. Issues of exclusion and inclusion occur at the intersection of social norms and power relations, which both researchers and participants are implicated in and engaged in reproducing (May & Fitzpatrick, 2019). In this sense, ethnographers are never fully outside or inside any context or community but in flux and in relationship with different members of those communities at any given moment (Naples, 1996).

As critical ethnographers then, we need to be less concerned with insider/outsider designations and more concerned with the quality and reciprocity of our ongoing and dynamic research (inter)relationships. As Michelle Fine observes, we must always "probe why, how, when, with whom and who is made vulnerable by the research, with an understanding that social researchers should always be the most vulnerable – not those being studied or 'left' behind once the research is complete" (2006, p. 88). Rethinking these tensions with postcolonial theory, we might rather see research relationalities in constant flux and tension. Thinking with this theory, Hoskins (2012) suggests, for example, that we move beyond the colonizer/colonized binary and work with notions of hybridity:

> Hybridity forecloses ideas and forms of purity encompassed in essentialist positions. Instead, new hybrid subjectivities emerge at the intersection of the coloniser – colonised displacing essentialised identities and rupturing colonial power and discourse.
>
> *(p. 87)*

Hoskins warns, however, that moving toward hybridity also risks the erasure of difference, especially when it is Indigenous peoples who are expected to do all the hybridizing. She instead advocates "a range of positions (evoking, refusing, and critiquing the binary) that are held in tension" (p. 87), and also simultaneously questioned.

Fine (1994) suggests a process of working "the hyphens" between self and other to "interrupt Othering" in qualitative research, arguing that many "researchers have spoken 'of' and 'for' Others while occluding ourselves and our own investments, burying the contradictions that percolate at the self-other hyphen" (p. 70). The hyphens are in-between spaces that don't assume we can know or overcome power relations; they encourage us to "probe how we are in relation to the contexts we study and with our informants, understanding that we are all multiple in those relations" (Fine, 1994, p. 72, see also Paris & Winn, 2014).

Jones and Jenkins (2008) argue that collaboration – in their case in a Pākehā (White) and Māori (Indigenous) research team – is not only about relationships but also about the researchers' respective relationalities both to difference and to one another. Hyphens are never innocent (Bhattacharya, 2015) but need to be worked, contested, negotiated, and reworked over time. Working the hyphens means dynamically addressing tensions in research relationships over time, working with and in these tensions rather than attempting to resolve them (Fitzpatrick & Allen, 2017).

Trust then between researchers and with communities is central. So too is establishing and maintaining accountability to the research participants, and their wider community, throughout the research process and beyond (this echoes Bakhtin's [1990] notion of answerability signaled earlier in the chapter). These emphases on relationality, accountability, and productive tensions can potentially provide the necessary ethical framework for non-minoritized researchers to work in minoritized educational contexts in ways that further socially just aims and do not cause (further) harm to participants and their communities (Hill & May, 2013). Linda Tuhiwai Smith (2012) again provides us with a useful way forward here with respect to what might constitute the key principles of such a framework via her discussion of the Indigenous *Kaupapa Māori research* model that she and other colleagues have developed in the New Zealand context.

Kaupapa Māori Research

Kaupapa Māori (Māori approach/philosophy) is a research model rooted in Indigenous epistemology that is specifically designed to centralize Māori cultural expectations, to incorporate Māori cultural values, and to satisfy the overarching need to achieve collective benefits for the participants involved. The ethical parameters that it outlines are also clearly applicable to a wide range of research contexts, research methodologies, and research participants – including, of course, those associated with ethnographic research.

A key feature of Kaupapa Māori research (KMR) is that, where possible, research in Māori contexts should be undertaken by Māori researchers. If non-Indigenous researchers are ever to be involved in such contexts, they must entirely be accountable to the Indigenous Māori research community with whom they are working. In both instances, the aim of KMR is to devolve power from the researcher(s) to the research group, or *whānau* (family) of interest. KMR considers the researcher as a participant member of the wider research group, and the research itself is driven through collaboration with the group as a whole. In such a context, accountability is to the people being researched, who also have joint ownership of the research project throughout. Hoskins argues that within such an approach there is "an imperative to relationship – not opposition, and to responsibility for others" (2012, p. 85).

To this end, KMR is shaped by four key initial questions, as precursors to the research, and five key principles underlying the research process itself. The four key questions to be satisfied before any research project proceeds can be summarized as follows:

- What (positive) difference is this research going to make for Māori?
- What meaningful interventions are going to result?
- How does the research support Māori cultural and language aspirations?
- Is the researcher merely telling Māori what they already know? (Smith, 1997)

During the research process itself, an additional five key principles provide researchers with the basis for maintaining high levels of ethicality when working within Indigenous – and, by extension, other minoritized – education contexts. These are: *initiation, accountability, legitimization, benefits*, and *representation* (Bishop, 2005):

- Initiation concerns "how the research process begins, and whose concerns, interests and methods of approach determine the outcomes" (Bishop, 2005, p. 112). On this basis, KMR seeks to incorporate Māori participation prior to, during, and following the research, and for Māori participants to play a central role in the research processes as a whole.

- Benefit seeks to ensure that all those involved in the research – the researcher, the research participants, and their wider community(ies) – work to achieve positive outcomes in relation to their part in the project. As a result, the principle rejects research projects that solely serve the interests of the researcher, as discussed previously.
- Representation aims to ensure that the information that is gathered through(out) the research process is an accurate depiction of the experiences and views of the participants, as well as their cultural values, beliefs, and practices. In this respect, research should be accurate and detailed, not simplified, conglomerated, or commodified. It should unravel complex (and, sometimes, competing) storylines, create spaces for dialogue, and make sense of the complex and shifting experiences and realities of the research participants and their research contexts (see also the next section).
- Legitimization concerns the authority that is claimed for the texts that are created from the research, whether these texts are written, oral, visual, and/ or multimodal. To accurately, fairly, and helpfully reflect the interests of the research participants and their Indigenous worldviews, epistemologies, and experiences, all research outputs need to have been collaboratively developed, vetted, and agreed by the wider research group (Bishop, 2005).
- Accountability refers to the overall control of the research process, the procedures, the means of evaluation, text constructions, and the ways of distributing any new knowledge, to ensure that the research benefits and enhances the research participants and their research communities. This includes, as Smith (2012) argues, disseminating research outcomes "back to the people in culturally appropriate ways and in a language that can be understood" (p. 15; see also Chapter 5).

Kaupapa Māori research is an exemplar then of an ethics of presence and relationality. Places and people cannot be reduced to data (see also Chapter 2), cannot be put at an analytical distance only, but must be preserved in the body of the researcher as lived, as real, and affective. This amounts to what Bernstein describes as "reciprocity in practice" (2019, p. 130). It also accords with Soyini Madison's (2019) notion of "response-ability" where, as a researcher, one is:

> [R]esponsible for providing an opportunity for others to also gain the *ability* to respond in some form. I bear witness, and in bearing witness, I do not have the singular "response-ability" for what I witness but the responsibility of invoking a response-ability in others to what was seen, heard, learned, felt, and done in the field and through performance.
>
> *(p. 101)*

This collective and relational endeavor is at the heart of Kaupapa Māori research and should likewise be in any critical ethnography in education.

Representation(s)

Kaupapa Māori research also usefully foregrounds the issue of representation(s) and, particularly, how we might deconstruct and decenter the singular, authoritative, authorial ethnographic voice. How do we think about representation and misrepresentation in research of the other in research texts? How do we approach issues of voice? How do we move from narration to co-construction, from narrative to dialogue? How do we construct ethnographic texts as collaborative, polyphonic, and/or multivocal? These are all crucial considerations in the ethics of representation. It is important to note here that when we use the term "representation", it is with the knowledge that research accounts are never representative of any kind of objective reality but that we do go about presenting (constructing) research texts and, in the process, we include the words of participants, descriptions of experiences and scenes, and we construct ethnographic materials that speak to the politics of place, people, and happenings (see Chapter 5 for a full discussion of fieldwork and ethnographic writing). As Webb argues "representation is also fundamental to everyday life. People practice representation all the time . . . it is how we understand our environments and each other" (2008, p. 2). Webb further notes that:

> each of us is produced through a complex mix of background, tastes, concerns, training tendencies, experiences . . . [that] do not give us a stable or permanent sense of being in the world, but one that is frequently confusing, and always subject to change.
>
> *(p. 2)*

Ethnographic representations are ethical and political. Hoskins reminds us that "who others are, is always in excess of what they are" (2012, p. 92) and that representations are ever and always partial:

> Making group representations of identity, while necessary for access to justice and decision making, should not attempt to reduce ourselves or others to merely, or only, a series of qualities or characteristics that at any given time constitute being Māori [Indigenous] or our social other: Pākehā [White]. In other words, cultural and social identities do not capture the whole of who one is.
>
> *(p. 92)*

As we discussed in Chapter 2, Palmer and Caldas argue that this task requires, in the first instance, an understanding that knowledge in critical ethnography must be "constructed and interpreted from the vantage point of the people whose voices are marginalized" (2017, p. 384). In a critique of self-referential forms of autoethnography, Madison similarly warns that "[w]hen the gaze is on one's own navel one cannot see the ground upon which one stands or significant others standing nearby" (2006, p. 321). In the 1980s, Conquergood (1985) was grappling with these same issues, albeit in specific relation to the performative dimensions of ethnography. He noted that ethical and moral issues in ethnographic performance are most evident in how ethnographers position themselves in relation to their research participants, along with the underlying intentionality that such positionings reveal. Conquergood critiques four unethical representational stances that can be evident in ethnographic fieldwork and performance. The *custodian's rip-off* is an unethical stance that commodifies any obtained research knowledge for self-gain, while the *skeptic's cop-out* engages in detachment and the othering of research participants. The *enthusiast's infatuation* becomes unethical when it trivializes the community's practices, while the *curator's exhibitionism* exoticizes and romanticizes the other.

Ortner (1995) provides a similarly important early critique when she cautions against what she terms the practice of "ethnographic refusal". For Ortner, this ethnographic refusal is exemplified via three key dimensions – sanitizing politics, thinning culture, and dissolving actors. A focus on the politics of domination and resistance in critical ethnographic accounts can "sanitize the internal politics of the dominated" (p. 179), while overly romanticizing them at the same time. A subordinated group's politics is thus more complex, wider reaching and, at times, more contradictory than often presented. Such a romanticized approach also often thins culture, providing a homogenized and reified account of a subordinated group's cultural practices. And, finally, an undue focus on domination and resistance can end up constructing subordinated individuals and groups as primarily reactive, rather than agentic. Each of these binaries can be contested with a robust attention to complex relationalities.

Both Conquergood and Ortner emphasize, instead, the importance of establishing and maintaining a relational and dialogic approach to ethnographic representation(s). Conquergood's fifth stance of *dialogical performance* is the ethical alternative to the four unethical representational stances highlighted earlier. This position specifically embraces the cacophony or harmony of different voices in the research context. It does not stop at just understanding the personal and the interrelationships with others in the doing of culture, he argues, but rather proceeds to engage in cultural politics, questioning power, and resistance.

Critical ethnographic researchers have since employed a wide range of writing and representational approaches that promote such dialogism and multivocality – including, among others, the use of poetry, writing as a play or literary story, or as split multivoiced texts – and we discuss these more fully in Chapter 5. In terms of the ethics of representation though, how we meaningfully acknowledge and foreground such multivocality constitutes a key, ongoing, ethnographic challenge. Macbeth (2001) describes such practices as examples of "textual reflexivity", which aim to problematize representational singularity, along with the linearity, reductionism, and conclusiveness of (too) much ethnographic storytelling. We need to maintain spaces for indeterminacy and uncertainty and for competing, often contradictory and unresolved, storylines – refusing to tie up all the threads or loose ends. Rather than merely constructing generalizations and identifying trends, writing against culture or particularizing the purpose of ethnography means focusing on the incoherence among and within the participants' stories, as well as the incoherence that exists within ourselves as researchers living in (and living out) postcolonial realities (Deiri, 2022).

This discursive opening up of representational stances and modes as an ethical priority of critical ethnographic work also aligns well – potentially, at least – with recent work in new materialism and posthumanism. New materialisms disrupt anthropocentric approaches that have the human subject as the unquestionable point of departure, rendering human experience as the fundamental condition in research (Johansson, 2016). Drawing on the Deleuzian notion of *agencement*, translated in English as assemblage (see Chapter 3), Barad (2007) argues that everything, both human and non-human, animate and inanimate, is inevitably entangled. Barad describes this process as "intra-action", "a dynamic and shifting entanglement of relations" (2007, p. 35; see also Chapter 2). There is no privileged position for the individual actor or the human subject, including the researcher, in such assemblages. Rather, "[t]he subject is radically decentered in the collective assemblage of enunciation" (MacLure, 2013, p. 660). These assemblages of people, discourse, matter, and nature are also, thus, not static or fixed. Assemblages constitute "a dynamic space and time of becoming, emerging, unfolding, and of moving, connecting, diverging" (MacLure, 2013, p. 660).

Within such dynamic, entangled, representational spaces, epistemological questions also necessarily take precedence by directing focus toward how meanings are shaped, and how knowledge is dynamically co/constructed (Lather & St. Pierre, 2013). The aim here is to decenter both language as the key (external) means of representation, and individual actors or human subjects, in the process. While the ethics of such work for (critical) ethnography remain relatively nascent, there are an increasing number of useful discussions on their implications – see, for example, Lather and St. Pierre (2013); MacLure (2013); St. Pierre (2011, 2015); Toohey (2018). And yet, this work also points to the ongoing ethical challenges raised by new materialist understandings. Lather (2007), for example, explains the trickiness of representation in new materialism in the following way:

> The tension between explanation and understanding . . . arises from both a focus on voices and an understanding that subjects are not transparent to themselves. Respecting the competence of commonsense and people's ability to give meaning to their everyday actions is both imperative and reductionist in reinscribing the ghost of presence. As I worked this tension over the last decade or so, I came to think that perhaps we are all unreliable narrators, researched and researcher alike, given the indeterminacies of language and the workings of power in the will to know. What resulted was a deliberately stumbling approach to the representation of ethnographic voice.
>
> *(p. 158)*

In this sense, representation is always fraught, partial, and shifting, but the products of our research remain deeply political and ethical.

Negotiating (Biomedical) Institutional Ethical Review Processes

To conclude this chapter, we turn to a brief discussion of institutional ethical review processes – These are known in the United States as "Institutional Review Board(s)" (IRB) but named differently elsewhere as ethics committees or ethical approval agencies. We will use IRBs as a useful descriptive shorthand. In a chapter on ethics, you might well ask why this section didn't come first since it might be the first ethical challenge that springs to mind for any (ethnographic) researcher. There are several reasons.

First, IRB procedures and requirements are well-documented and detailed elsewhere, including in relation to critical ethnographic work (see Madison, 2019 for a useful overview), and so we do not wish to rehearse them here. Second, as we have tried to emphasize throughout this chapter, the ethics of critical ethnographic work permeate *all* aspects of the research – from beginning to end and beyond (see also Chapter 8). Given this, as Guillemin and Gillam argue, we need to move from an understanding of ethics as a procedural mechanism to one of "ethics in practice" (2004, p. 261). The first vignette in this chapter, for example, clearly highlighted the limits of cultural advisory frameworks in preventing potentially exploitative and unethical practices from subsequently occurring. Nor does it absolve researchers from grappling with the messy reality of these practices before, during, and after the fieldwork is complete. Third, placing a discussion of IRBs here – as an afterword, rather than a foreword – allows us to *délinéarisé* (unbundle) the chapter in a visual way, de-emphasizing the procedural in favor of process(es). And fourth, we want to focus solely, in what follows, on how IRBs most often apply a highly problematic biomedical model of ethics to social sciences research in general, and critical (ethnographic) research, in particular. To illustrate this last point, we provide one final vignette from Stephen's research here:

> In 2017, I (Stephen) proposed to undertake a new ethnographic research project in a Māori-medium high school program in Auckland, New Zealand. The possibility of pursuing such a project rested on my 30-year involvement as a White ally and advocate in Indigenous Māori language education contexts (see, e.g. Hill & May, 2011, 2013). This was, in turn, the result of establishing close, trusted/ing and accountable relationships with Māori academic and professional colleagues over that time. The other reason for considering this as a potential ethnographic research project was the pre-existing relationship I had with this particular school. My children had all been through the school and I had been an active advocate and

supporter of the school's Māori-medium program. I was also, at the time, a member of the school's governing board.

Realizing that my position on the governing board might present an issue for my university ethics committee, I had sought in advance from the governing board permission to recuse myself from any issues pertaining to the Māori-medium program. I was also prepared to stand down from the board for the duration of the research (at that time, anticipated to be one year) should the university ethics committee require it. Without diminishing the importance and necessity of these provisos, they were deemed by the school's governing board to be sufficient for managing the research process in the Māori-medium program. And so too did I. The school board also recognized that such research could not be undertaken, in the first instance, without a pre-existing relationship of trust and engagement with those involved in the program itself – a key feature of Kaupapa Māori research, discussed above.

Despite these provisos, and the explicit support of the governing board, the university ethics committee initially refused point blank to endorse the research project. This was on the basis not just of my role on the governing board, which I was prepared to relinquish, but the longstanding relationship I had with the school itself. The committee viewed this as a conflict of interest in and of itself and noted that they would only approve such an ethnographic study if it was conducted in a school with which I had no previous relationship. Added to this, they viewed the critical ethnographic research approach adopted as insufficiently delineated, requiring of me also a formalized scientized Observation Schedule, rather than the more open-ended classroom observations and engagement that I had proposed. What followed was nine months of debate with the ethics committee, including numerous written responses, and two formal meetings with the committee chair, before ethics permission was finally granted.

What was most striking to me about the committee's position was that it was not actually concerned at any point with research ethics per se, but rather with a much narrower procedural conception of risk management. With respect to my school board position, the ethics committee clearly misunderstood the difference between governance and management – implying that my board role, even if it was relinquished (as I was prepared to do), could jeopardize teachers and students in the program. And yet, there are strict measures in place for such governing boards with respect to ensuring they do not, at any time, stray into operational school matters. More broadly, and more problematically, the committee viewed my pre-existing relationship with the school as an obstacle in itself. There was no understanding of the importance of pre-existing relationships in working in Māori educational contexts, nor the related irony that approaching another school "cold" to undertake such research would almost certainly have been refused in the first instance on that basis. The attempt to impose a positivist Observation Schedule also revealed a fundamental lack of understanding, or appreciation, of the tenets of critical qualitative research.

In the end, I eventually persuaded the committee to grant the ethics application, which they still did only reluctantly. In so doing, I had to resign permanently from the governing board and, by that time, also had to delay the project to the following school year. That said, I did at least win one battle, by successfully arguing against the use of a formalized Observation Schedule in the ethnographic research project.

What this vignette highlights is the subsumption by a narrowly defined procedural ethics – based on an inappropriate biomedical model – of a broader, interdisciplinary, research ethics in practice. The university ethics committee couched its initial refusal in terms of the potential abuse of power that my governing board role, and even my relationship with the school, might involve. This was the point/position they continually returned to over the subsequent nine months of debate and negotiation. While ostensibly well-meaning, this position construed any pre-existing relationships within a school as high risk, by definition. This position ignores the longstanding disciplinary practices of educational research within schools (e.g., think of action research projects by teachers) that view such interrelationships as normal and necessary, albeit with suitable provisos to ensure against abuse of power. Allied with this was the ethics committee's fundamental lack of understanding about the ethical implications of working within an Indigenous Māori context, as well as the methodological tenets of critical, qualitative social sciences research.

This position reflects a longstanding complaint against IRBs worldwide. The American Association of University Professors, for example, asserts that the approach taken by many IRBs "was established and has evolved within a clinical and biomedical framework that does not fit [social sciences] research" (2000, p. 267). In this respect, the biomedical approach to ethics is clearly predicated on individualistic conceptions that result in a reductionist view of both research access and participation. Access in biomedical terms is construed as primarily physical access to a research site. In contrast, the understanding of access in ethnographic research constitutes, as we have seen, a process of establishing, and then successfully maintaining, social relationships. As Atkinson (2015) argues, following Murphy and Dingwall (2007), the iterative nature of ethnographic research:

> [M]eans that access is always tentative and conditional, that "consent" is always relational and sequential, rather than based on a one-off contractual agreement, and that ethnographic researchers will never find it possible to specify at the outset [as biomedical ethics regimes require] all that their research will involve.
>
> *(p. 179)*

While not wanting to dismiss the importance of, or obvious need for, engaging with institutional ethical review procedures, we agree with Guillemin and Gillam when they observe that "[i]t appears that ethics at the procedural level [have] been imposed on qualitative research from outside" (2004, p. 268). Given this, we may need to be ready, in advance, to contest these IRB procedures if they demonstrably fail to recognize the key tenets and processes of critical ethnographic fieldwork. Indeed, as Atkinson concludes, it is incumbent upon us "to insist to multiple audiences that the intellectual commitments of ethnographic research are profoundly ethical, in ways that are not even approximated by bureaucratic protocols" (2015, p. 186). In short, when engaging with IRBs as a critical ethnographer, forewarned is forearmed!

References

American Association of University Professors (AAUP). (2000). *Protecting human beings: Institutional review boards and social science research*. AAUP.

Atkinson, P. (2015). *For ethnography*. Sage.

Bhattacharya, K. 2015. Diving deep into oppositional beliefs: Healing the wounded transnational, de/colonizing warrior within. *Cultural Studies <=> Critical Methodologies, 15*(6), 492–500.

Bakhtin, M. (1990). *Art and answerability: Early philosophical essays*. University of Texas Press.

Barad, K. (2007). *Meeting the universe halfway: Quantum physics and the entanglement of matter and meaning*. Duke University Press.

Bell, R. C., Martinez, M., & Rubio, B. (2022). Dialogical relationships and critical reflexivity as emancipatory praxis in a community based educational program. In S. May & B. Caldas (Eds.), *Critical ethnography, language, race/ism and education*. Multilingual Matters

Bernstein, K. (2019). Ethics in practice: Answerability in complex, multi-participant studies. In D. Warriner & M. Bigelow (Eds.), *Critical reflections on research methods: Power and equity in complex multilingual contexts* (pp. 127–142). Multilingual Matters.

Bishop, R. (2005). Freeing ourselves from neo-colonial domination in research: A Kaupapa Maori approach to creating knowledge. In N. Denzin & Y. Lincoln (Eds.), *The Sage handbook of qualitative research* (pp. 109–138). Sage.

Bourdieu, P. (1990). *The logic of practice*. Polity Press.

Chiseri-Strater, E. (1996). Turning in upon ourselves: Positionality, subjectivity, and reflexivity in case study and ethnographic research. In P. Mortensen & G. E. Kirsch (Eds.), *Ethics and responsibility in qualitative studies of literacy* (pp. 115–133). National Council of Teachers of English.

Coles, J. (2022). Beyond silence: Disrupting antiblackness through BlackCrit ethnography and black youth voice. In S. May & B. Caldas (Eds.), *Critical ethnography, language, race/ism and education*. Multilingual Matters

Conquergood, D. (1985). Performing as a moral act: Ethical dimensions of the ethnography of performance. *Literature in Performance, 5*(2), 1–13.

Deiri, Y. (2022). Multilingual radical intimate ethnography. In S. May & B. Caldas (Eds.), *Critical ethnography, language, race/ism and education*. Multilingual Matters.

Delgado-Gaitan, C. (1993). Researching change and changing the researcher. *Harvard Education Review, 64*(4), 389–411.

Dumas, M. J., & ross, k. m. (2016). 'Be real black for me": Imaging BlackCrit in education. *Urban Education, 51*(4), 415–442.

Emirbayer, M., & Desmond, M. (2012). Race and reflexivity. *Ethnic & Racial Studies, 35*(4), 574–599.

Fabian, J. (1990). Presence and representation: The Other and anthropological writing. *Critical Inquiry, 16*, 753–772.

Fields, J. (2008). *Risky lessons: Sex education and social inequality.* Rutgers University Press.

Fine, M. (1994). Working the hyphens: Reinventing self and other in qualitative research. In N. K. Denzin & Y. S. Lincoln (Eds.), *Handbook of qualitative research* (pp. 70–82). Thousand Oaks, CA: Sage.

Fine, M. (2006). Bearing witness: Methods for researching oppression and resistance – A textbook for critical research. *Social Justice Research, 19*(2), 83–108.

Fitzpatrick, K., & Allen, J. M. (2017). Tensions in ethnographic research. *The Ethnographic Edge, 1*(1), 47–59.

Flaherty, C. (2017, April 25). Past as prologue. *Inside Higher Ed.* https://www.insidehighered.com/news/2017/04/25/controversy-over-alice-goffman-leads-pomona-students-say-her-alleged-racial

Geertz, C. (1973). Thick description: Toward an interpretative theory of culture. In *The interpretation of cultures* (pp. 3–30). Basic Books.

Goffman, A. (2015). *On the run: Fugitive life in an American city.* Picador.

Guillemin, M., & Gillam, L. (2004). Ethics, reflexivity, and "ethically important moments" in research. *Qualitative Inquiry, 10*(2), 261–280.

Hill, R., & May, S. (2011). Exploring biliteracy in Māori-medium education: An ethnographic perspective. In T. McCarty (Ed.), *Ethnography in language policy* (pp. 161–184). Routledge.

Hill, R., & May, S. (2013). Non-indigenous researchers in indigenous language education: Ethical implications. *International Journal of the Sociology of Language, 219*(1), 47–65.

Hoskins, T. K. (2012). A fine risk: Ethics in Kaupapa Maori politics. *New Zealand Journal of Educational Studies, 47*(2), 85–99.

Jackson, J. (2004). An ethnographic flimflam: Giving gifts, doing research, and videotaping the native subject/object. *American Anthropologist, 106*(1), 32–42.

Johansson, L. (2016). Post-qualitative line of flight and the confabulative conversation: A methodological ethnography. *International Journal of Qualitative Studies in Education, 29*(4), 445–466.

Jones, A., & Jenkins, K. (2008). Rethinking collaboration: Working the indigene-colonizer hyphen. In N. K. Denzin, Y. S. Lincoln, & L. T. Smith (Eds.), *Handbook of critical indigenous methodologies* (pp. 471–486). New York, NY: Sage.

Lather, P. (2001). Postbook: Working the ruins of feminist ethnography. *Journal of Women in Culture and Society, 27*(1), 199–227.

Lather, P. (2007). *Getting lost: Feminist efforts toward a double(d) science.* State University of New York Press.

Lather, P., & St. Pierre, E. A. (2013). Post-qualitative research. *International Journal of Qualitative Studies in Education, 26*(6), 629–633.

Lewis-Kraus, G. (2016, January 12). The trials of Alice Goffman. *The New York Times Magazine.* https://www.nytimes.com/2016/01/17/magazine/the-trials-of-alice-goffman.html

Macbeth, D. (2001). On "reflexivity" in qualitative research: Two readings and a third. *Qualitative Inquiry, 7*(1), 35–68.

MacLure, M. (2013). Researching without representation? Language and materiality in post-qualitative methodology. *International Journal of Qualitative Studies in Education, 26*(6), 658–667.

Madison, D. S. (2006). The dialogic performative in critical ethnography. *Text and Performance Quarterly, 26*(4), 320–324.

Madison, D. S. (2019). *Critical ethnography: Method, ethics, and performance* (3rd ed.). Sage.

Markham, A. (2005). The methods, politics and ethics of representation in online ethnography. In N. Denzin & Y. Lincoln (Eds.), *The Sage handbook of qualitative research* (3rd ed., pp. 793–820). Sage.

May, S. (1997). Critical ethnography. In N. Hornberger (Ed.), *Research methods and education. Encyclopedia of language and education* (1st ed., Vol. 8., pp. 197–206). Kluwer.

May, S., & Fitzpatrick, K. (2019). Critical ethnography. In P. Atkinson, S. Delamont, A. Cernat, J. W. Sakshaug, & R. A. Williams (Eds.), *Sage research methods foundations.* Sage. http://dx.doi.org/10.4135/9781526421036831954

Murphy, E., & Dingwall, R. (2007). Informed consent, anticipatory regulation and ethnographic practice. *Social Science and Medicine, 65*(11), 2223–2234.

Naples, N. (1996). A feminist revisiting of the insider/outsider debate: The "outsider phenomenon" in rural Iowa. *Qualitative Sociology* 19(1), 83–106.

Noblit, G., Flores, S., & Murillo, E. (Eds.). (2004). *Postcritical ethnography: An introduction.* Hampton.

Ortner, S. (1995). Resistance and the problem of ethnographic refusal. *Comparative Studies in Society and History, 37*(1), 173–193.

Paechter, C. (2012). Researching sensitive issues online: Implications of a hybrid insider/outsider position in a retrospective ethnographic study. *Qualitative Research, 13*(1), 71–86.

Palmer, D., & Caldas, B. (2017). Critical ethnography. In K. King, Y-J. Lai, & S. May (Eds.), *Research methods in language and education. Encyclopedia of language and education* (3rd ed., pp. 381–392). Springer.

Paris, D., & Winn, M. T. (Eds.). (2014). *Humanizing research: Decolonizing qualitative inquiry with youth and communities.* Sage.

Patai, D. (1994). When method becomes power. In A. Gitlin (Ed.), *Power and method* (pp. 61–73). Routledge.

Penehira, M., Smith, L. T., Green, A., & Aspin, C. (2011). Mouri matters: Contextualising mouri in Māori health discourse. *AlterNative: An International Journal of Indigenous Peoples, 7*(2), 177–187.

Pillow, W. (2003). Confession, catharsis, or cure? Rethinking the uses of reflexivity as methodological power in qualitative research. *International Journal of Qualitative Studies in Education, 16*(2), 175–196.

Popkewitz, T. S. (1998). The culture of redemption and the administration of research. *Review of Education Research, 68*(1), 1–34.

Shankman, P. (2009). *The thrashing of Margaret Mead: Anatomy of an anthropological controversy.* University of Wisconsin Press.

Smith, G. (1997). *Kaupapa Maori as transformative practice* [Unpublished PhD thesis]. University of Auckland.

Smith, L. (2012). *Decolonizing methodologies: Research and indigenous people* (2nd ed.). Zed Books.

St. Pierre, E. (2011). Post-qualitative research: The critique and the coming after. In N. K. Denzin & Y. S. Lincoln (Eds.), *Sage handbook of qualitative research* (4th ed., pp. 611–635). Sage.

St. Pierre, E. (2015). Refusing human being in humanist qualitative inquiry. In N. Denzin & M. Giardina (Eds.), *Qualitative inquiry – past, present, and future: A critical reader* (pp. 103–120). Routledge.

Subedi, B. (2006). Theorizing a 'halfie' researcher's identity in transnational fieldwork. *International Journal of Qualitative Studies in Education, 19*(5), 573–593.

Toohey, K. (2018). The onto-epistemologies of new materialism: Implications for applied linguistic pedagogies and research. *Applied Linguistics, 40*(6), 937–956.

Vanderstaay, S. L. (2005). One hundred dollars and a dead man: Ethical decision making in ethnographic fieldwork. *Journal of Contemporary Ethnography, 34*(4), 371–409.

Van Maanen, J. (2011). *Tales of the field: On writing ethnography* (2nd ed.). University of Chicago Press.

Villenas, S., & Foley, D. (2011). Critical ethnographies of education in the Latino/a diaspora. In R. Valencia (Ed.), *Chicano school failure and success: Past, present and future* (3rd ed., pp. 175–196). Routledge.

Webb, J. (2008). *Understanding representation.* Sage.

Weis, L., Fine, M., & Dimitriadis, G. (2009). Towards a critical theory of method in shifting times. In M. Apple, W. Au, & L. Armando Gandin (Eds.), *The Routledge international handbook of critical education* (pp. 437–448). Routledge.

5

BEING AND DOING CRITICAL ETHNOGRAPHY

Ethnographic Writing and Fieldwork

To engage in ethnographic inquiry, to do critical ethnography, requires us to be, and to be bold. It invites us to step out and to leap off: to begin, to start somewhere, on something. To do ethnography, you must become an ethnographer. To become an ethnographer, you must undertake ethnographic fieldwork. There are many ways to do this, but it requires embodied action. It also requires an ethnographic imagination that is not limited to/by a preoccupation with particular methods. Critical ethnography is a methodology, underpinned by ontologies and theories, not a prescriptive set of un- or under-contextualized methods, employed in recipe fashion.

Critical ethnography then involves being and doing. Being is most important, and it requires an ethnographer to see, feel, and move with ethnographic sensibilities and critical awareness. To *be* an ethnographer is to experience – in the body – the field/s that one is curious about; it is deeply relational, responsive, and emotional. Being involves ethnographic sensibility, an attention to people, place, embodiment, things, context, and a deep listening and noticing. All ethnography is relational and an ethnographer has to try to grapple with their own ego, their presumptive knowledge of context, and cultivate openness to the new, the absurd (Atkinson, 2019), the ordinary, the chaotic, as well as to patterns, language, body movements, how spaces are constructed, and many other things. A sensory approach can be helpful here (see Pink, 2015). Then (at the same time) one must also "do". The doing can be about reading, writing, observing, engaging, drawing, taking photos, interviewing, talking with, listening, interacting, and many other actions.

In this chapter, we reflect on various ways of *being* and *doing* that arise out of ethnographic fieldwork. But we want to conceptualize these beings and doings in line with, in response to, and in conversation with, theory. We do so because

DOI: 10.4324/9781315208510-5

we maintain that ethnography is a broad approach to research, and that critical ethnography (of the kind we propose) requires an engagement with ontology and epistemology and, therefore, with critical social theory. We also maintain that critical ethnography's eclectic use of methods is consonant with critiques of the (over)systematization of research methods (as discussed in Chapter 3). Ethnographers have always had an organic approach to methods – they do not know exactly what specific methods they will use or engage with until they are in the field. In this sense, methods can be approached in a way that is responsive, rather than strictly intentional. While ethnographers are certainly not ignorant about distinct methods, and their relative merits and possibilities, one never actually knows what methods will be right, purposeful, connected, practical, or productive until the project has begun.

Rooted in anthropology, ethnographers have typically taken a ground-up approach to fieldwork, letting the field and its subjects (or objects) speak. The field speaks in words, movements, rituals, relationships, feelings, intuitions, smells, sounds, tastes. It speaks in the arrangement of things, and interactions between and with animals, places, events, and objects, and it speaks through the geographies of buildings, streets, landscapes, and wide-open spaces. Ethnographers have, thus, always been concerned with the more-than-human. While posthumanism and new materialisms have certainly shifted the ontological gaze, ethnographers have always noticed the relationships in the field between people and other objects/actors, as well as structures, even if they maintained an anthropocentric ontology (for further discussion on this, see Chapter 3). Many ethnographers demonstrate that this methodology does not need to be so limited (e.g., Pedersen, 2013; Hamilton & Taylor, 2017; Hickey-Moody, 2020). Critical ethnographers experience the field through attending to power relations and in conversation with theory. We suggest that the field and theory work in dynamic relationship with each other. In critical ethnography, theory and method(s) coalesce to form ethnographic fieldwork and practice.

Critical Ethnography as Methodology (Rather Than Method)

Like all ethnography, critical ethnography requires the researcher to gain deep, lived understandings of a context and to reflect on the meanings of cultures within that context. This requires significant time in the field trying to understand what Willis refers to as "the social creativity of a culture" (1977, p. 121). Ethnographers employ a range of actual methods, depending on the focus and the site; these can include field notes, visual artifacts (such as photos and artwork), interviews, observations, participation, and a range of visual and arts-based methods. Documents such as official policies and email conversations, statutes, websites, newsletters, and the like can also be included. Contemporary ethnographers are increasingly using participant-generated research methods and engaging participants as co-researchers, videographers, photographers, diarists, and inter-viewers (see Pink, 2021; Pink et al., 2016). Ethnography in this sense is not bound by any rigid methodological rules. Rather, it draws on a range of methods and is flexible – dependent on practicality, the research foci, and relationships between participants and researchers. This is possible in ethnography, as a range of methodological tools can be used within a broad framework and, crucially, wider social and political contexts can be analyzed alongside and in relation to specific contextual incidences (May & Fitzpatrick, 2019).

Given this, we do not attempt to explain in detail here the various approaches to ethnographic methods or fieldwork, about which there are already a myriad of texts (see e.g., Atkinson, 2015, 2019; Atkinson et al., 2001; Blommaert & Jie, 2021; Coffey, 2018; Delamont, 2016; Madison, 2019). Instead, we suggest that – under the broad methodology of critical ethnography – more specific methods might be thought of as responses to the challenges and possibilities of doing ethnographic fieldwork and as particular ways to approach the interrogation of power-laden relationalities.

Methods then become leaping-off points for ethnographic doings. How any-one approaches their own project will depend on the inquiry they are undertak-ing, the ethico-onto-epistemologies (Barad, 2007) with which they engage, the practicalities of context, as well as the relationalities of the field. Barad (2007) argues that there is no separation between the self and the world. So, ethics is inextricably tied to being and knowing, and therefore, to knowledge production. Writing, we argue, is therefore, an ethical undertaking that is inseparable from ontology and epistemology (see also Geerts & Carstens, 2019).

Being inspired by the loosening of method (as discussed in Chapter 3), we think that ethnographers might work with ontology and field/context (in dynamic articulation), keep in mind a broad set of tenets (see Chapter 2), and then, perhaps, view their methodological doings and happenings as points to leap off from: as responses to the field; as theoretical relationalities; as ways to inquire. These may not be (and probably are not) all planned in advance because they will rely on the context of the research and the relationships (and relationalities) encountered therein. We do understand that ethics review boards require plan-ning specific methods, but we favor keeping these broad and expansive so that a range of options is available (see also Chapter 4).

In this chapter, we will discuss examples of work that has inspired us, to show (instead of tell) what ethnographic beings and doings – writing, fieldwork, and other methods – might and can involve. These examples will also highlight how a critical ethnographer must always be alert to relations of power. This might begin with considering in/equalities and in/exclusions, but in the messiness of ethno-graphic fieldwork and practice, these categories will unavoidably get challenged and nuanced; contradictory and unstable power relations will emerge. Remaining open to the mess is important. Lather argues that all ethnographic practice is partial, incomplete, and bewildered so that "we often do not know what we are seeing, how much we are missing, what we are not understanding, or even how to locate those lacks" (2001, p. 217). This practice of "not-knowing" (which she draws from Derrida's notion of double effacement) is a move to displace mastery so that the ethnographer is immersed in the project, while simultaneously questioning the bounds of the project's possibilities and the limits of their own knowing. She asks:

> Given contemporary demands for practices of knowing with more to answer to in terms of the complexities of language and the world, what would be made possible if we were to think of ethnography as a space surprised by difference into the performance of practices of not-knowing? Meaning, reference, subjectivity, objectivity, truth, tradition, ethics: What would it mean to say "yes" to what might come from unlocking such concepts from regularizing and normalizing? In making room for something else to come about, how do we stop confining the other within the same? This is about the ethics of not being so sure, about deferral while entire problematics are recast and resituated away from standard logics and procedures.
>
> *(Lather, 2001, pp. 218–219)*

We take from this that a challenge for critical ethnographers is to engage with the complexities of the field, with notions of power and ethics and relationalities, and then also to trouble these, to remain unsure, to question the basis of our assumptions and our own representations of our work. In this, processes of writing are of central consideration. And so, in this chapter, we dedicate significant attention to ethnographic writing, centralizing it to show what writing can do, why it is important, and why it requires intense attention (to detail, to word choice, to construction, to context, to craft). We conclude the chapter with some brief observations about field/work – the intersection of field and work (method) – as well as, perhaps, the over preoccupation with the ethnographic interview as a key ethnographic method.

Ethnographic Writing

To write is to write and rewrite, edit and delete, and rewrite again. It is a creative engagement, a letter to the reader. Writing is, in many ways, the central concern of the ethnographer (although we acknowledge the possibilities of other forms of ethnographic production, including arts-based, performative, and visual methods); the principal means by which to draw in the reader (Delamont, 2016). Writing is also partial, wholly constructed, and a process which enables troubling while also potentially obscuring its own production. Producing ethnographic texts may enable engagement with Lather's (2001) practice of not-knowing, but it also risks covering up its creative mess in a search for the neat, complete, and coherent text.

And so, we begin, consciously, to talk about the problem of what to do (of method) by talking about writing: writing as inquiry (Richardson, 2003); writing as creative-relational inquiry (Wyatt, 2019); writing as central ethnographic practice (Atkinson, 2019); writing as performativity (Pollock, 1998); and writing as a bridge to possibility (Poulos, 2014). And, most importantly for critical ethnography, writing as a political act, as a practice of not-knowing (Lather, 2001). While writing is not the only productive output, it is certainly dominant and continues to have the greatest salience in academic texts (as well as in novels, blogs, short stories, poetry, and narrative). It tends to be enhanced and extended, rather than replaced in ethnographic publications, by other forms, such as visual art, photographs, digital recordings, dance, and other movement practices. We certainly do not want to diminish these other forms, but, we admit, writing is, indeed, still an essential and central ethnographic practice. Writing is a craft, an art, a discipline, and (hopefully) a pleasure. It might be difficult, but it is always relational. Writing needs an audience, it craves one. With reference to the relational, Wyatt aims for "writing that does; a writing that aspires to intervene in the everyday of the personal/social/political" (2019, p. 9). Drawing on the French feminist writer and philosopher, Hélène Cixous, he conceptualizes writing as a gesture that is "fragile but not futile. . . . Writing is the movement we make towards the other and towards the world" (p. 19). It is also "an act of resistance to the pressure to stay silent, to do nothing" (p. 20). Poulos suggests that writing is essential, both to life and ethnographic practice: "If you want to be successful as an ethnographer . . . you have to write. And write. And write some more" (2014, p. 347). Atkinson observes that "as social researchers, we all have to write" (2019, p. 2).

Any approach to writing is a matter of ethico-onto-epistemology (Barad, 2007), as well as style and purpose. While many ethnographers view writing as an organic process – which it is or can be – it is also a political one. What we choose to write about, what we include and exclude, are all produced by the social, political, and relational contexts we inhabit. How we write, what we attend to, and what we say, *matters*. bell hooks (2015) reminds us that, if our research is to make any difference, then it is pointless to only communicate with a few relatively privileged academics. She notes that textual practices are important in this regard:

> Combining personal with critical analysis and theoretical perspectives can engage listeners who might otherwise feel estranged, alienated. To speak simply with language that is accessible to as many folks as possible is also important. Speaking about one's personal experience or speaking with simple language is often considered by academics and/or intellectuals (irrespective of their political inclinations) to be a sign of intellectual weakness or even anti-intellectualism.
>
> *(hooks, 2015, p. 77)*

hooks challenges us to resist inaccessible language, which creates social boundaries. How we write (and who we write for) can and does, inevitably, include or exclude. Reflecting on his life at a university, post World War II, Geertz commented that "[o]ne might be lost or helpless, or racked with ontological anxiety; but one could try, at least, not to be obtuse"[1] (2000, p. 7). This is an important reminder for writer ethnographers that there is an audience and there is a politics in communicating with them. Geertz also argued that "[a]nthropology . . . involves a seriously divided life. The skills needed in the classroom or at the desk and those needed in the field are quite different" (2000, pp. 15–16). Atkinson (2019) likewise asserts that:

> [F]ieldnotes are inscriptions of attention, engagement and memory. They exist only because we transform phenomena into textual representations. By the same token, they achieve their significance because of recurrent acts of attention, reflection and imagination. They have no value or significance in themselves unless and until they are animated by our intellectual work: in transmuting notes into ideas, and transforming those ideas into further textual forms.
>
> *(p. 35)*

Rinehart (1998) notes that the process of translating experience into written form is not easy:

> Lives, true enough, can be seen as compartmentalized and fragmented: To handle the chaos of contemporary life, many of us have learned the skill of compartmentalizing, of classifying experience into neat, scientific components. But raw experience, I contend, comes at a rush. It is only after the effects of life have washed over us that we reconstitute them as belonging to this or that category. Life is magical and complex and multifaceted, and that is how ethnographers using a fictionally derived method might learn to "report" it.
>
> *(p. 201)*

Writing is a creative act of translation and communication, an attempt to reach out to a reader. We write to understand our own experiences, to record a version of what we see, and hear, and feel, and smell. Pollock imagines writing "at the brink of meaning, poised between abjection and regression". She argues that "writing as doing replaces writing as meaning; writing becomes meaningful in the material, dis/continuous act of writing" (1998, p. 75). Writing is always partial and incomplete; there is always more. Lather argues that we might attend to "where the text becomes a site of the failures of representation, and textual experiments are not so much about solving the crisis of representation as about troubling the very claims to represent" (2001, p. 201). Braidotti views writing as "a method for transcribing cosmic intensity into sustainable portions of being" (2013, p. 166). This is a particularly evocative way to communicate how powerful writing is. There are many approaches and no one right way. In what follows, we explore some of the key ethnographic writing possibilities.

Types of Ethnographic Writing

Sara Delamont (2016, p. 39) suggests that there are four types of writing for ethnographers to engage in. Each concerns the very purpose of writing. First is "[w]riting the data". Writing, she states, "makes up the basic data of ethnography: fieldnotes, interview transcripts . . . conventional documents or online text". Second is "[w]riting to be reflexive", which has many different approaches, such as a "field diary or reflexive journal in which the researcher records their reactions to the experiences of data collection and analysis". She suggests that researchers keep an "out of the field" diary journal as well, to record their thoughts, reflections, and insights. Third, Delamont explains is "[w]riting to aid analysis", which is about the process of analyzing and theorizing the research materials. Finally, her fourth category is "[w]riting for others to read", which refers to all research communications, including books, articles, and social media announcements. Delamont's four types of writing highlight purpose and audience as important considerations and position writing as both a process and a product, a way of thinking, and a way of analyzing as well as representing. Audience has been a key consideration of feminist research as a move to include, communicate, and trouble the masculinist voice of science. So too should it be in critical ethnographic fieldwork. This is quite a systematized way to think about writing that is consistent with realist ontologies. Other ontologies offer different possibilities (for further discussion of how different social theories impact ethnographic practice, see Chapter 3).

Tales

Atkinson (2019) differentiates between realist writing and other more creative forms. Van Maanen (2011) argues that all research is a process of telling tales, and names realist tales, confessional tales, and impressionist tales as three possible approaches. Each of these is informed and formed by the ontologies of the writing and of the study. Realist writing positions the author in the background and uses an impersonal and detached tone. According to Atkinson, realist ethnography "reflects a taken-for-granted textual style. It reflects the kind of writing that is common in much non-fiction reportage, and indeed shares features with realist fiction too" (2019, p. 67). Realist writing attempts to convey "what actually 'happened' and can function as a 'readerly' text, while more 'writerly' texts might be needed in order to do justice to the complexities of quotidian activity" (2019, p. 85). In this sense, realist texts tend to obscure their own production and to present the research setting and analysis as self-evident, rather than highly constructed and crafted. The craft itself, and the messiness of the research site and the research process, is obscured in favor of a cleaned up and tidy account.

Confessional tales seek to make the fieldwork and the process of its production more transparent than is apparent in realist writing. These include autobiographic detail and authorial ownership (the use of "I" in the text) and typically provide more context to realist tales (e.g., being placed alongside a realist account) (Van Maanen, 2011). Impressionist tales, Van Maanen's third category, draw from the art movement. He describes this kind of writing as focused on specific moments and stories, up close accounts of memorable and colorful scenes:

> The impressionists of ethnography are also out to startle their audience. But striking stories, not luminous paintings, are their stock-in-trade. Their materials are words, metaphors, phrasings, imagery, and most critically, the expansive recall of fieldwork experience. When these are put together and told in the first person as a tightly focused, vibrant, exact, but necessarily imaginative rendering of fieldwork, an impressionist tale of the field results.
> *(Van Maanen, 2011, pp. 101–102)*

Impressionistic writing is thus dramatic, evocative, and emotive. Van Maanen (2011) notes that, to any of these tales, ethnographers can apply different modes of analyses and theory.

Sparkes (2002) adds to Van Maanen's trio four more kinds of "tales": autoethnography, ethnodrama, poetic representations, and fictional representations. All of these consider the onto-epistemology and form of qualitative writing, and Sparkes (2002) encourages researchers to think of themselves as storytellers. Autoethnography – a significant field in its own right – combines aspects of autobiography with ethnography. As Ellis et al. observe, it "is an approach to research and writing that seeks to describe and systematically analyze (graphy) personal experience (auto) in order to understand cultural experience (ethno)" (2011, p. 273). Ethnodrama involves the development of a written theatrical script that comprises significant sections of ethnographic narrative in dramatized form. It is performative writing aimed at reaching a wider audience and enhancing narrative impact (McMahon, 2016; Caldas, 2022). Poetic representations draw on poetry to represent the author's experience, the words of participants, and to evoke ethnographic scenes. There are many ways to use poetic writing in ethnography (see e.g., Faulkner, 2016; Fitzpatrick & Fitzpatrick, 2021).

Fictional representations involve the writer in constructing fictional accounts from experience and imagination. These might be inspired by actual research but make no claims to be empirical texts as such. In this, authors have license to embellish, imagine, and extrapolate. Creative nonfiction and creative fiction are used by some authors (for further discussion and examples, see Clough, 2002; Wyatt, 2007). Ellis (2000) uses the term "ethnographic short story" and "methodological novel" (Ellis, 2004). Others have employed fiction (or faction) writing to create research novels (e.g., Bruce, 2016; Sleeter, 2020). Crucially, these researchers employ fiction and creative methods to write about and against issues of social injustice. In *The Inheritance*, for example, Christine Sleeter (2018) creates the character Denise, a teacher and a woman who benefits directly from an American Indian tribe being forcibly removed from their ancestral lands. The book explores the white guilt of the character, and her attempts to grapple with her responsibilities as a teacher to make these histories known. Tanner (2016) uses collaborative fiction to explore notions of whiteness and privilege. She combines youth participatory action research with drama to co-create a play about whiteness and racism. In another example, Bruce (2016) draws on decades of her own and others' research in women's sport to inform a novel about elite sport, gender, media, and commercialization. Such examples imagine possible futures, create characters that readers care about, and introduce research themes in personal and evocative ways. They take ethnography to its possible ends, challenging definitions of research and modes of research writing. While these are not necessarily forms of critical ethnography, they show that writing is always partially a fiction; it is always representing the thing, it is not the thing itself.

Atkinson (2019) argues that many contemporary accounts claim to be "new" writing or experimental writing forms that decenter the author, use arts-based methods, and engage in messy lived texts. He cautions against overclaiming in this regard and argues that:

> [T]oo many contemporary authors fail to engage fully with either modernist or postmodern literary models, instead resorting to what I call sentimental realism. Far from "decentring the author", they reinstate an author and privilege her or his subjectivity. They display, therefore, a failure of literary nerve.
>
> *(p. 107)*

Atkinson points out that, in fact, the modernist writing of the early 20th century was already using discursive forms, such as stream of consciousness and multiple perspectives (as in the work of Virginia Woolf, James Joyce, and others). He argues that experimental, literary, and surrealist styles of writing have thus always been part of ethnographic endeavor, including writing from the perspectives of non-human actors:

> There is nothing new in an aesthetics of ethnography. Indeed, from realist roots, through surrealist and modernist developments, ethnography has always enjoyed a close affinity with diverse forms of literary and artistic representation.
>
> *(p. 110)*

Atkinson wonders whether surrealist accounts might challenge the tendency for rationalist ethnographic texts, and he challenges ethnographers to be bolder in their writing. Regardless of style, however, we have a responsibility to make our writing *good*, to craft it so that it compels the reader, so that it inspires imagination, so that it engages emotion, and elucidates issues of privilege, in/justice, dis/advantage, the absurd, the interesting, the strange, and the everyday. To this end, many writers employ story and narrative.

Stories and Narrative

> a story is born and lives in the space between the storyteller and the audience. The storyteller cannot hold their story too tightly to themselves. To live, it must have room to grow.
>
> . . . .
>
> It lives in the telling.
> *We* live in the telling.
> But that is telling.
> We are creatures of words. We are creatures of imagination. We live on the edges of dreams and the margins of thought. We live in the whisper of the page.
>
> (Hereaka, 2019, p. 27)

In order to communicate the rich, embodied, and complex nature of ethnographic experience, many writers have represented their research as story or narrative. There are many different approaches to this work. Van Maanen notes that ethnography exists "somewhere in academic limbo-land (or purgatory) as a storytelling institution possessing a good deal of scholarly legitimacy whose works are commissioned and approved by the leading educational institutions of the day" (2006, p. 13). McDrury and Alterio (2003) remind us that:

> Storytelling is a uniquely human experience that enables us to convey, through the language of words, aspects of ourselves and others, and the worlds, real or imagined that we inhabit. Stories enable us to come to know these worlds and our place in them, given that we are all, to some degree, constituted by stories: stories about ourselves, our families, friends and colleagues, our cultures, our place in history.
>
> *(p. 31)*

Clandinin and Connelly (2000) maintain that narrative is a powerful way to both communicate and interpret experience. Narrative invokes the storytelling traditions of many cultures and so is familiar and engaging as well as accessible. Well-written narratives contain what Denzin (1997) has called verisimilitude – the sense that what is relayed is authentic, without making claims to truth. Atkinson (2019) notes that ethnographies:

> [D]epend for their analytic and argumentative force on establishing story-lines and narrative threads. There are no recipes for finding and spinning such a story. And no amount of thematic coding, sorting and moving extracts of data will help us do so. On the other hand, finding "stories" that carry the analysis will do far more than any such procedural management of field data.
>
> *(p. 88)*

Atkinson instructs ethnographers to "[s]top coding and start thinking about your narrative resources!" (p. 88). Narrative writing is also political. It can be more accessible but is, like all writing, a reinterpretation, reinscription, a representation. Choosing which stories to tell, which characters to centralize, and which moments to highlight are authorial choices that carry responsibility. Narratives can risk constructing participants as autonomous, coherent, "understandable", and stable subjects (Blumenreich, 2004). Shifting cultural contexts, and complex, unstable identities, can be more difficult to present as story. Narrative authors can also risk making themselves into a god-like figure, one who drives the narrative but is invisible to the reader (Clandinin & Connelly, 2000).

The *beyond bullying project* (https://beyondbullyingproject.com/) provides an exemplar of inclusive, political, accessible narrative practices. It employed a story booth to invite people to tell their own stories. Working with a physical booth in schools, and then with a digital booth online, the project invited young people to share a story about lesbian, gay, bisexual, transgender or queer gender, and sexuality in their lives. The project constructed the booth as a safe space for self-recording; the researchers were not present, and people were simply invited to tell their stories. The stories are available on the website, which also invites more storytelling. One of the stories is titled "I Was the Tomboy":

> My story is going to be about my sexuality.
>
> And being bullied about it. So probably about like my eighth-grade year, I started to realize that um-, the way I looked at other girls, like I noticed that girls are pretty. And I didn't dress girly, like other girls. I was kind of a boyish kind of girl. I was the tomboy. I loved sports. I played football, played volleyball, and right now in my sophomore year, I'm playing softball. In my eighth-grade year, I had decided to come out. The first person I told was my friend, L. She accepted me. She was a real cool friend. And I loved her for that.
>
> But other kids, they just, they didn't accept the fact that I liked girls. Even though I still like boys, too. Bisexual is the term. But I mean, I think

people are special the way they are. I have friends who are gay, who are transgender, and I love them all because they love me. So, eighth-grade year was hard. When I came into my freshman year I met a new friend. And we had a lot of good memories together cause, you know, he was also bisexual. So, we had a nice mutual understanding cause we knew what each other was going through. And I don't know, I think it's because it was high school and a lot of kids had a lot of understanding of what the term bisexual was and there was people who accepted the fact that I was bisexual.

(https://beyondbullyingproject.com/project/bbp-stories-i-was-the-tomboy/)

The project employed digital forms of storytelling to allow participants to narrate their own accounts in their own words. It also includes accounts written by the research team about how the storytelling project created encounters in the schools:

Randee, a mixed-race, gregarious, slightly awkward first-year student. Randee seemed to wander through the school, not settle into any class, activity, or course of study – neither hiding nor trying to leave. Our booth, meant to collect stories of lesbian, gay, bisexual, transgender, and queer (LGBTQ+) sexuality and gender from students, teachers, and staff over two weeks, became her temporary home base. On that first day, she expressed interest in telling a story about losing friends when she came out as a lesbian in grade 8. Evan, a racially mixed, gay staff member in the school's Wellness Center and a leader on LGBTQ+ issues at West High, greeted Randee when he brought another student to the booth to tell a story. Evan played an active role in supporting students like Randee – queer and on the edge of the school community. Having spent months trying to convince Randee to attend class, Evan pointed to her and said to our team, "This is what truancy looks like". Indeed, across our two weeks at West High, several teachers came to the booth, found Randee, and walked her back to class. For her part, Randee insisted, "I don't feel like [school's] for me". Evan speculated later that "gay boys" head downtown to escape school and hang out with street-involved gay youth, but "queer girls" stick around, walk other girls to class, and flirt. We watched Randee do just that: escort young women to and from our booth and, later, offer to accompany us to our presentations about the project in classes. In her interview, she described avoiding her own classes even as she regularly attended her friend's health class because the friend did not want to go alone.

(Gilbert et al., 2018, p. 164)

The researchers in this project, Gilbert et al. (2018), note that there are a myriad of accounts of the problems and failures of LGBTQI+ students in schools. The being and doing of this project – and the possibilities of storytelling – allow them to see other possible stories regarding Randee. They argue that:

> [T]o see her identity only through concerns about academic failure is to obscure the desires and relationships that queerness makes possible for Randee and the school's role in supporting and undermining those multiple and contradictory desires and relationships.
>
> *(p. 164)*

The researchers conclude that "telling and hearing stories allow people to author the self and to recognize intersecting lives of people, families, and communities, even as those same stories gesture toward spaces beyond current social and linguistic conventions" (pp. 164–165).

Stories are powerful. They bring the reader into direct emotional contact with participants. The stories we tell in research have impact. How we present and represent stories is important. Gilbert et al. (2018) have presented their participants' stories in the *beyond bullying project* powerfully, in their own words, and with sound files accompanying the texts. Others retell stories, carefully crafting the scene or the narrative to draw the reader in. Atkinson (2019) discusses the impact of graphic presence, writing an account of a specific event or moment in a way that makes the reader feel like they were actually there. This requires literary devices and writerly craft. Writing is a craft; a construction and a telling. Pollock reminds us that "[p]erformative writing is an important, dangerous, and difficult intervention into routine representations of social/performative life" (1998, p. 75). Telling stories – our own and others – is an ethical act and a messy, slippery process. Pollock notes that writing "moves with, operates alongside, sometimes through, rather than above or beyond, the fluid, contingent, unpredictable, discontinuous rush of (performed) experience – and against the assumption that (scholarly) writing must or should do otherwise" (p. 81). Stories are unbound and writing is, in part, unpredictable. Some 35 years ago, Clifford and Marcus (1986), in their influential edited collection that for the first time explored ethnographic writing as invention (rather than as an objectively real account), noted that all writing is partial truth, defined as much by what is left out as by what is included. Clifford, for example, insists in the Introduction that "ethnographic truths are thus inherently partial – committed and incomplete" (1986, p. 7). Atkinson (2019) notes that:

> There is an important and intricate relationship between our engagement with a given social world and our reconstruction of those social realities into textual forms. In the real world of research, these divisions – into fieldwork, analysis and writing – are spurious. They are simultaneous aspects of the research process, and their synchronicity is a particular feature of

ethnographic research. But we have to make some such distinctions in order to examine those complementary facets of the research process.

(p. 2)

Writing quality is an ongoing and contested issue. Clifford asks, "should not every accurate description be convincing?" (1986, p, 4) and Coffey (2018) notes that "ethnography has always been a literary endeavour" (p. 97). Pelias (2018) insists that we must learn from literature in order to be good writers and there is, indeed, a history of literary approaches to ethnographic writing (Bochner & Ellis, 2002). Van Maanen (2006) uses the term "textwork" to describe the importance of the craft of writing. He explains that "[t]extwork is a suturing together of two words meant to convey that writing is a labor-intensive craft and represents a good deal of what we do as intrepid ethnographers" (p. 14). Editing is also as important as writing in terms of inquiry. For Clough (2009):

> We are always working at the very boundaries of visibility, where imagina-
> tion must take over . . . and when we arrive – though it is seldom that;
> more, rather, a pause – we hold only vapid certainties. . . . This is, of
> course, a state of affairs which art happily shares with physics, and it is only
> we in the middle of that continuum of enquiry who endlessly and neuroti-
> cally rehearse our whining methodological discomforts.
>
> *(p. 347)*

All of the storying examples that we have drawn on thus far are still clearly situated within Western literary traditions and this is, of course, an ethnocentric and incomplete rendering of these possibilities. Other culturally located/distinct storying conventions add to the potential criticality of ethnographic fieldwork and practice, while also highlighting the cultural locatedness of voice and representation, along with the means to "speak back" to dominant discourses. Latinx scholars, for example, have drawn on the "cultural repertoires of practice" (Gutierrez & Rogoff, 2003) of Latinx families, including *consejos* (advice-giving narratives) and *historias* (stories) in their ethnographic writings. Black storywork, arising out of BlackCrit, and developed out of critical race theory's notion of counter-storying, is another key example. As discussed in Chapter 3, Coles highlights how Black storywork "captures the youth's critical collective storying rooted in their own words to bridge the contradictions between their lived experiences and distorted anti-Black narratives" (2020, p. 4). Multimodalities are also an integral focus of these critical renderings, characterized by a combination of collective storying layered with dialogue, freestyle rapping, writing, reading, drawing images, sharing photos, clothing (e.g., #BlackLivesMatter shirts), social media posts, and dancing (Coles, 2022). Pacific scholars draw on the process of *talanoa* (Vaioleti, 2006; Sualii-Sauni & Fulu-Aiolupotea, 2014) – a research practice that is centered on Pacific cultural practices and epistemologies – as "an analytical framework that enables dialogic practices to advance thinking and understanding and provide ample opportunities for individual and collective learning" (Baice et al., 2021, p. 80). Talanoa is culturally located, relies on relationalities, and "honours ethics of care and generosity, respect, reciprocity, negotiation, and encouragement" (p. 80).

Writing stories and narratives, and research accounts of any kind, is thus an ethical, cultural, and political act, one in which we are caught between the aesthetics and emotionalities of "good writing" and the culture and politics of which and whose stories to tell. The decisions we make impact both how readable our texts are, and how impactful the subject matter is. Tullis Owen et al. (2009) argue that the way we construct texts alters the very arguments we might make. Our writing is formed by the field as much as by the theory and, also, by their very intersection.

Writing With and Through Theory

St. Pierre (2018) argues that reading theory leads to living/writing theory. For her, after engaging with Derrida and Deleuze:

> Deconstruction happens. The text undoes itself. The movement of writing takes over, and the writer, the person . . . loses control and finds herself barely able to keep up in the thinkingwriting as words appear on the computer screen she could not have thought without writing. This writing does not begin in recognition (Ah, I recognize that – that's what that is! I'll describe it.). This writing is adventure, experimentation, pushing through toward what? Toward the unintelligible, toward Derrida's *différance*, Deleuze's pure difference, perhaps toward a different world.
>
> *(p. 605)*

For St. Pierre, the writing and the theory and the being are one, interwoven at the intersection of writer, writing, and theory. Ethnographers have, however, traditionally viewed the "field" as external to the researcher. Atkinson (2019) argues that social theory can too strongly direct research agendas so that:

> Fashionable theorists of today and of the recent past are often characteristic of continental European social thought. This strand of thinking is striking for the breadth of its scope, the power of its language, and its totalising tendency. By totalising, I mean that it somehow invites not the touchstone of empirical evidence, but commands loyalty and even devotion. Research can thus be assimilated to whatever "theory" is in vogue, with the research a mere instantiation of the pre-existing ideas. Consequently, too many students and younger scholars find themselves searching for "a theory" and a theorist to whom they can align themselves. They can depend upon – in

the sense of leaning on – the grand narratives of a Foucault, a Deleuze, a Bourdieu, a Butler, or a Haraway. Now do not misunderstand: famous theorists have productive ideas. But they do not have all the answers. Worse, adherence to them can lead to premature closure of research. Instead of informing the exploration of social worlds and worlds of ideas, the chosen "theory" can prove to be a Procrustean bed: everything is forced into a predictable shape in order to fit the pre-existing ideas.

(pp. 87–88)

These two arguments are worth considering in some detail in relation to how theory is approached in ethnographic writing. For St. Pierre (poststructuralist and new materialist ontology), there is no separation between the theory, the researcher, and the field. The theory becomes the writing, becomes the field, and all are in dynamic intra-action (Barad, 2007)[2] with each other. A deep understanding of Derrida or Deleuze writes its way into the text, is the text, co-writes the text. For Atkinson, the field and the theory are two different realities. The latter is used to understand the former, but the former also must be understood on its own terms and with its own voice. Both these perspectives provide different ways to approach research, each informed by different ontologies. The researcher's ontological position then informs how writing is undertaken, conceptualized, and brought into being.

Critical ethnography must be a process of dynamic interaction between the field and theory/ies. While critical ethnography requires critical theories, these need not be totalizing, or wholly construct what one experiences in the field. Theory will, indeed, inform the possibilities of thinking and engagements, and it also simultaneously obscures what we see, hear, and experience. One can't unthink theory though; reading theory changes how we think and who we are. Engaging in fields also changes how we are and how we think. In some ways, these are all inseparable. We live the field as much as we live the theory. We are part of both in inextricable ways. And it is from our being in both, in all this multiplicity, that we write. The ways of trying to understand writing that we narrate in this chapter are just a framework for trying to understand a somewhat mystical process. Even when we are trying to be intentional, the writing has its own life force, at the intersection (always) of field and theory and life and being. Some researchers engage these intensities as a process between writers, as an active engagement in-between.

Collaborative Writing

Another approach to writing is via collaboration, and there is significant work detailing different approaches to this kind of co-production (e.g., see Speedy, 2012, Speedy et al., 2010; Davies & Gannon, 2006; Diversi & Moreira, 2018). This is also a political act and decision and is approached in a myriad of ways, depending on context. Some ethnographers co-write with community members and participants. This is particularly the case in ethnographies that engage community members as co-researchers and those that engage participatory methods (Cammarota & Fine, 2010). In this, research questions and foci may be set by the co-researchers. Mazzei and Jackson (2012; see also Gale & Wyatt, 2009) write about collaborative writing, not as the connecting of two "I's", but as a materialist production of something that is (in)between:

> Part of what we have learned . . . is that writing between-the-two in the threshold is not a process of working individually to contribute to the whole but is a process of producing something not possible outside the space of the threshold where the "two" produce thinking not possible otherwise.
>
> *(p. 451)*

If we combine this idea with hooks' (2015) insistence that our writing must be accessible to community members for whom academic work is often not available, then the politics of collaborative writing with others outside the academy is a conscious political act. It is not necessarily an easy undertaking, but collaborative writing with community members means that "writing between-the-two" reaches ontologically further. We conceptualize this idea with Bourdieu's notion of field. The field is the social and cultural context, within which habitus is (dynamically) formed. Writing with someone who is located in a different cultural field (or a different intersection of fields) is powerful because it allows for a greater range of ontological possibilities in the intersection of fields and habitus. In a powerful account of autoethnography and poetry as decolonizing practice, Virginia Tamanui and Esther Fitzpatrick (2021) conceptualize their writing relationship as a friendship, a collaborative autoethnography, a conversation between two women, one Indigenous, one White; one outside the academy, one in the academy:

> Much like the conversations we shared in our local café, this work too is interrupted by quotes that resonate, poems in the making, tangential thoughts, as we weave ourselves into relationship. It is a collaborative autoethnography, a duoethnography, a storying of our becoming friendship. It is a living poem, stories in entanglement with others, always in the process of being/becoming bicultural.
>
> *(p. 183)*

Tamanui and Fitzpatrick argue that ancestry matters for ontology, and they invoke both their biological ancestors and their "ancestors of the mind", the ontologies that haunt their writing and thinking together. In this piece, the ancestors are both Māori (Indigenous) and Pākehā (White) within the New Zealand postcolonial context in which they live and write, and they argue with each other, they wrestle in their chapter for vocality. In the process, Derrida's notion of hauntology is both summoned and challenged. Tamanui, for example, writes to Fitzpatrick, stating:

> I never meant all that but you looked to find a way to connect . . . to fulfil
> a bicultural expectation that you have. What I mean is that you are so good
> at claiming things that aren't yours and shifting what it means to someplace
> else – shifting what I meant. . . . In the turn to escape blood and land
> through thought did you hear ME say hauntology? In fact, I said I don't
> like hauntings but here we are.
>
> *(Tamanui & Fitzpatrick, 2021, p. 186)*

Tamanui and Fitzpatrick's co-telling maps the contestation inherent in post/colonial relationships, a clashing and jostling of theoretical and ontological relationalities. A wrestling with the past and its difficult present articulations. They illustrate these relationalities throughout their collaborative account, inviting the reader to imagine them discussing, writing, turning away and back. They also use poetry to examine their complex, postcolonially situated relationship and observe that "[w]ithout poetry we can't speak. It is our breath" (p. 188). The decision to use poetry is also political. It decenters the dominance of prose in academic writing. It opens space and uncertainty. They use Māori and English to write, demonstrating bicultural engagement through the metaphor of weaving a *tukutuku* (woven panel):

> You arrive
> And gently pass me the flax,
> Through the veil.
> "Te Puia girl" you name me.
> Tuku tuku
> I pull you pull.
> The words lash together,
> Tuhi tuhi.
> Weaving together,
> A sleeping house for humanity.
>> How easy it is to misunderstand.
>> We return to preparing the fibres,
>> Finding each other again.
>> Tuku tuku,
>> I pull you pull.
>> Settling into the rhythms,
>> Settling into the repetitions
>> Time before and after.
> If I stuff up a lash
> We start again.
>
> *(Tamanui & Fitzpatrick, 2021, p. 195)*

Poetic form here becomes the representation of the spaces between (more on poetry later). In a different way, Gale and Wyatt (2009) work with Deleuze and Guattari to imagine and live their collaborative writing "between-the-two" of them. Theory is central to this endeavor:

> We draw upon the work of Deleuze to provide us with an appropriate figure that will give sense to the way in which the form and content of our book unfolds. The figures created by Deleuze reject the arborescent structure that books traditionally use: the tree with its branches and leaves reaching out for light (enlightenment) and its system of roots around the central tap root probing down into the earth searching for stability, working to establish strong foundations. In place of this traditional model, with its central core and firm trunk-like body, Deleuze proposes, through the application of principles of multiplicity, connection and heterogeneity, a model of the rhizome.
>
> *(p. 6)*

Collaborative writing isn't easy. Tamanui and Fitzpatrick caution that "[w]e never really grasped the time, energy, and emotion that would unfold, and who else would be involved" (2021, p. 188). They insist that an existing friendship is an important foundation for this work. Mazzei and Jackson (2012) state that:

> We then engage in the process of adding words, thoughts, questions, and examples to the emerging creation. Indeed, when we first began writing together, we could more easily identify our own words or thoughts in the final document, but as we have continued to work together, this becomes more and more difficult and, more importantly, unnecessary. This exemplifies the "in-between-ness" of the threshold – a space in which the machinic and productive forces of words, thoughts, questions, and examples function immanently in their becoming . . . [these] words and thoughts produced in the threshold no longer belong to one of us (as if they ever did) but are produced by the force that we make and that makes (and unmakes) us.
>
> *(pp. 454–455)*

The notion of voice within collaborative writing then is also political. For Tamanui and Fitzpatrick (2021), transparency of authorial voice is central to the politics of writing across relationalities of biculturalism in New Zealand's post-colonial context, what Michelle Fine (1994) calls "working the hyphens" (see Jones & Jenkins, 2008; see also Chapter 4). For Mazzei and Jackson (2012) and Gale and Wyatt (2009), the voices become blurred, interwoven, a new emergence at the intersection of the two. We have experienced the latter too with this co-authored book; its inevitably iterative construction, further expanded and extended by regular interruptions and delays over the few years of writing. And through it all, we have simultaneously had to negotiate/mediate the changing, often complex, dynamics between the personal, political, and academic dimensions of our own relationship in the writing of it.

We have dedicated significant attention in this chapter to writing, given its significance to/in navigating the interstices of theory, methodology, and ethnographic representation(s). But we now briefly turn to thinking about the intersections between field *and* work (method) – particularly, how the field shapes what we end up doing in any given ethnographic study, and how this is unavoidably theoretical. For this, we first need to consider what a field actually is, or what it might be.

Field/Work

> "I found myself facing that most brutal and inescapable . . . fact of the anthropological life: fieldwork"
>
> (Geertz, 2000, p. 9)

As with ethnographic writing, ethnographic fieldwork must always be informed by the theory/methodolody nexus. In our own critical ethnographic work, for example, we have previously drawn on Bourdieu's generative sociological model and concepts in order to work our methods in ways that are ontologically consistent with the theories applied (see e.g., Fitzpatrick, 2013; May, 1994). This avoids what Bourdieu et al. describe as the "mania for methodology", which "makes it possible not so much to achieve the economy of thought that all method permits, but rather to economize on thought about method" (1991, p. 62). Rigid and prescriptive approaches to methodology, they observe, simply enable researchers to "see more and more in less and less" (p. 62). Bourdieu et al. (1991) are essentially arguing here that we cannot dislocate the *how* of method from the *where* and *why* of context, culture, and politics, which are, inevitably, shaped by the field(s) in which we live and work. These fields not only include the research context but also our personal, professional, academic, and disciplinary locations, along with their complex intersections. This makes for a dynamic engagement with field and method. On the one hand, fields shape our engagement (what we do) with ethnographic research – via, for example, accepted methodological conventions and parameters. On the other hand, what we end up doing potentially (re)shapes the field(s) in which we work (Fitzpatrick & May, 2015). As Dillabough observes of the latter, we need to "uncover the degree to which . . . representations and their associated methodological approaches . . . may be seen as processes at work in shaping the cultural field" (2008, p. 203).

In traditional anthropological and ethnographic research, the ethnographer defined the field, went about living and experiencing the context and site of research, and then wrote about it. However, if we adopt the more dynamic/

intersectional view of the relationship between field and method and theory that we argue for here, the spatiotemporal boundaries of fields immediately become more slippery – more difficult to demarcate or define. St. Pierre (2018) sums this fluidity up well in her critical reflection on her own doctoral study:

> I wondered what exactly counted as an interview. Ohio State's Institutional Review Board had given me permission to interview the old women in my hometown who met my sample selection criteria, but it had not given me permission to interview an old school friend I met downtown whom I talked with as we ate hot dogs sitting at the same drugstore counter where we'd sat eating hot dogs as high school students. Could I use that data and data from all the other unapproved conversations I had during fieldwork to write with?
>
> My hometown was officially the field of my study, the natural setting. But my school friend and I both remarked during that lunch that we felt we were in the past as much as the present. When was the field? During fieldwork, I was, indeed, in the past – present – future – time was untimely. I'd been studying that small tobacco town since I moved there from Yankee country as a child of five. It had borne my never-ending scrutiny because I had been the Other there, never quite fitting. I had 35 years of field notes and interviews to work with, and, as I wrote, I strayed far from "official" data, overwhelmed with a lifetime of the real. So I made the field as I wrote. I laid out the field in sentence after sentence in all the writing spaces I could find. There could never be an "audit trail" from official data in interview transcripts and field notes to the sentences I wrote. I suppose my study wasn't valid.
>
> *(p. 606)*

In contemporary research, the notion of field is even more tricky to pin down, not least because our physical worlds are now so interspersed with the digital. In(between) digital worlds, as Blommaert and Jie observe, "[a]lgorithms shape what we could call 'relational architectures', and as soon as we . . . enter the online algorithmic universe, we are absorbed into these relational architectures" (2021, p. 87). Digital interactions, as usual daily practice for most people, mean that we engage relationalities across multiple digital platforms, each of which frames our interactions in direct ways, and each of which is linked to wider political worlds of surveillance, big data, advertising, monitoring, and feedback loops. We have relationships that are wholly digital and physically distanced. But what even is distance, when we can see, hear, connect, and feel each other so clearly across and within digital worlds? Temporalities shift in digital landscapes – digital objects are ever present and never over or gone.

Except when they disappear, and we can't get them back. Digital connections have necessarily changed the ways in which we undertake ethnographic fieldwork, since they both complicate "*what* we (can) observe and *who* is involved in what we observe" (Blommaert & Jie, 2021, p. 91; emphasis in original). In online spaces, we engage not only just as researchers but also "as ordinary users entirely absorbed into the intrastructural system configured by technologies" (p. 95).

These complex dynamics, and how we are situated within and respond to them, highlight the broader point that "ethnographic fieldwork is undoubtedly a matter of existential as well as methodological commitment" (Atkinson, 2019, p. 65). Van Maanen (2006) expands on this by observing that:

> Fieldwork of the immersive sort is by and large definitional of the trade. Yet fieldwork practices are also biographically and situationally varied – spectacularly so. Studies differ in terms of working style, place, pace, time and evidentiary approaches. They also vary by textual styles and, like fieldwork approaches, they change over time as new ways of doing old things and old ways to do new things emerge and establish a hold on at least some ethnographers.
>
> *(p. 14)*

Fieldwork can involve many ways of being and doing for ethnographers. Being in the field can be challenging and exhausting, as well as exciting and invigorating. It can also be boring, quotidian, and repetitive. And at times, the long term and immersive nature of ethnographic fieldwork can generate a deeply embodied inertia.

Immersion in the field creates experiences that are, in and of themselves, of research interest. Presence in itself creates relations and possibilities for inquiry. Ethnographers also tend to consciously create specific opportunities for interrogations or explorations by starting conversations, seeking certain experiences, asking for responses, requesting documents, comments, and group engagements. One may invite participants to respond verbally, online, in writing, or through arts-based mediums (sculpture, poetry, dance, visual art, photos). These more specific and consciously sought "methods" can be planned or spontaneous. They require the researcher to overcome their inertia and everyday engagement in the field and take a risk, ask a question, invite a poetic response, host a group discussion, ask participants to take photos, etc. Nevertheless, these methods remain informed – or should be – by our ontological positioning, theoretical engagements, and methodological commitments. The dynamic intersections of theory, field, and method, thus, provide a myriad of potential engagements that critical ethnographers can respond to through(out) their research, highlighting its generative and eclectic nature.

A Note on the Ethnographic Interview

We finish this chapter with a cautionary note on the (over)use of the ethnographic interview. It is a method that is regularly drawn on in ethnographic fieldwork – so much so that it is now largely viewed as synonymous with it. Soyini Madison observes, for example, that the ethnographic interview is the key means by which interviewer and interviewee can be "in partnership and dialogue as they construct memory, meaning, and experience together" (2019, p. 35). Madison proceeds to argue that:

> The beauty of this method of interviewing is in the complex realms of individual subjectivity, memory, yearnings, polemics, and hope that are unveiled and inseparable from shared and inherited expressions of communal strivings, social history, and political possibility. The interview is a window to individual subjectivity and collective belonging.
>
> *(p. 35)*

We do not want to discount the significance of the ethnographic interview as a methodological staple of fieldwork. However, we do want to highlight some key concerns regarding its use. As Kvale observes, researchers using interviews "attempt to understand the world from the subjects' points of view and to unfold the meaning of their lived world. The interviews give voice to common people, allowing them to freely present their life situations in their own words" (2006, p, 481). Kvale points out, however, that the interview itself is at times mistakenly represented as an emancipatory experience, when often it is quite the opposite. In this respect, and contra Madison, interviews, if used interrogatively and unreflexively, often simply reinforce/sediment unequal power relations between the researcher and research participants. Oakley (1981) first raised this issue some 40 years ago:

> [I]nterviewers define the role of interviewees as subordinates; extracting information is more to be valued that yielding it; the convention of interviewer-interviewee hierarchy is a rationalization of inequality; what is good for interviewers is not necessarily good for interviewees.
>
> *(p. 40)*

As Clandinin and Connelly (2000) acknowledge, this inteviewer–interviewee hierarchy also leads to an unavoidable degree of falsity and formality in research interactions. Focus groups, which can provide a more relaxed, interactive context, have been offered as a useful alternative here, particularly if participants are involved in designing the questions (McClelland & Fine, 2008). However, focus groups too may be subject to many of the hierarchies inherent in interviews (Johansson, 2016; see also later).

Perhaps of greatest concern, though, is that many researchers claim that their research is ethnographic simply *because* it includes interviews (and/or focus groups). However, as Blommaert and Jie assert,

> there is nothing intrinsically ethnographic about an interview, and doing interviews does not make your research ethnographic . . . interviews can be thoroughly non-ethnographic: when they are decontextualised, massacred, and reduced to something that never happened in a real interaction.
>
> *(2021, p. 41)*

Moreover, they note, it is critical to understand that in an ethnographic fieldwork context "not all there is to be found out can be found out by *asking*" (p. 45). Atkinson (2015) expands on this critique when he argues that:

> [W]e seem to have lost the understanding that the conduct of ethnography involves an intensive period of engagement ("participant observation") in a given social milieu. Too often we discover the studies that have been called "ethnographic" are nothing of the kind, but are based entirely on interviews, and contain absolutely no engagement with a "field" of social activity.
>
> *(p. 12)*

For Atkinson, this overreliance on the interview is, in fact, the very antithesis of the ethnographic imagination, since it doesn't necessarily tell us anything useful about the nuances of social action and social organization – indeed, it may well occlude them. Certainly:

> [A] series of interviews with separate informants does not constitute an eth-nographic study of their everyday social worlds. It can tell us little about social action within a given setting. It can tell us nothing about how peo-ple actually engage with one another. It tells us little or nothing about the achievement of social order within a given setting. Moreover, dealing in interviews primarily, or as the sole source of data, too often glosses over the nature of the interview itself. The interview is itself a social encounter. Inter-view-derived narratives and accounts are performances in their own right.
>
> *(p. 60)*

Like any speech act, interviews have their own distinct characteristics, including the language(s) in which they are conducted – most often unreflexively in Eng-lish, or the dominant national language, the language of the researcher, and/or monolingually (see Chapter 6). All of these characteristics, and how they reflect and construct the power relations among research relationships, and within the wider sociohistorical, sociocultural, sociolinguistic, and sociopolitical contexts in which they are situated, bear specific, ongoing, critical, and reflexive scrutiny.

Importantly, interviews – like any method – need to cohere with the theoretical approach, and ethnographers need to consider how they align (or not) ontologically. St. Pierre points out that most poststructuralist theories displace the speaking subject in favor of attending to the discursive and what "people say in ordinary conversation mostly echoes, repeats, dominant discourse" (2016, p. 79).

These various criticisms of the ethnographic interview have led some to argue instead for more open-ended conversations. Fine and Weis (2003) advocate, for example, for the use of "extraordinary conversations" which, when used in schools with students, can open up closed spaces and allow students greater freedom to express and explore issues of power and in/equity. That said, conversations still have their own internal hierarchies and are subject to hegemonic relationships and cultural normativities, like any other exchange. And so, as a final exemplar, we return to recent developments in post-qualitative methodologies that directly address this ongoing issue.

Johansson, for example, draws on the work of Deleuze and Guattari to argue that traditional interviews and focus groups, which reflect "majority discourses" or "established ways of talking and thinking", should be replaced by the "confabulative conversation" (2016, pp. 458–459). Johansson draws here on the two meanings of confabulation. The first is its everyday meaning of an informal conversation. The second, from the world of psychiatry, describes confabulation as the use of invented stories that are unconsciously used to fill gaps between memories, often in the form of vivid fantasies and dreams, blurring out distinctions between realities and what is experienced. For her, then, the confabulative conversation in ethnographic fieldwork:

> [A]ims to blur out distinctions between the actual and the virtual, making the virtual as real as the actualized, thus opening for possibilities to regard dreams, fantasies, and speculations as valuable and legitimate. . . . In the understanding of this confabulative conversation, no distinction is made between what is said and what is. Language is not seen as representations or expressions of something located outside the verbal, instead language is ontological, with abilities to change the subjects through lines of becoming. Thus, ontological movements are producing becomings, but in accordance with Deleuze and Guattari's ontology of immanence, it also produces [new] possibilities for knowledge.
>
> *(p. 460)*

This position returns us to the key argument we have made throughout this chapter. Any/all ethnographic writing and fieldwork, if it is to be critical and reflexive, must remain underpinned by a wider, dynamic, recognition of onto-epistemological diversity, openness, and, above all, *uncertainty*. We do not undertake critical ethnographic fieldwork and writing to find, and then outline, "the answers". We do so to open up their possibilities.

Notes

1. We assume that Geertz intended the word "abstruse" here.
2. As we first discussed in Chapter 2, Barad (2007) understands intra-action as a dynamic intensity between all people, things, and phenomena; intra-actions are co-constituting and make the self inseparable from the world (see also Geerts & Carstens, 2019).

References

Atkinson, P. (2015). *For ethnography*. Sage.

Atkinson, P. (2019). *Writing ethnographically*. Sage.

Atkinson, P., Coffey, A., Delamont, S., Lofland, J., & Lofland, L. (Eds.). (2001). *Handbook of ethnography*. Sage.

Baice, T., Lealaiauloto, B., Meiklejohn-Whiu, S., Fonua, S. M., Allen, J. M., Matapo, J., . . . Fa'avae, D. (2021). Responding to the call: talanoa, va-vā, early career network and enabling academic pathways at a university in New Zealand. *Higher Education Research & Development, 40*(1), 75–89.

Barad, K. (2007). *Meeting the universe halfway: Quantum physics and the entanglement of matter and meaning*. Duke University Press.

Blommaert, J., & Jie, D. (2021). *Ethnographic fieldwork: A beginner's guide* (2nd ed.). Multilingual Matters.

Blumenreich, M. (2004). Avoiding the pitfalls of 'conventional' narrative research: Using poststructural theory to guide the creation of narratives of children with HIV. *Qualitative Research, 4*(1), 77–90.

Bochner, A., & Ellis, C. (Eds.). (2002). *Ethnographically speaking: Autoethnography, literature, and aesthetics*. AltaMira Press.

Bourdieu, P., Chamboredon, J., & Passeron, J. (1991). *The craft of sociology: Epistemological preliminaries*. Walter de Gruyter.

Braidotti, R. (2013). *The posthuman*. Polity Press.

Bruce, T. (2016). *Terra ludus: A novel about media, gender and sport*. Springer.

Caldas, B. Becoming an "avocado": Embodied rescriptings in bilingual teacher education settings—A critical performance ethnography. In S. May & B. Caldas (Eds.), *Critical ethnography, language, race/ism and education*. Multilingual Matters.

Cammarota, J., & Fine, M. (Eds.). (2010). *Revolutionizing education: Youth participatory action research in motion*. Routledge.

Clandinin, J., & Connelly, M. (2000). *Narrative inquiry: Experience and story in qualitative research*. Jossey Bass.

Clifford, J. (1986). Introduction. In J. Clifford & G. Marcus (Eds.). *Writing culture: The poetics and philosophy of ethnography* (pp. 1–26). California University Press.

Clifford, J., & Marcus, G. (Eds.). (1986). *Writing culture: The poetics and philosophy of ethnography*. California University Press.

Clough, P. (2002). *Narratives and fictions in educational research*. Open University Press.

Clough, P. (2009). Finding God in Wellworth high school: More legitimations of storymaking as research. *Ethnography and Education, 4*(3), 347–356.

Coffey, A. (2018). *Doing ethnography*. Sage.

Coles, J. (2020). A BlackCrit re/imagining of urban schooling social education through Black youth enactments of Black storywork. *Urban Education*, 1–30. https://doi.org/10.1177/0042085920908919

Coles, J. (2022). Beyond silence: Disrupting antiblackness through BlackCrit ethnography and Black youth voice. In S. May, & B. Caldas (Eds.). *Critical ethnography, language, race/ism and education*. Multilingual Matters.

Davies, B., & Gannon, S. (2006). *Doing collective biography: Investigating the production of subjectivity*. Open University Press.

Delamont, S. (2016). *Fieldwork in educational settings: Methods, pitfalls and perspectives* (3rd ed.). Sage.

Denzin, N. K. (1997). *Interpretive ethnography: Ethnographic practices for the 21st century*. Sage.

Dillabough, J. (2008). Exploring historicity and temporality in social science methodology. A case for methodological and analytical justice. In K. Gallagher (Ed.), *The methodological dilemma: Creative, critical and collaborative approaches to qualitative research* (pp. 185–218). Routledge.

Diversi, M., & Moreira, C. (2018). *Betweener autoethnographies: A path towards social justice*. Routledge.

Ellis, C. (2000). Creating criteria: An ethnographic short story. *Qualitative Inquiry, 6*(2), 273–277.

Ellis, C. (2004). *The ethnographic I: A methodological novel about autoethnography*. AltaMira Press.

Ellis, C., Adams, T. E., & Bochner, A. P. (2011). Autoethnography: an overview. *Historical social research/Historische sozialforschung*, 273–290. https://www.jstor.org/stable/23032294

Faulkner, S. L. (2016). *Poetry as method: Reporting research through verse*. Routledge.

Fine, M. (1994). Working the hyphens: Reinventing self and other in qualitative research. In N Denzin & Y. Lincoln (Eds.), *Handbook of qualitative research* (pp:70–82). Sage.

Fine, M., & Weis, L. (2003). *Silenced voices and extraordinary conversations: Re-imagining schools*. Teachers College Press.

Fitzpatrick, E., & Fitzpatrick, K. (Eds.). (2021). *Poetry, method and education research*. Routledge.

Fitzpatrick, K. (2013). *Critical pedagogy, physical education and urban schooling*. Peter Lang.

Fitzpatrick, K., & May, S. (2015). Doing critical educational ethnography with Bourdieu. In M. Murphy & C. Costa (Eds.), *Theory as method in research: On Bourdieu, social theory and education* (pp. 101–114). Routledge.

Gale, K., & Wyatt, J. (2009). *A nomadic inquiry into collaborative writing and subjectivity*. Cambridge Scholars Publishing.

Geerts, E., & Carstens, D. (2019). Ethico-onto-epistemology. *Philosophy Today, 63*(4), 915–925. https://dio.org/10.5840/philtoday202019301

Geertz, C. (2000). *Available light: Anthropological reflections on philosophical topics*. Princeton University Press.

Gilbert, J., Fields, J., Mamo, L., & Lesko, N. (2018). Intimate Possibilities: The Beyond Bullying Project and stories of LGBTQ sexuality and gender in US Schools. *Harvard Educational Review 88*(2), 163–183. https://doi.org/10.17763/1943-5045-88.2.163

Gutierrez, K., & Rogoff, B. (2003). Cultural ways of learning: Cultural traits or repertoires of practice. *Educational Research, 32*, 19–35.

Hamilton, L., & Taylor, N. (2017). *Ethnography after humanism: Power, politics and method in multi. species research*. Springer.

Hereaka, W. (2019). Prologue. In W. Ihimaera & W. Hereaka (Eds.), *Pūrakau: Māori myths retold by Māori writers* (pp. 22–29). Penguin Random House New Zealand.

Hickey-Moody, A. C. (2020). New materialism, ethnography, and socially engaged practice: Space-time folds and the agency of matter. *Qualitative Inquiry, 26*(7), 724–732.

hooks, b. (2015). *Talking back: Thinking feminist, thinking black*. Routledge.

Johansson, L. (2016). Post-qualitative line of flight and the confabulative conversation.: A methodological ethnography. *International Journal of Qualitative Studies in Education, 29*(4), 445–466. https://doi.org/10.1080/09518398.2015.1053157

Jones, A., & Jenkins, K. (2008). Invitation and refusal: A reading of the beginnings of schooling in Aotearoa New Zealand. *History of Education, 37*, 125–144.

Kvale, S. (2006). Dominance through interviews and dialogue. *Qualitative Inquiry, 12*(3), 480–500.

Lather, P. (2001). Postbook: Working the ruins of feminist ethnography. *Signs: Journal of Women in Culture and Society, 27*(1), 199–227.

Madison, D. (2019). *Critical ethnography: Method, ethics, and performance* (3rd ed.). Sage.

May, S. (1994). *Making multicultural education work*. Multilingual Matters.

May, S., & Fitzpatrick, K. (2019). Critical ethnography. In P. Atkinson, S. Delamont, A. Cernat, J. Sakshaug & R. Williams (Eds.), *Sage research methods foundations*. Sage Publications. http://dx.doi.org/10.4135/9781526421036831954

Mazzei, L. A., & Jackson, A. Y. (2012). In the threshold: Writing between-the-two. *International Review of Qualitative Research, 5*(4), 449–458.

McClelland, S. I., & Fine, M. (2008). Writing on cellophane: Studying teen women's sexual desires, inventing methodological release points. In *The methodological dilemma: Creative, critical and collaborative approaches to qualitative research* (pp. 232–260) Taylor and Francis.

McDrury, J., & Alterio, M. (2003). *Learning through storytelling in higher education: Using reflection, and experience to improve learning*. Kogan Page.

McMahon, J. (2016). Creative analytical practices. In B. Smith & A. Sparkes (Eds.). *Routledge handbook of qualitative research in sport and exercise* (pp. 302–315). Routledge.

Oakley, A. (1981). Interviewing women – a contradiction in terms. In H. Roberts (Ed.), *Doing feminist research* (pp. 30–61). Routledge and Kegan Paul.

Pedersen, H. (2013). Follow the Judas sheep: Materializing post-qualitative methodology in zooethnographic space. *International Journal of Qualitative Studies in Education, 26*(6), 717–731. https://doi.org/10.1080/09518398.2013.788760

Pelias, R. J. (2018). *Writing performance, identity, and everyday life: The selected works of Ronald J. Pelias*. Routledge.

Pink, S. (2015). *Doing sensory ethnography*. Sage.

Pink, S. (2021). *Doing visual ethnography* (4th ed.). Sage.

Pink, S., Horst, H., Postill, J., Hjorth, L., Lewis, T., & Tacchi, J. (2016). *Digital ethnography: Principles and practice*. Sage.

Pollock, D. 1998. Performing writing. In P. Phelan & J. Lane (Eds.), *The ends of performance* (pp. 73–103). New York University Press.

Poulos, C. N. (2014). Writing a bridge to possibility. *International Review of Qualitative Research, 7*(3), 342–358.

Richardson, L. (2003). Writing: A method of inquiry. In Y. Lincoln & N. Denzin (Eds.), *Turning points in qualitative research: Tying knots in a handkerchief* (pp. 379–396). AltaMira Press.

Rinehart, R. (1998). Fictional methods in ethnography: Believability, specks of glass, and Chekhov. *Qualitative Inquiry, 4*(2), 200–224.

Sleeter, C. (2018). *The inheritance: A novel*. CreateSpace Independent Publishing Platform.

Sleeter, C. (2020). *White Bread: Anniversary edition*. Brill Sense.

Sparkes, A. (2002). *Telling tales in sport and physical activity: A qualitative journey*. Human Kinetics.

Speedy, J. (2012). Collaborative writing and ethical know-how: Movements within the space around scholarship, the academy and the social research imaginary. *International Review of Qualitative Research, 5*(4), 349–356.

Speedy, J., Bainton, D., Bridges, N., Brown, T. Brown, L., Martin, L. Sakellariadis, A., Williams, S., & Wilson, S. (2010). Encountering "Gerald": Experiments With meandering methodologies and experiences beyond our "selves" in a collaborative writing group. *Qualitative Inquiry, 16*(10), 894–901.

St Pierre, E. (2016). Practices for the 'new' in the new empiricisms, the new materialisms, and post qualitative inquiry. In N. Denzin, & M. Giardina (Eds.), *Qualitative inquiry and the politics of research* (pp. 75–96). Routledge.

St. Pierre, E. (2018). Writing post qualitative inquiry. *Qualitative Inquiry, 24*(9), 603–608. https://doi.org/10.1177/1077800417734567

Sualii-Sauni, T. M., & Fulu-Aiolupotea, S. M. (2014). Decolonising Pacific research, building Pacific research communities and developing Pacific research tools: The case of the talanoa and the faafaletui in Samoa. *Asia-Pacific Viewpoint, 55*(3), 331–344. https://doi.org/10.1111/apv.12061

Tamanui, V., & Fitzpatrick, E. (2021). The tukutuku panel is never bare: Weaving bicultural relationships through poetic performances. In E. Fitzpatrick & K. Fitzpatrick (Eds.), *Poetry, method and education research* (pp. 183–206). Routledge.

Tanner, S. J. (2016). Accounting for whiteness through collaborative fiction. *Research in Drama Education: The Journal of Applied Theatre and Performance, 21*(2), 183–195.

Tullis Owen, J., McRae, C., Adams, T., & Vitale, A. (2009). truth troubles. *Qualitative Inquiry 15*(1), 178–200.

Vaioleti, T. (2006). Talanoa research methodology: A developing position on Pacific research. *Waikato Journal of Education, 12*, 21–34. https://researchcommons.waikato.ac.nz/bitstream/handle/10289/6199/Vaioleti%20Talanoa.pdf

Van Maanen, J. (2006). Ethnography then and now. Qualitative Research in Organizations and Management. *An International Journal, 1*(1), 13–21.

Van Maanen, J. (2011). *Tales of the field: On writing ethnography* (2nd ed.). University of Chicago Press.

Willis, P. (1977). *Learning to labor: How working class kids get working class jobs*. Columbia University Press.

Wyatt, J. (2007). Research, narrative and fiction: Conference story. *Qualitative Report, 12*(2), 318–331.

Wyatt, J. (2019). *Therapy, stand up, and the gesture of writing: Towards creative-relational inquiry*. Routledge.

6

LANGUAGE, RACE/ISM, AND IN/EQUITY IN EDUCATION

Critical Ethnographic Approaches[1]

Here we explore the pivotal role that critical ethnography can play in understanding, critiquing, and contesting the confluence of language, race/ism, and in/equity in education. This combination of factors disproportionately and negatively affects linguistically minoritized students' experiences of, and success in, education. As a precursor to, and illustration of just what is at stake here, we begin with a vignette, followed by a brief personal narrative about the two schools that have most influenced Stephen's views on race/ism and in/equity in education:

> It is 10 September 2018, and I (Stephen) find myself sitting in and observing in Te Whānau Whāriki (WW), the Indigenous Māori language immersion program at Te Kura o Ritimana, Richmond Road Primary School, in Auckland, New Zealand. The classroom day begins, as always, with two students from the program being responsible for leading *whaikōrero* (formal speech), *karakia* (blessing) and *waiata* (song) for all. The first classroom session to follow focuses on *pānui* (reading). The three *kaiako* (teachers) work collectively, rather than individually – in this instance, each leading/facilitating a particular reading group. Students from across the program are divided into three groups based on current reading levels in Māori, rather than strictly based on age/level. The pedagogies used include group work and scaffolded learning (by both teachers and students), with emphasis placed throughout on the multimodal interconnections between reading and exploratory talk in Māori. It is just one of the many innovative pedagogical practices evident in Te Whānau Whāriki and the wider school, with its long and successful history of critical bilingual and multicultural approaches to bilingual teaching and learning. This history now stretches to some 30-odd years – much of which I have also had the pleasure and

DOI: 10.4324/9781315208510-6

privilege of being involved in as a researcher and friend of the school. It is also strikingly different from the usual pedagogies adopted in "mainstream" (English-medium) schools in New Zealand, where Indigenous Māori and other linguistically minoritized students tend to fare much less well.

School 1: Diverse Students, Institutional Homogeneity (The Usual)

The predominantly negative experiences of schooling for Māori and Pacific students in mainstream New Zealand schools were clearly apparent in the first school I taught in. It was the mid-1980s, and I had chosen to begin my teaching career at this school in Petone, a then still predominantly working-class suburb of Wellington, New Zealand, because it was a low socioeconomic, ethnically and linguistically diverse high school. It was, both figuratively and literally, on the wrong side of the railway line – in fact, the school grounds abutted the Petone railway line, separating it physically from the (slightly) more salubrious suburbs on the other side. I was young, idealistic, committed to social justice and diversity and, above all, wanted to make a difference in education, and for my students. If I'm honest, this specifically chosen school context was also the antithesis of my own resolutely and relentlessly White monocultural and monolingual background, which I was increasingly desperate to both repudiate and renounce.

Most of the students at the school were ethnically and linguistically minoritized students – predominantly Māori students and Pacific students. They were challenging, at times, but also wonderfully engaging, talented, smart, and so obviously (and often proudly) culturally located. Many of them were bilingual or multilingual. I had high hopes and aspirations for them – aspirations which, over time, I found increasingly difficult to fulfill. Many of these students continued to leave school as soon as they could; very few of those who remained went on to higher education; and, while the school's student population continued to reflect a vibrant ethnic and linguistic diversity at the individual level, the only space in which such diversity was institutionally recognized and valued was in *te reo Māori* (Māori language) classes and in the Māori and Pacific students' *kapa haka* (cultural performance) group. Even here though, there were issues: for example, te reo Māori was still viewed as a low status (even remedial) language subject option by the school's administrators and some teachers, in sharp contradistinction to other language subjects, such as French and German. And while Māori and Pacific cultures were acknowledged elsewhere in the school, these were limited largely to ceremonial and/or celebratory occasions.

As a result of these, often dispiriting, early experiences of teaching, I began to think that perhaps schools – and all those within them – couldn't make any (significant) difference to the educational and life trajectories of ethnically and linguistically minoritized students, after all. It was a sobering, even crushing, reassessment of my initially naïve assumptions about the (supposedly) transformative power of education.

School 2: Recognizing Diversity Systemically (The Unusual)

It was upon returning to postgraduate study some years later that I first became aware of Richmond Road Primary School. Through a number of unexpected serendipities (see May, 1998), I ended up undertaking a three-year critical ethnography of the school from 1990 to 1992. This was to be the focus of my dissertation and, subsequently, my first book (May, 1994). Richmond Road was the first urban elementary school in New Zealand, and perhaps also one of the first of its kind internationally (Cazden, 1989; Corson, 1990), to focus extensively on bilingual/immersion education as an avenue for furthering educational and wider social justice aims for linguistically minoritized students. In the 1980s, Richmond Road implemented a radically reconceptualized educational program to better serve the educational needs of its predominantly Māori and Pacific students.

Richmond Road's broader philosophy centered on critical multiculturalism (see May, 1999a; May & Sleeter, 2010), developing and institutionalizing a whole-school recognition of cultural and linguistic diversity, with bilingual provision at its core. It was the first urban school in New Zealand to establish multiyear-level bilingual classrooms (in Māori, Samoan, and subsequently, in the 1990s, French). The bilingual programs provided a partial immersion approach (at least 50% medium of instruction in the target language) – broadly equivalent pedagogically to the subsequent development of dual language programs in the United States. They were explicitly predicated on an additive approach to bilingualism – viewing the achievement and/or maintenance of student bilingualism, via the use of minoritized languages as mediums of instruction, as a core educational and wider societal value. As the late Jim Laughton, the visionary principal who established these programs at Richmond Road, observed in a position paper on their development:

> There are many children at Richmond Road School whose mother tongue is not English. Submerged unavoidably in a strange language from school entry these children are particularly vulnerable. It is the school's task to ameliorate that condition – to show them respect, to encourage pride in their identity by including their languages and cultures to a significant degree. . . . In short, to facilitate educational advancement from a solid platform of self-knowledge, self-assurance and an acknowledged first language competence.
>
> *(cited in May, 1994, p. 114)*

Richmond Road's bilingual programs were also predicated on a student-centered approach and the related reciprocity of teaching and learning, exemplified by the principle "everyone who has knowledge teaches" (May, 1995). Both developments were underpinned by the school's extensive engagement with critical educational theory and practice – including regular staff interaction at the time with my own Bourdieusian analysis over the course of the three-year critical ethnographic study (May, 1998; Fitzpatrick & May, 2015).

I titled my 1994 book on Richmond Road, *Making multicultural education work*, to highlight how it can do so, structurally, epistemically, and pedagogically within a critical multicultural and additive bilingual framework. However, the title also alluded ironically to the fact that multicultural education seldom actually works – highlighting how rare such school examples are. Nonetheless, Richmond Road restored, for me, a belief in the *possibilities* of radical, transformative change via schooling – particularly with respect to the institutionalized recognition of ethnic and linguistic diversity. The school has continued to reinforce this belief for me ever since, and I have remained actively engaged, albeit episodically, with the school's ongoing efforts to this end. In 2006, I was involved in an action research project, led by teachers in the school, that reflected critically and developmentally on the school's long history of bilingual teaching and learning. And in 2018, as foregrounded in the vignette, I was once again involved in researching the school. This time it was to review its three bilingual programs – including Te Whānau Whāriki, the Māori immersion program where it all began – in terms of best practices in bilingual/immersion teaching and learning.

Critical Ethnography: Making the Connections; Examining the Disjunctures

I begin with these two juxtaposed school examples because they have fundamentally shaped, and continue to shape, my own ongoing engagement with issues of language, race/ism, and education, along with the inequities that still so often attend them. However, the two schools also highlight, for me, the possibilities that critical ethnography affords in exploring, critiquing, and contesting these issues. If I could have applied the theoretical and methodological knowledge of critical ethnography that I later acquired to my first school, I might have been able to better understand, and contest, the systemic inequities that still constructed the school's ethnically and linguistically diverse students in predominantly deficit terms. This was most obvious, retrospectively, in the ongoing disconnect between students' own individual ethnicities and bi/multilingual[2] repertoires, and the institutionalized (non)recognition of these within the school.

Critical ethnography would also have been useful here in highlighting how these school processes are inevitably underpinned by wider educational and related public policies that promote monolingualism in the dominant societal language as a principal aim (Gramling, 2016; May, 2016), and which are often situated in conjunction with highly racialized views of linguistically minoritized individuals and groups (May & Caldas, 2022). The latter is most often seen in the nomenclature regularly adopted to describe such students and almost always referenced in deficit terms with respect to the dominant language – most often,

English. This includes students in so-called "mainstream" (dominant, most often national, language) compulsory education contexts, as well as so-called Limited-English-Proficient (LEP) students, English Language Learners (ELLs), English Second Language (ESL), and English Foreign Language (EFL) students in both compulsory education and tertiary contexts. All these terms highlight the normative ascendancy of English, either nationally or in relation to English as the current world language.

Foregrounding these wider historical, social, and cultural inequities through critical ethnography might also have led me to apply a far greater degree of critical reflexivity to my own well-meaning, but often naïve, misguided, and misdirected, "missionary" intentions as a beginning teacher. These were grounded in a commitment to social justice, but were still inevitably shaped (and occluded) by my personal positionality – coming from a monolingual, relatively privileged background (May, 1998), being cisgender, and being sociohistorically and socioculturally *situated* as a member of the White ethnic majority in a postcolonial state "historically embedded in colonial flows of power" (Bell et al., 2022).

Meanwhile, via my critical ethnography of Richmond Road, I began to see how schools can potentially make a difference, and just what that entails, by critically exploring the often complex – and, at times, contradictory and competing – interstices between ethnicity, language, education, racism, and related in/equities. Bearing in mind Berlant's (2011) caution about "cruel optimism" (see Chapter 1), and thus not wanting to overstate the possibilities of change here, critical ethnography can nonetheless provide the (potential) basis for exploring resistances and alternatives to existing discriminatory educational processes and practices toward linguistically minoritized students. These include (re)centering students' dynamic bi/multilingualism within the school, along with employing these as a direct counter to, and subversion of, monolingual conceptions of language use. It also includes highlighting the institutional responses that overtly – and in Richmond Road's case, *systemically* – (re)value the languages and cultures of minoritized students.

Such critical ethnographic work is necessarily interdisciplinary, while also traversing a wide range of different language education contexts within (and across) different national domains. The former includes, among others, the fields of education, applied linguistics, sociolinguistics, anthropology, cultural studies, and sociology. The latter includes a range of related language education contexts and associated points of research focus, such as bilingual language development and use, bilingual and multilingual education programs and pedagogy, biliteracy, language revitalization, Indigenous language education, and critical multicultural and antiracist education approaches that focus centrally on bi/multilingualism.

As we will see, specific theoretical sources and influences in this critical ethnographic work on language and education are also wide-ranging. They include the use of interactional sociolinguistics, which explores how students communicate in face-to-face contexts to highlight bi/multilingual students' often-transgressive linguistic practices within education (Alim, 2004; Paris, 2011; Rampton, 2006). This focus on students' dynamic bilingual language use has also been more recently examined with respect to the related notion of "translanguaging" (García, 2009; García & Li Wei, 2014). Bourdieusian ethnographic analyses of linguistic habitus, capital, and fields in education (see Grenfell et al., 2012; Grenfell & Pahl, 2018) foreground both the reproduction and reinforcement of monolingual language education for bi/multilingual students, as well as the potential for critical bilingual alternatives (May, 1994; Palmer, 2011). Latinx cultural and educational studies focus on students' existing "funds of knowledge" (González et al., 2005), alongside postmodernist and postcolonial critiques of education highlighting the linguistic and wider marginalization of Latinx students within US education, in particular (Villenas & Foley, 2002, 2011). Latinx studies, as well as key critical ethnographies of African American students, also draw directly on Critical Race Theory (CRT), Black Critical Theory (BlackCrit), Latino Critical Race Theory (LatCrit), and raciolinguistics (see Alim et al., 2020; Bernal, 2002; Dumas & ross, 2016; Flores & Rosa, 2015; Rosa & Flores, 2017) to explore the racialized construction of bilingual students and the impact of linguistically discriminatory processes toward them in US education (Baker-Bell, 2020; Malsbary, 2014; Paris, 2011).

Tribal Critical Race Theory (Brayboy, 2005; McCarty, 2022) explores these same issues specifically in relation to Native American (and other Indigenous) students. Likewise, there is a long history of engagement with Indigenous epistemologies, language practices, and language education policies as a basis for educational and wider social change (Hermes et al., 2012; Smith, 2012). These Indigenous epistemologies, language policies and practices underpin advocacy for, and the implementation of, Indigenous education initiatives worldwide. Such initiatives aim to contest the ongoing cultural and linguistic assimilation of Indigenous peoples in dominant language educational contexts, along with the related entrenchment of wider educational and social inequities for Indigenous peoples (Hill & May, 2011; McCarty, 2014).

With this background in mind, we can now turn to a more detailed examination of *what* and *how* critical ethnography can contribute usefully to explicating the links between language, ethnicity, race/ism, and in/equity.

What Does (Critical) Ethnography Do for Work in Language, Race/ism, and Education?

Critical ethnography provides a materials-rich and theory-driven approach to questions of language representation and practices within education. As Monica Heller observes of this:

> Ethnographies . . . allow us to see how language practices are connected to the very real conditions of people's lives, to discover how and why language matters to people in their own terms, and to watch processes unfold over

time. They allow us to see complexities and connections, to understand the history and geography of language. They allow us to tell a story.

(2008, p. 250)

These ethnographic stories have often focused in depth on the discriminatory representation, exclusion, and/or repudiation of the language varieties of linguistically minoritized students within schools, alongside the often unquestioned valorization of dominant national languages, and/or international languages (such as English), which are also invariably the dominant language(s) of school instruction. In this sense, critical ethnographies of language and education provide a macro critique of the quest for linguistic homogeneity and the normalization of institutionalized monolingualism within modern nation-states – the product of the "the desirous and quixotic dream" (Gramling, 2016, p. 9) of the nationalism of the last few centuries (see also Bauman & Briggs, 2003; May, 2012). This analysis sits alongside a related critique of the commodification and depoliticization of the globalization of English (May, 2015; Pennycook, 1994), exemplified in the ongoing rapid expansion of the ESL/EFL teaching industries worldwide (Phillipson, 2010), exploring the implications of both via micro analyses of their often exclusionary consequences within classrooms.

Or, more accurately perhaps, critical ethnographies of language and education provide a *multiscalar* approach to these issues. They recursively link language ideologies with respect to the relative value of languages – what Liddicoat (2013) describes as linguistic "hierarchies of prestige" – with actual language use, curriculum policy, and related pedagogical practices. In turn, these issues are situated within broader processes of globalization and racialization that, more often than not, position the often bi/multilingual linguistic repertoires of linguistically minoritized students as having little or no value. In so doing, dichotomizations between macro and micro language and education policies, monolingualism and bi/multilingualism, localization and globalization, and the related normalized uses (and perceived usefulness) of so-called local and global language varieties, are both usefully challenged and deconstructed. In this sense, critical ethnographic work makes overt the links between wider historical and contemporary patterns of linguistic inequity in specific relation to individual, family, classroom, and educational language practices – charting the often discriminatory pressures evident within these various language domains for students.

Voice and Repertoire

The origins of this kind of research can be traced back to the 1960s and the emergence of the related fields of linguistic ethnography and educational linguistics. Championed by the noted sociolinguist Dell Hymes, ethnographic approaches to language and education within these traditions focused on the illumination of "diverse ways of speaking" (1980, p. 20) and their *validation* within a wider humanizing, democratizing, and anti-hegemonic research stance. What this Hymesian approach foregrounded was the notion of "voice", in conjunction with its inherent pluralization via the related notion of linguistic "repertoires". Voice can be described as "the capacity to make oneself understood in one's own terms, to produce meanings under conditions of empowerment" (Blommaert, 2013, p. 22) – something which, as we shall see, still regularly eludes linguistically minoritized students in education. Linguistic repertoires "are an organized complex of specific resources, such as [language] varieties, modes, genres, registers, and styles" (p. 13). All of us have access to these complex linguistic repertoires. However, such repertoires often differ markedly both within and across social, racial/ethnic, and linguistic groups, depending on wider socialization processes and related opportunities for, or constraints on, language use in specific contexts. For linguistically minoritized students, they also often include bi/multilingual competencies – although, again, the opportunities for such competencies to be recognized and used invariably depend on the wider social and educational contexts in which students find themselves.

Linguistic Diversity as Deficit or Resource?

Critical ethnography is thus particularly apposite for exploring the diversity, complexity, contradictions, contest, and (dis)continuities inherent within the actual language practices of students, along with the varied – often discriminatory, sometimes emancipatory – institutionalized educational responses to them. A key point of focus in this work has been the construction of the linguistic diversity of students as (more often) a deficit or (far less often), a resource. The best of this ethnographic work concurrently explores the dynamic, complex dialectic between these two conceptions, as they are situated within educational settings, and related professional (teacher/student) engagement and institutionalized policies and practices. The work is necessarily theoretically eclectic, drawing on a range of critical traditions, as highlighted earlier, while their points of focus inevitably tend to fall on a continuum. At one end is a primary focus on the linguistic discrimination and related marginalization of linguistically minoritized students in educational settings. At the other end is a focus on the processes of dynamic bi/multilingualism – or, more accurately, the use of students' complex bi/multilingual repertoires – as a *counter-insurgent* means of language identity, celebration, and reclamation. For heuristic purposes, and to the degree that we can, we will chart these different emphases separately in what follows.

Linguistic Discrimination and Exclusion in Education

> "Don't act dumb, like ESL students".
>
> (quoted in Talmy, 2009, p. 243)

English Second Language (ESL) programs, both in compulsory schooling and in tertiary contexts worldwide, have been a particular point of focus for exploring and critiquing the deficit positioning of linguistic minority students in critical ethnographic work. Drawing on his two-and-a-half-year critical ethnography of ESL students in a Hawaiian public high school, Talmy (2009), for example, traces how ESL students were encouraged by teachers to participate "respectfully" in the classroom. Such respect was, however, intrinsically linked to monolingual English language teaching and learning norms, in apparent contradistinction to the students' own emergent English abilities and language backgrounds. In the process, the students' bi/multilingualism, and their communicative and pragmatic competence as emergent bilinguals, were either ignored or, as encapsulated by the teacher's comment earlier, specifically derided. The result, not surprisingly, was that the ESL students in these classes – a diverse group of students, comprising a fifth of the school's overall population – often felt they "learned nothing" in their ESL classes. However, as Talmy concludes:

> [T]hey and their classmates [actually] learnt plenty, or at least, there was plenty made available for them to learn: the assimilationist aims of ESL, the deficit-oriented (language) ideologies constituting the stigma of ESL, the valorization of the mainstream [English-medium classrooms], the power of the L2 [second language] teacher to mediate classroom participation through local definitions of respect, the acceptability of so grossly and openly disrespecting ESL.
>
> *(p. 250)*

Ibrahim's (1999) critical ethnography of the experiences of migrant African students in an urban, French immersion high school in Ontario, Canada, similarly highlights how teachers regularly construct students' language backgrounds in deficit terms. In Ibrahim's study, there is an added irony, since the focus of teachers often remained on English language ability – widely used by students outside the classroom – despite it being a French-medium schooling context. As one of Ibrahim's participating students, Asma, observes:

> If you don't speak English, like . . . my Grade 7 [teacher said], "Oh, so she doesn't speak! Oh, we are sorry, you can explain to her, she doesn't understand English, *la petite*. Can you [help]?" They think we are really stupid, that we are retarded, that we don't understand the language. Now I know English, I speak it all the time. I show them that I understand English [laughs], I show them that I do English. Oh, I got it, it gives me great pleasure.
>
> *(p. 359)*

The emphasis on linguistic performativity (*doing* English), highlighted in Asma's comment, is a key feature of Ibrahim's study – what he terms more broadly the "ethnography of performance" (p. 350), drawing on, among others, the work of Butler (1990). This is because his ethnography was one of the first to explore how students identified with Black (African American) English, primarily via their active engagement with rap and hip hop, as a result of, and a counter-response to, their highly racialized experiences at this school – of which more later. Meanwhile, both Ibrahim's and Talmy's critical ethnographic studies illustratively foreground the racialized experiences, and the related dismissal of students' linguistic repertoires, as an all too regular discriminatory feature of schooling (see also, e.g., Malsbary, 2014; Zentella, 1997).

This focus on linguistic discrimination, and the repudiation of the language backgrounds of students, builds on earlier, important work in linguistic ethnography. Most notable here, perhaps, are Shirley Brice Heath and Susan Philips's pivotal studies. Heath's still-influential book, *Ways with words* (1983), was a decade-long ethnographic exploration of the language practices of children among three communities in the Piedmont Carolinas in the United States: Roadville (a working class White community), Trackton (a working class Black community), and Maintown (a middle class Black and White community). Heath's title is significant here for two reasons. The pluralization of "ways" highlights the multiple language practices evident across the three communities, differentiated by both race and class. Meanwhile, the "ways with words" metaphor itself extends the Hymesian notion of "ways of speaking", discussed earlier, to encompass and directly explore its relationship to the acquisition of literacy and related academic success.

Heath found that Trackton and Roadville children were less academically successful, primarily because of their familial language and literacy practices being viewed by teachers as "divergent" from those expected at school – Trackton because of the predominant use of "Black English Vernacular" and Roadville because of differing, class-based communicative practices. Maintown students were more successful because their middle-class language practices were most closely aligned with those of the school, although middle-class African American students still did not accrue the same level of educational benefit as their White peers, highlighting the ongoing intersectionality of race, class, and language in relation to academic achievement.

Susan Philips (1983) combined macroanalysis and microethnography with long-term, in-depth participant observation and interviewing to explore the language practices of Native American children in the Warm Springs Reservation in the US state of Oregon. As with Heath, she found that these children's "styles of learning" and communicative "participation structures" in the home differed, at times markedly, from those of the school. Warm Springs children were socialized at home into communicative practices that emphasized listening and observing rather than talking and speaking up, and in voluntary, rather than involuntary, group participation. This contrasted with the emphasis their teachers placed on regular and public verbalization in class as a required demonstration of (successful) learning – a key language practice identified with White, middle-class language practices. Consequently, the reluctance of Warms Springs children to speak in class resulted in subsequent low levels of achievement in verbal competency tests, and a related deficit construction by teachers of their language practices.

The confluence of critical ethnographic studies, such as Talmy's and Ibrahim's, and linguistic ethnographies such as those of Heath and Philips, highlights the regular mismatch between the communicative practices of students from different class and/or racial/ethnic groups and those of the school, where the latter, in fact, represent (and occlude) White middle-class language practices as the norm. As Reyes observes, these studies effectively "reveal how ethnic majority groups establish and maintain power by having their speech norms legitimized in institutional settings, such as classrooms. Mainstream practices become accepted as 'normal', 'proper', and 'standard'" (2010, p. 413).

In contrast, Indigenous and other linguistic minority language practices, and their communicative participation structures, are pathologized and/or dismissed. However, a related development in critical ethnographic work on language and education has been a shift in focus from the disjunctures among these home and school language practices, and their discriminatory consequences for linguistic minority students, toward what schools (and teachers, in particular) can do to (more effectively) bridge them. In so doing, these studies highlight how validating and using home language practices can become a key pedagogical resource for more successful teaching and learning in the classroom for linguistic minority students.

Funds of Knowledge

One key framework that has emerged in this regard, and which has since been widely used in critical ethnographic work, focuses on students' and their families' "funds of knowledge". Originally developed by Moll et al., funds of knowledge describe "the historically accumulated and culturally developed bodies of knowledge and skills essential for households and individual functioning and well-being" (1992, p. 133). Its initial conceptualization arose from Moll et al.'s exploration of the family resources of Mexican American families in Tucson, Arizona, and how these could be used as a basis for local curricular reform.

The researchers elicited everyday household knowledge and practices from local Mexican American families and then engaged teachers in the ethnographic study of these family practices. Following from this, teachers developed a more relevant and contextualized curriculum for students from those families. A key dimension of funds of knowledge in Moll et al. (1992) and subsequent studies (González et al., 2005; Moreno, 2002; Vasquez et al., 1994) are the often fluid and blurred bi/multilingual language practices, and related transnational cultural practices within these linguistic minority Latinx families and communities – what Gutierrez and Rogoff (2003) describe as "cultural repertoires of practice". Such cultural repertoires of practice for Latinx families, for example, include *consejos* (advice-giving narratives) and *historias* (stories), both of which differ from normative school-based language practices (Vasquez et al., 1994; Villenas & Foley, 2011; see also Chapter 5).

Funds of knowledge have often been used in conjunction with the development of what have come to be known as asset or resource pedagogies, which specifically acknowledge and value the practices of linguistic minority students, seeing these "as resources and assets to honor, explore, and extend" (Paris & Alim, 2014, p. 87). Such asset pedagogies include culturally relevant, culturally responsive, and, most recently, culturally sustaining pedagogies. It is beyond the scope of this chapter to engage with the development of these pedagogies over time in any further detail (see Missingham, 2017 for a useful overview), except to say that each development is increasingly informed by critical race theory (CRT), to which we will return. However, by way of brief example, Alim and Paris assert that culturally sustaining pedagogy "asks us to reimagine schools as sites where diverse, heterogeneous [student] practices are not only valued but sustained" (2017, p. 3), and that, in so doing, it seeks "to perpetuate and foster – to sustain – linguistic, literate, and cultural pluralism as part of schooling for positive social transformation" (p. 2).

Bilingual Education

Another key means by which such educational (and wider social) transformation can perhaps be achieved is via the successful development and implementation of bilingual education. Bilingual education has the potential, not only to (re)value students' bi/multilingualism as a basis for teaching and learning, but also to act as a broader counternarrative to the ideology of monolingualism that still underpins much educational delivery worldwide (May, 2014). Critical ethnographies that focus on bilingual education programs thus provide important, rich, and much-needed pedagogical alternatives to the regular linguistic marginalization and discrimination of bi/multilingual students discussed in the preceding sections. These ethnographies encompass a focus on both individual school programs and system-wide educational and language policy developments promoting additive forms of bilingual education.

We discussed earlier Stephen's three-year ethnographic study of Richmond Road School (May, 1994) and so will not revisit it again. Other ethnographic studies of progressive bilingual school contexts include Freeman's (1998) account of Oyster Bilingual School in Washington DC, which drew upon a theoretical combination of ethnography and critical discourse analysis to explore the school's trail blazing Spanish – English dual-language program. Teresa McCarty's (2002) 20-year ethnographic engagement with Rough Rock Demonstration School in the Navajo reservation in Arizona is another key exemplar – charting the school's efforts to maintain, and where necessary, revitalize Navajo via the establishment of a Navajo language immersion program within the school. McCarty situates her ethnographic account within the wider context of community-led Indigenous language revitalization efforts which, in the case of Rough Rock, included establishing a publishing center for Navajo curricula, offering initial literacy instruction in Navajo, and providing additional summer camps for students, teachers, and elders to share in research, storytelling, dramas, and art projects on local themes (see also, McCarty & Nicholas, 2012).

Indigenous language education has provided a rich locus for critical ethnographic work – although, interestingly, to date much of this work has been situated primarily within the field of language policy rather than education, per se. Hill and May (2011, 2013a, 2013b), for example, have explored ethnographically the role of Māori language immersion pedagogies in relation to both Indigenous language revitalization and their educational effectiveness in improving academic outcomes for Indigenous Māori students in New Zealand. Drawing on an ethnography of *Rakaumangamanga*, a combined Māori-medium elementary and high school, they highlight how a high-level additive immersion program in Māori (81%–100% of the school day), alongside a structured approach to the acquisition of academic English, results in the successful achievement of bilingualism and biliteracy for students (the vast majority of whom are first language English speakers or have Māori as their heritage language). Achieving biliteracy is also a key indicator for the wider academic achievement that these students experience over time.

The effectiveness of additive Indigenous language education programs has also been explored at the macro level of language policy development and via multi-site ethnographic analyses. One of the earliest and most influential of these was Nancy Hornberger's (1988) ethnographic study of bilingual education policy and practice in Puno, Peru, exploring the critical role of local schools in Quechua language revitalization. Hornberger's study was one of the first to highlight how official language policies can open what she later described as "ideological and implementational spaces" for the development of bi/multilingual education at the local level (Hornberger, 2006). However, whether these policies are enacted effectively, or not, inevitably rests with the decisions of local actors, the degree of local support, and the related development and implementation of effective pedagogies and practices in those local contexts. Subsequent studies have continued to explore the interstices of ethnography and language policy development with respect to these macro – micro dialectics in a range of Indigenous language education initiatives internationally, albeit again primarily in relation to the field of language policy (see Hornberger, 2008; May, 1999b, 2013; May & Aikman, 2003; McCarty, 2011).

Dynamic Bilingualism and Everyday Language Practices

These studies consistently highlight the crucial role of bilingual education in the maintenance and/or revitalization of Indigenous and other minoritized languages

(May, 2017). However, additive bilingual programs, as their description suggests, still tend to compartmentalize languages – treating them as accretive and discrete. This reflects, in turn, an ongoing monolingual perspective of language learning, even in bilingual education contexts. Monica Heller (1999, 2006) was one of the first to explore this conundrum directly. Heller examined the broader language policy imperatives underpinning French immersion schooling in Canada via a critical ethnography of a French immersion high school in Toronto. She highlighted how the school's strict emphasis on separating languages of instruction, along with its wider aim of achieving an elite, "balanced" bilingualism, in the formal language varieties of French and English, created tensions for students in relation to their own language use. Indeed, she found that students' everyday bi/multilingual language practices were far more fluid, dynamic, informal, and transgressive than the formal bilingual education context the school accounted for or allowed. Ibrahim (1999), whom we discussed earlier, also highlights these differences in his focus on the everyday use of Black (African American) English among migrant African students in another French immersion high school in Toronto.

Ibrahim drew specifically (although Heller did not) on Ben Rampton's (1995) notion of "language crossing" – a key concept that has since informed much sociolinguistic work on bi/multilingual language use. Rampton explored this concept in his ethnographic study of London youth – charting how the young people in his study would regularly cross into a new ethnicity via the use of language practices associated with another ethnic group. Drawing on interactional linguistics (how communication occurs in everyday face-to-face contexts), and methodologically via the use of omni-directional microphones, he explored "the ways that [London] youngsters of Asian and Anglo descent used Caribbean-based Creole, the ways Anglos and Caribbeans used Punjabi", and "the way . . . 'stylised Asian English' . . . was used by all three" (1995, p. 489).

Rampton's (1995) study was neighborhood-based, but it has provided an important conceptual and methodological benchmark for subsequent school-based ethnographies focused on language crossing, including in his own later work. Rampton (2006), for example, adopts the same broad conceptual and methodological parameters to explore language practices ethnographically among students in classrooms in Central High, a multiethnic and multilingual London secondary school. By this, he argues:

> [C]lassrooms emerge as sites where day-in-day-out, participants struggle to reconcile themselves to each other, to their futures, to political edicts and to the movements of history, where vernacular aesthetics often provide as much of the momentum as the transmission of knowledge, where the curriculum cohabits with popular music and media culture, where students make hay with the most unrewarding subjects, and where participants

wrestle with the meaning of class stratification, their efforts inflected with social ambivalence (and sexual desire).

(pp. 3–4)

Rampton examines the students' use of stylization – drawing on Bakhtin's (1981) description of this practice as the production of "an artistic image of another's language" (p. 362). As Rampton observes, "these accent shifts represent moments of critical reflection on aspects of educational domination and constraint that become interactionally salient on . . . particular occasion[s]" (2006, p. 27). These are most clearly demonstrated in Rampton's study in students' regular movement between exaggerated posh (Received Pronunciation/British Standard English) and Cockney (working-class London) accents, both with teachers and each other. In so doing, the students address (and critique) issues of social class, class subjectivities, and related social positioning and power relations, within their classroom and in wider educational contexts.

Language crossing has also since been explored in the United States via the work of, among others, Mary Bucholtz, Angela Reyes, and H. Samy Alim. Bucholtz (1999, 2001) focuses on the language use of "White kids" in a San Francisco Bay Area school. She explores how some students used Black English to identify with Black cultural practices, and associated conceptions of coolness, while others used "super-standard" English, and a related "nerd" identity, to specifically distance themselves from these same cultural practices. Reyes (2007) combines ethnography and critical discourse analysis to examine how Southeast Asian American students in the United States form their identities in relation to circulating stereotypes (both positive and negative) of Asian American pan ethnicity. Via the use of an after-school video project in an alternative education setting, she investigates how these students both critique, and yet also internalize, constructions of Asian Americans as "foreign". On the one hand, the students criticize how "mainstream" media films depict Asian newcomers with mock Asian accents and martial arts stereotypes. On the other hand, the students utilize similar Asian stereotypes and "mock Asian English" in their own videos, particularly in order to differentiate themselves from those they describe as F.O.B ("fresh off the boat"). As Reyes observes, while they resented the stereotype of all Asian Americans as foreigners, "the teens tended to authenticate depictions of recently arrived Asian immigrants as familial reality, allowing them to justify the recirculation of Asian newcomer portrayals in their own teen-created videos" (p. 60).

H. Samy Alim's (2004) ethnographic study of the linguistic practices of African American students at an alternative Northern California high school, Sunnyside High, explores the students' varied uses of African American English, which Alim termed Black Language (BL), in relation to the influence of hip hop, and related language style shifting. Alim found that BL was a prominent feature of student language use, but that style shifting was also clearly apparent, particularly when these high school students interacted with students from a prestigious local university. The high school students' varied language practices thus provide a counternarrative to those teachers in the study who continued to view BL in homogenous and racialized terms vis-à-vis American Standard English. The analysis is further informed by Alim's own personal knowledge and command and use of these student language registers, which allows him to interact authentically with the students throughout the course of the study.

Recent Theoretical Orientations: CRT, Translanguaging, and Superdiversity

Alim, along with Django Paris (Alim & Paris, 2017; Paris & Alim, 2014), has also been at the forefront of exploring the bi/multilingual language practices of students via CRT and ethnography. Paris's ethnographic study in South Vista, a small charter high school in the California Bay Area, is a key exemplar in this regard. He focused on a small group of African American, Latinx, and Pacific youth, exploring

> their ways with language and text and their forging of ethnic and linguistic identities in the face of continued segregation and racism, in the face of poverty, in the face of a changing community, and in the midst of their high school years.
>
> *(2011, p. 2)*

Paris pays particular attention to these students' "multiethnic youth space – a social and cultural space centered on youth communication within and across communities" (p. 16). He explores a continuum of language and textual practices associated with this youth space, ranging from those that maintain ethnic and linguistic exclusion to those that inhabit "common ground" (p. 18), thus establishing ethnic and linguistic solidarity among students.

Regarding the latter, Paris extends Rampton's notion of language crossing to examine students' language *sharing*. Language sharing focuses on the ratification across ethnic boundaries of momentary and sustained uses of language normally associated with particular ethnic groups (e.g., the use of BL by African American students or Spanish among Latinx students). A key exemplar of language sharing includes what Paris describes as "flowed texts" (2011, p. 127): rap performance texts shared among students that blur and reconstitute the boundaries between students' everyday oral and literate practices. Paris observes that these flowed texts could potentially have been drawn upon as a resource for, and/or bridge to, the teaching of school-based academic literacies but, as with most such bi/multilingual language practices, were not recognized or mobilized by teachers in any way. As he concludes, "by silencing the linguistic and textual economy of multiethnic youth space, we are silencing knowledge about language, literacy and plurality" (p. 159), both in classrooms and in wider society.

The consistent overlooking of everyday bi/multilingual language practices has also been highlighted in recent related ethnographic work framed by understandings of superdiversity (Blommaert, 2013; Vertovec, 2007), raciolinguistics (Flores & Rosa, 2015; Rosa & Flores, 2017), and translanguaging (García, 2009; García & Li Wei, 2014). Superdiversity explores the complex and fluid language practices evident among multiethnic and multilingual populations in major cities worldwide, resulting from increasing migration and transmigration, along with the increasing use of technology to traverse transnational spaces. Raciolinguistics foregrounds the normative influence of Whiteness in the ongoing racialized construction of linguistic minority language practices. Translanguaging explores the pedagogical consequences of drawing on students' dynamic and fluid language practices as a basis for teaching and learning.

Methodological Innovations

Along with new developments in critical theory, ethnographic work in language and education has also demonstrated a number of key methodological innovations. Paris's (2011) ethnography, for example, was specifically framed within what he terms a humanizing research stance, which "involve[s] dialogic consciousness-raising and the building of relationships of dignity and care for both researchers and participants" (p. 9). This emphasis on reciprocity and positionality is a key feature of other critical ethnographic work in this area – see, for example, Hill and May's (2013a) discussion of these issues in relation to ethnographic work in Indigenous language contexts. Paris's study also drew on a combination of methodological approaches, including discourse analysis, the ethnography of communication, linguistic anthropology, and quantitative sociolinguistics. Again, this builds on earlier critical ethnographic work in the language and education field that specifically combines qualitative and quantitative analyses (see e.g., Alim, 2004; May, 1994; Zentella, 1997).

Innovative methods have also featured in critical ethnographic work in this field. These include Rampton's (1995, 2006) use of omni-directional microphones to capture everyday language use in real time, and in both formal classroom and informal youth spaces, as well as his use of retrospective participant commentaries where he asked participants to comment on recorded interactions. Alim (2004) extended the traditional sociolinguistic interview method via his use of the "semi-structured conversation (SSC)" (p. 27), where he asked his participants to engage in a conversation among themselves about preselected topics, based on his own ethnographic insights. Alim argued that SSCs were methodological advancements that allowed for more free-flowing "natural" interactions to occur.[3] The use of counter-stories has been a prominent feature of recent critical ethnographies on language and education that draw on a CRT/BlackCrit framework (see e.g., Caldas, 2018; Kinloch et al., 2017; Malsbary, 2014), as has the use of *historias* and *testimonios* (Nuñez & García-Mateus, 2022; Villenas & Foley, 2011) in LatCrit.

Caldas (2018, 2022) also foregrounds the use of drama and performance ethnography in her explorations of bilingual student teachers' identity and advocacy development. Finally, the role and use of photo methods, social media, and digital ethnography, while still relatively underutilized, is gaining traction in critical ethnographies focused on language and education (see Boucher, 2017; Gallagher et al., 2013; James & Busher, 2013; Reyes, 2007; Thorne & May, 2017).

All these developments highlight both the ongoing saliency and significance of critical ethnography as a key methodological contribution in exploring questions of language, race/ism, in/equity, and education. This is especially so in light of the ongoing dominance of the ideologies of public and educational monolingualism, which continue to shape and constrain the education that linguistically minoritized students experience – foisting the dominant language on these students, while concomitantly ignoring and/or disavowing their individual bi/multilingual language repertoires (May, 2014). These monolingual ideologies within education are further exacerbated by the increasingly pervasive influence of English as the currently ascendant world language. The hegemony of English acts here to sediment existing linguistic hierarchies at all levels: from the macro (via globalization and nation-state language policies), the meso (local education policies; school boards) to the micro (tertiary and compulsory education classrooms). Critical ethnographies that focus on the racialized experiences of linguistically minoritized students in education aim to address, and contest, the silencing of bi/multilingual students at all three levels – not only by supporting their "diverse ways of speaking" but also in their "speaking back to power".

Notes

1. This is revised version of a chapter that was initially published as: May, S. (2022) Critical ethnography, language, race/ism and in/equity in education: Charting the field. In S. May & B. Caldas (Eds.), *Critical ethnography, language, race/ism and education*. Multilingual Matters.
2. Bilingualism and multilingualism are a continuum, rather than a clear demarcation – hence, the use of bi/multilingual.
3. This has clear resonances with the use of story booths in the *Beyond bullying project* (https://beyondbullyingproject.com/), discussed in chapter 5.

References

Alim, H. S. (2004). *You know my steez: An ethnographic and sociolinguistic study of styleshifting in a Black American speech community*. Duke University Press.

Alim, H. S., & Paris, D. (2017). What is culturally sustaining pedagogy and why does it matter? In D. Paris & H. S. Alim (Eds.), *Culturally sustaining pedagogies: Teaching and learning for justice in a changing world* (pp. 1–21). Teachers College Press.

Alim, H. S., Reyes, A., & Kroskrity, P. (Eds.). (2020). *The Oxford handbook of language and race*. Oxford University Press.

Baker-Bell, A. (2020). Dismantling anti-Black linguistic racism in English language arts classrooms: Toward an anti-racist Black language pedagogy. *Theory into Practice*, 1–14.

Bakhtin, M. (1981). *The dialogic imagination: Four essays* (M. Holquist, Trans.). University of Texas Press.

Bauman, R., & Briggs, C. (2003). *Voices of modernity: Language ideologies and the politics of inequality*. Cambridge University Press.

Bell, R. C., Martinez, M., & Rubio, B. (2022). Dialogical relationships and critical reflexivity as emancipatory praxis in a community based educational program. In S. May & B. Caldas (Eds.), *Critical ethnography, language, race/ism and education*. Multilingual Matters.

Berlant, L. (2011). *Cruel optimism*. Duke University Press.

Bernal, D. (2002). Critical race theory, Latino critical theory, and critical raced-gendered epistemologies: Recognizing students of color as holders and creators of knowledge. *Qualitative Inquiry, 8*(1), 105–126.

Blommaert, J. (2013). *Ethnography, superdiversity and linguistic landscapes*. Multilingual Matters.

Boucher, M. (2017). The art of observation: Issues and potential of using photo-methods in critical ethnography with adolescents. *International Journal of Adult Vocational Education and Technology, 8*(2), 1–15.

Brayboy, B. M. J. (2005). Toward a tribal critical race theory in education. *The Urban Review, 37*(5), 425–446. doi:10.1007/s11256-005-0018-y

Bucholtz, M. (1999). You da man: Narrating the racial other in the production of white masculinity. *Journal of Sociolinguistics, 3*(4), 443–460.

Bucholtz, M. (2001). The whiteness of nerds: Superstandard English and racial markedness. *Journal of Linguistic Anthropology, 11*(1), 84–100.

Butler, J. (1990). *Gender trouble: Feminism and the subversion of identity*. Routledge.

Caldas, B. (2018). "More meaningful to do it than just reading it": Rehearsing praxis among Mexican-American/Latinx pre-service teachers. *Teaching Education, 29*(4), 370–382.

Caldas, B. (2022). Becoming an "avocado"; Embodied rescriptings in bilingual teacher education settings – a critical performance ethnography. In S. May & B. Caldas (Eds.), *Critical ethnography, language, race/ism and education*. Multilingual Matters.

Cazden, C. (1989). Richmond road: A multilingual/multicultural primary school in Auckland, New Zealand. *Language and Education, An International Journal, 3*, 143–166.

Corson, D. (1990). *Language policy across the curriculum*. Multilingual Matters.

Dumas, M., & ross, K. (2016). "Be real Black for me": Imagining BlackCrit in education. *Urban Education, 51*(4), 415–442.

Fitzpatrick, K., & May, S. (2015). Doing critical educational ethnography with Bourdieu. In M. Murphy & C. Costa (Eds.), *Theory as method in research: On Bourdieu, social theory and education* (pp. 101–114). Routledge.

Flores, N., & Rosa, J. (2015). Undoing appropriateness: Raciolinguistic ideologies and language diversity in education. *Harvard Educational Review, 85*, 149–171.

Freeman, R. (1998). *Bilingual education and social change*. Multilingual Matters.

Gallagher, K., Wessels, A., & Ntelioglou, B. (2013). Becoming a networked public: Digital ethnography, youth and global research collectives. *Ethnography and Education, 8*(2), 177–193.

García, O. (2009). *Bilingual education in the 21st century: A global perspective*. Blackwell/Wiley.

García, O., & Li Wei. (2014). *Translanguaging: Language, bilingualism and education*. Palgrave Macmillan.

González, N., Moll, L., & Amanti, C. (Eds.). (2005). *Funds of knowledge: Theorizing practices in households and classrooms*. Lawrence Erlbaum.

Gramling, D. (2016). *The invention of monolingualism*. Bloomsbury Academic.

Grenfell, M., Bloom, D., Hardy, C., Pahl, K., Rosswell, J., & Street, B. (2012). *Language, ethnography and education: Bridging new literacy studies and Bourdieu*. Routledge.

Grenfell, M., & Pahl, K. (2018). *Bourdieu, language-based ethnographies and reflexivity: Putting theory into practice*. Routledge.

Gutierrez, K., & Rogoff, B. (2003). Cultural ways of learning: Cultural traits or repertoires of practice. *Educational Research, 32*, 19–35.

Heath, S. (1983). *Ways with words: Language, life, and work in communities and classrooms*. Cambridge University Press.

Heller, M. (1999). Heated language in a cold climate. In J. Blommaert (Ed.), *Language Ideological Debates* (pp. 143–170). Mouton de Gruyter.

Heller, M. (2006). *Linguistic minorities and modernity* (2nd ed.). Longman. (Original work published 1999)

Heller, M. (2008). Doing ethnography. In Li Wei & M. G. Moyer (Eds.), *The Blackwell guide to research methods in bilingualism and multilingualism* (pp. 249–262). Blackwell.

Hermes, M., Bang, M., & Marin, A. (2012). Designing indigenous language revitalization. *Harvard Educational Review, 82*(3), 381–402.

Hill, R., & May, S. (2011). Exploring biliteracy in Māori-medium education: An ethnographic perspective. In T. McCarty (Ed.), *Ethnography in language policy* (pp. 161–184). Routledge.

Hill, R., & May, S. (2013a). Non-indigenous researchers in indigenous language education: Ethical implications. *International Journal of the Sociology of Language, 219*(1), 47–65.

Hill, R., & May, S. (2013b). Balancing the languages in Māori-medium education in Aotearoa/New Zealand. In V. Zenotz, D. Gorter, & J. Cenoz (Eds.), *Minority languages and multilingual education* (pp. 171–189). Springer.

Hornberger, N. (1988). *Bilingual education and language maintenance: A Southern Peruvian Quechua case*. Foris.

Hornberger, N. (2006). Nichols to NCLB: Local and global perspectives on U.S. language education policy. In O. García, T. Skutnabb-Kangas, & M. Torres-Guzmán (Eds.), *Imagining multilingual schools: Languages in education and glocalization* (pp. 223–237). Multilingual Matters.

Hornberger, N. (Ed.). (2008). *Can schools save Indigenous languages?* Palgrave Macmillan.

Hymes, D. (1980). *Language in education: Ethnolinguistic essays*. Center for Applied Linguistics.

Ibrahim, A. (1999). Becoming Black: Rap and hip-hop, race, gender, identity, and the politics of ESL learning. *TESOL Quarterly, 33*(3), 349–369.

James, N., & Busher, H. (2013). Researching hybrid learning communities in the digital age through educational ethnography. *Ethnography and Education, 8*(2), 194–209.

Kinloch, V., Burkhard, T., & Penn, C. (2017). When school is not enough: Understanding the lives and literacies of Black youth. *Research in the Teaching of English, 52*(1), 34–54.

Liddicoat, A. (2013). *Language-in-education policies: The discursive construction of intercultural relations*. Multilingual Matters.

Malsbary, C. (2014). "Will this hell never end?": Substantiating and resisting race-language policies in a multilingual high school. *Anthropology & Education Quarterly, 45*(4), 373–390.

May, S. (1994). *Making multicultural education work*. Multilingual Matters.

May, S. (1995). Deconstructing traditional discourses of schooling. *Language and Education, 5*, 1–29.

May, S. (1998). On what might have been: Some reflections on critical multiculturalism. In G. Shacklock & J. Smyth (Eds.), *Being reflexive in critical educational and social research* (pp. 159–170). Falmer Press.

May, S. (Ed.). (1999a). *Critical multiculturalism: Rethinking multicultural and antiracist education*. RoutledgeFalmer.

May, S. (Ed.). (1999b). *Indigenous community-based education*. Multilingual Matters.

May, S. (2012). *Language and minority rights: Ethnicity, nationalism and the politics of language* (2nd ed.). Routledge.

May, S. (2013). Indigenous immersion education: International developments. *Journal of Immersion and Content-Based Education, 1*(1), 34–69.

May, S. (2014). *The multilingual turn: Implications for SLA, TESOL and bilingual education*. Routledge.

May, S. (2015). The problem with English(es) and linguistic (in)justice. *Critical Review of International Social and Political Philosophy, 18*(2), 131–148.

May, S. (2016). Language, imperialism and the modern nation-state system: Implications for language rights. In O. García & N. Flores (Eds.), *Oxford handbook on language and society* (pp. 35–53). Oxford University Press.

May, S. (2017). Bilingual education: What the research tells us. In O. García, A. Lin, & S. May (Eds.), *Bilingual/multilingual education. Encyclopedia of language and education* (3rd ed.). Springer.

May, S., & Aikman, S. (2003). Indigenous education: Addressing current issues and developments. *Comparative Education, 39*(2), 139–145.

May, S., & Caldas, B. (Eds.). (2022). *Critical ethnography, language, race/ism and education*. Multilingual Matters.

May, S., & Sleeter, C. (Eds.). (2010). *Critical multiculturalism: Theory and praxis*. Routledge.

McCarty, T. (2002). *A place to be Navajo: Rough Rock and the struggle for self-determination in indigenous schooling*. Routledge.

McCarty, T. (Ed.). (2011). *Ethnography and language policy*. Routledge.

McCarty, T. (2014). Ethnography in educational linguistics. In M. Bigelow & J. Ennser-Kananen (Eds.), *The Routledge handbook of educational linguistics* (pp. 23–37). Routledge.

McCarty, T. (2022). Critical ethnographic monitoring and chronic raciolinguistic panic: Problems, necessities, possibilities, and dreams. In S. May & B. Caldas (Eds.), *Critical ethnography, language, race/ism and education*. Multilingual Matters.

McCarty, T., & Nicholas, S. (2012). Indigenous education: Local and global perspectives. In M. Martin-Jones, A. Blackledge, & A. Creese (Eds.), *The Routledge handbook of multilingualism* (pp. 145–166). Routledge.

Missingham, B. (2017). Asset-based learning and the pedagogy of community development. *Community Development, 48*(3), 339–350.

Moll, L. C., Amanti, C., Neff, D., & Gonzáles, N. (1992). Funds of knowledge for teaching: Using a qualitative approach to connect homes and classrooms. *Theory into Practice, 31*, 132–141.

Moreno, J. (2002). The long-term outcomes of Puente. *Educational Policy, 16*(4), 572–587.

Nuñez, I., & García-Mateus, S. (2022). Interrogating our interpretations and positionalities: Chicanx researchers as scholar activists in solidarity with our communities. In S. May & B. Caldas (Eds.), *Critical ethnography, language, race/ism and education*. Multilingual Matters.

Palmer, D. (2011). The discourse of transition: Teachers' language ideologies within transitional bilingual education programs. *International Multilingual Research Journal, 5*(2), 103–122.

Paris, D. (2011). *Language across difference: Ethnicity, communication, and youth identities in changing urban schools.* Cambridge University Press.

Paris, D., & Alim, H. S. (2014). What are we seeking to sustain through culturally sustaining pedagogy? A loving critique forward. *Harvard Educational Review, 84*(1), 85–100.

Pennycook, A. (1994). *The cultural politics of English as an international language.* Longman.

Philips, S. (1983). *The invisible culture: Communication in classroom and community on the Warm Springs Indian Reservation.* Waveland.

Phillipson, R. (2010). *Linguistic imperialism continued.* Routledge.

Rampton, B. (1995). *Crossing: Language and ethnicity among adolescents.* Longman.

Rampton, B. (2006). *Language in late modernity: Interaction in an urban school.* Cambridge University Press.

Reyes, A. (2007). *Language, identity and stereotype among Southeast Asian American youth: The other Asian.* Lawrence Erlbaum Associates.

Reyes, A. (2010). Language and ethnicity. In N. H. Hornberger & S. L. McKay (Eds.), *Sociolinguistics and education.* Multilingual Matters.

Rosa, J., & Flores, N. (2017). Unsettling race and language: Toward a raciolinguistic perspective. *Language in Society, 46,* 621–647.

Smith, L. T. (2012). *Decolonizing methodologies: Research and indigenous peoples* (2nd ed.). Zed Books.

Talmy, S. (2009). A very important lesson: Respect and the socialization of order(s) in high school ESL. *Linguistics and Education, 20*(3), 235–253.

Thorne, S., & May, S. (Eds.). (2017). *Language and technology. Encyclopedia of language and education* (3rd ed.). Springer.

Vasquez, O., Pease-Alvarez, L., & Shannon, S. (1994). *Pushing boundaries: Language and culture in a Mexicano community.* Cambridge University Press.

Vertovec, S. (2007). Super-diversity and its implications. *Ethnic and Racial Studies, 30,* 1024–1054.

Villenas, S., & Foley, D. (2002). Chicano/Latino critical ethnography of education: Borderlands cultural productions from *la Fonterra.* In R. Valencia (Ed.), *Chicano school failure and success: Past, present and future* (2nd ed., pp. 195–226). RoutledgeFalmer.

Villenas, S., & Foley, D. (2011). Critical ethnographies of education in the Latino/a diaspora. In R. Valencia (Ed.), *Chicano school failure and success: Past, present and future* (3rd ed., pp. 175–196). RoutledgeFalmer.

Zentella, A. C. (1997). *Growing up bilingual: Puerto Rican children in New York.* Blackwell.

7

GENDER, SEXUALITY, AND (CRITICAL) EDUCATION ETHNOGRAPHY

This chapter focuses on the field of gender and sexuality studies in education. Critical ethnographic methodologies have been used in a range of ways over time to interrogate and expose complex relations of power at the intersection of genders and sexualities. In education contexts, these most commonly focus on sites of compulsory schooling but have also included prisons, online environments, higher education, and community education. Ethnographic studies focused on gender and sexuality tend to be rooted in feminism and a range of social theories is used by scholars to further methodological issues and challenge onto-epistemologies. In the last 30 years, these theoretical directions have included work drawing on hegemonic masculinities (Connell, 1995), biopower, governmentality and discourse (Foucault, 1978), the heterosexual matrix (Butler, 1999), phantasy (Ahmed, 1999), and queer theory (Sedgwick, 1990). Many feminist researchers have employed or been inspired by psychoanalysis (for example, via the work of Kristeva, 1982, 1990, 2000). More recently, gender and sexuality scholars are exploring the possibilities of new materialisms and posthumanism (Braidotti, 2019; Haraway, 1989, 2006; Barad, 2007), while many are still informed by post-structuralism (via the theory of Derrida, Deleuze, and others). As a result, the significant contributions of feminist work, and feminist ethnography in particular, have impacted the field of gender and sexuality in fundamental ways.

Feminism in contemporary times is in a period of, perhaps unprecedented, salience; gender binaries are being questioned in the public realm, and a diversity of gender and sexual identities are being acknowledged in public discourse. In this, the very bases of the "heterosexual matrix" (Butler, 1999), and the related "sex-gender-sexuality constellation" (Youdell, 2005; see also Chapter 3), are not only being called into question but also actively disrupted. Work on trans identities and experiences is evidence of this.[1] In schools, young people are questioning

DOI: 10.4324/9781315208510-7

gender norms and heteronormative exclusions and exploring notions of sexual citizenship (e.g., Aggleton et al., 2019; Rasmussen et al., 2016). In many places, the agentic gender and sexual expressions of young people are in direct tension with the cultural contexts of schooling and the conservative tendencies of educational institutions, while also finding unique expression therein.

Researching gender and sexuality in education (especially in schools) then creates unavoidable methodological, theoretical, and ethical challenges and possibilities, and researchers have employed critical ethnography in various ways to engage with these complexities. For example, schools can be seen as institutions that tend to reproduce dominant cultural boundaries and, thus, as more likely to reinforce rather than challenge gender binaries and heteronorms. While some ethnographic studies do suggest this, others show that schools are also wild places where many different kinds of gender and sexuality expressions occur; expressions that are neither consistent nor easily categorized (Gilbert, 2014; Quinlivan, 2013). Conversations about sexuality in schools can be received (or perceived) as risky and disruptive to views of children and youth as (ideally) asexual, and of schools as spaces of cognitive (rather than embodied) learning and development (Robinson & Davies, 2017). Diverse gender performances and queer subjectivities can collide directly with how most schools impose gender binaries and norms through uniforms, toilets, and other material and symbolic categorization mechanisms (Riggs & Bartholomaeus, 2018; Graham et al., 2017). Sexuality education is treated as a suspect area of academic study in schools. When it is taught explicitly, it is often seen as controversial and risky, and so constraints on content, purpose, and pedagogy are evident (Carmody, 2015; Fields, 2008; Gilbert, 2014; Leahy, 2014; Allen & Rasmussen, 2017). But school sites are also imbued with digital landscapes that transcend schooling boundaries (Ringrose, 2012; Albury & Byron, 2018). And so, at the same time as they are often denied full access to sexuality education in schools, young people are actively seeking education about sex online (Ragonese et al., 2017; Evers et al., 2013).

Discussing sex and sexuality in school-based research projects can by uncomfortable (Ollis et al., 2019), and international research suggests that young people are rarely consulted about programme content, while notions of risk and safety dominate practice (Allen, 2005, 2007a, 2007b). Heteronorms rule at the expense of diversity, some key content (e.g., pleasure, pornography, social medias, religion) tends to be missing from the curriculum (Shipley, 2017; Allen et al., 2013; Allen & Rasmussen, 2017) and teachers can be unsure how to engage with the digital spaces familiar to young people (Albury, 2013). Researching gender and sexuality in education is thus fraught because, as Gilbert puts it, there are unavoidable "underlying antagonisms between the wildness of sexuality and the purposes of schooling" (2014, p. xiii).

Gender and sexualities research in education settings thus requires ethnographers to engage with issues of researcher positionality, private versus public identity positions, the silencing and surveillance of gender positioning, as well as the "risks" associated with perceptions about how adults (should or could) talk with children and young people about sex and sexuality. Researchers also have to contend with how schools gatekeep access and reputation, the perceptions of parents and communities about young people's sexualities, whether they should learn about this at school, what they should learn, and related moralisms. Additionally, potential tensions arise when ethnographers ask young people about their identities, desires, and sexual experiences. There are also related risks around the visibility of nonhetero and non-cis identities in school settings, especially as research has shown that LBGTQI+ students experience higher levels of bullying and exclusion at school (Kosciw et al., 2009; Hillier et al., 2010; Clark et al., 2013). Further sensitivities arise if research includes a focus on issues such as sexual violence, digital intimacies, consent, gender identities, sexual relationships, bullying, and explicit sexual materials online. Added to all this is the tension of how research itself produces particular kinds of sexual subjectivities (Jones, 2013). Given all the aforementioned complexity, critical ethnographic methods have enabled researchers to employ particular kinds of inquiries into gender and sexuality in education settings. Schools, as one example, are diverse and unruly places where – despite tendencies to impose categorizations – contradictory happenings eventuate and differentiated networks and discourses are operating. Ethnographic studies can explore such messy contradictions and multiplicities.

In this chapter, we first explore how gender and sexuality ethnographies have been fundamentally informed by feminist (and) poststructuralist approaches to research, then impacted by queer imaginaries, and, increasingly, by new materialist theories. In the second part of the chapter, we show how some of the key tenets of critical ethnography create particular affordances for researching gender and sexuality in education settings. We focus strongly here on how the temporalities and spatialities of ethnography enable a robust and ethical engagement with many of the tensions noted earlier, including enabling relationships, reciprocity, negotiation, and responsivity to contexts. Throughout, we pay attention to the importance of theory, and draw on examples of research projects which are broadly ethnographic. Not all the authors we draw on here would (or do) name their studies as "critical" but, consistent with our approach in this book, we view this work as critical if it engages broadly with relations of power. In this sense, contemporary critical ethnography – at least in the way we are reimagining it here – includes feminist ethnography, along with other ethnographic approaches that seek to interrogate how genders and sexualities are meaningful and productive sites of articulation.

Feminist Ethnography

Feminist ethnography has its own history and has fundamentally impacted the fields of gender/sexuality studies and education more broadly. Space does not allow us to rehearse the history of feminist ethnography here (for an excellent overview, see Davis and Craven, 2016). Rather, we make a few important observations about how it has broadly impacted the field, before discussing the insights that educational ethnographies in gender and sexuality have produced (see also our discussion of feminist poststructuralism in Chapter 3).

According to Davis and Craven (2016), feminist ethnography:

> [A]ttends to the dynamics of power in social intersection that *starts* from a gender analysis. By gender analysis we mean that a feminist ethnographic project takes into account all people in a field site/community/organisation and pays particular attention to gender by honing in on people's statuses, the different ways in which (multiple) forms of privilege allow them to wield power or benefit from it, and the forces and processes that emerge from all of the above.
>
> *(p. 9; emphasis in original)*

Feminist ethnography is not only about the research foci though. But also, crucially, about the methods and approach to conducting research, including how questions are framed (and by whom) and how fieldwork, analyses, and writing are undertaken. Feminist methods are necessarily relational (Desmond, 2014; Lather, 2007) and pay attention to histories of feminist scholarship (Davis and Craven, 2016). Youdell observes that "feminist ethnography has been concerned with the nature and status of its representations, what is included and what is left out, and the inclusions and silences as the author speaks" (2010, p. 92). She argues that many feminists have drawn on poststructuralism, which has "also troubled ethnography, moving from concerns with authenticity and reciprocity to processes of subjectivation in research and representation" (p. 92). Feminist work has made a number of important interventions in ethnography. It has challenged the centrality of White heteromale identities (McRobbie, 1991) and various objectivist stances (Fine, 1994), colonizing and racialized inquiries (Madison, 2009, 2019), as well as shifting ethnographic imaginaries beyond truth claims and toward a praxis of getting lost (Lather, 2012). Nancy Naples' (1996) challenge to the insider/outsider dichotomy (commonly referred to in traditional anthropological and ethnographic work) is a good example of how feminists have used theory to disturb and disrupt ethnographic language, positioning, and practice. Many ethnographic texts advise ethnographers to immerse themselves in a social and cultural setting and acquire "insider status" in order to gain "authentic" accounts (Hammersley, 1992; Tedlock, 2000). Naples (1996) troubled this assumption by explaining that:

> [I]n this feminist revisiting of the insider/outsider debate, I argue that [this] distinction masks the power differentials and experiential differences between the researcher and the researched. . . "outsiderness" and "insiderness" are not fixed or static positions, rather they are ever-shifting and permeable social locations that are differentially experienced and expressed by community members.
>
> *(p. 84)*

Naples (1996) drew here on poststructuralist conceptualizations of researcher positionality and, in so doing, exposed and deconstructed the assumed neutrality of researchers and related attempts at a distanced approach to researcher identity. Accepting the insider/outsider dichotomy ignores the complexity of human relationships and cultures, and the responsibility of the researcher for reciprocity, relationality, and connection (a point we return to later). It also denies the porosity of research sites, the fluidity of researcher subjectivity, and the ethical problems with attempting to "merge" into the cultural milieu of a research setting (see also Chapter 4). Abidin (2020) argues that, in digital ethnography, researcher subjectivity becomes even more fluid and so "digital and physical presence and self-presentation frequently shift along spectrums of conspicuousness" (p. 72).

In general terms, feminist approaches to research have influenced critical ethnographers, and all qualitative researchers, to move toward greater reflexivity, analyses of power in research relationships, and away from "the masculinist voice of abstraction and universalization" (Lather, 1998). Queer work is, likewise, pivotal to this discussion and also engages a dynamic reflexivity.

The Impact of Queer

Valocchi argues that queer theory has impacted ethnographic inquiry in a range of ways and suggests that: "[t]he power of the ethnography lies in the variable interplay between the imitation of norms and signifiers of class, on one hand, and the resource limitations rooted in material conditions, on the other" (2005, p. 763). Valocchi argues that ethnographic methods are especially useful for exploring queer projects because such research:

> [R]equires a sensitivity to the complicated and multilayered lived experiences and subjectivities of individuals, to the social settings within which these experiences and subjectivities take shape, and to the larger cultural, discursive, and institutional contexts of these lives where resources are allocated, images created, and taxonomies are given power. Ethnographic methods, with their emphasis on how individuals create meaning, seem best suited to this enterprise.
>
> (p. 767)

Rooke notes that a queer approach goes beyond a research focus on queer lives but still requires a dedicated engagement with queer theory to question "the stability and coherence of the ethnographic self and the performativity of this self in writing and doing research" (2009, p. 150). For Youdell, doing queer "is about interrogating how discourses of sex and sexuality are implicated in processes of subjectivation that constitute subjects who are sexed and sexualised in particular ways" (2010, p. 88). She argues that "[a] central project of queer in this framework is resisting these processes through practices that unsettle the meanings of these discourses and deploy other discourses that have been subjugated or disallowed" (p. 88). Queer work in ethnography draws on the work of Eve Sedgwick, Judith Butler, Michel Foucault, and others. Drawing on Miller's (1988) notion of the "open secret" and Sedgwick's (1990) "epistemology of the closet", Talburt (1999) noted that:

> [F]or gay men and lesbians the open secret creates an unknowing of the meanings of their sexuality in even seemingly desexualized circumstances. Their interlocutors occupy positions of some degree of power, for their knowledges, "real" or imagined, play a role in shaping the dynamics of exchanges and constructing the actions of the gay or lesbian subject/object of knowledge.
>
> *(p. 526)*

In a queer re-reading, Youdell (2010) reflects on an earlier ethnographic project and her own uncomfortable subjectivities as a queer and/or not-queer researcher in a school setting. She unearths remembered emotional landscapes that were silenced (or not recorded at the time), including a series of encounters with a student, "Molly", and the edges of coming out at the school (see also Chapter 3). Employing an "uncomfortable reflexivity" (Pillow, 2003), she concludes that:

> [T]he ambivalence, incompleteness, discomfort and dislocation of uncomfortable reflexivity and the uncanny seem to offer a different sort of queer – one which retains practices of troubling as a central concern but which also looks to what exceeds this framework politically, affectively and psychically.
>
> *(p. 98)*

Youdell hints at the idea that such messy and incomplete reflexive accounts are more possible now, in the times both after poststructuralism and after queer, although she contends that she feels both after queer and before queer simultaneously in relation to such research encounters. Talburt argued that queer approaches to research "[i]f taken seriously . . . would shift ethnography's purposes from representation of gay and lesbian subjects and experiences to analysis of practices as they are constructed in social and institutional locations" (1999, p. 526). Youdell (2010), indeed, takes up this challenge. She draws on Talburt to reframe the purpose of research beyond the politics of identity, and toward a greater understanding of how complex cultural and political contexts circumscribe subjects in particular ways, and in continually destabilizing analyses. She argues that "ethnography continues to offer detailed present tense representations of 'real life', albeit 'life' that is no longer claimed as 'real'" (p. 92). Importantly then, queer ethnography requires a difficult and ongoing engagement with researcher positionality and ontologies over time. It acknowledges that readings in any given time are unstable and messy, and that we might (and should) revisit out analyses and interpretations. Multiplicities are central to this, along with a resistance to resolving tensions.

Talburt's (1999) own study, for example, focused on a lesbian woman faculty member at a university in the United States. The teacher, "Julie", also identified as Catholic and a feminist, and she taught a religious studies class at a liberal university. This results in an intersectional ethnographic account of irresolvable multiple subject positions. Talburt recounts how irreverent Julie is when teaching about Christianity and how the students read her embodiment as inconsistent with the study of religion. She explains that "Julie's body offers students a text, albeit not transparent, to interpret, particularly as her words and authoritative manner combine with her appearance to defy conventional notions of femininity and Christianity" (p. 535). She concludes that:

> Queer theory pushes the limits of ethnography, even critical ethnography that seeks to understand the formation of subjectivities and practices in relations of power, in that it explicitly draws presences from discursive silences as it questions the constitution and effects of social and institutional norms.
>
> *(p. 537)*

She goes on to suggest:

> Queer ethnography thus may not have as a central goal the accretion of knowledge as do critical inquiries into race, class, and gender; rather, it may reconfigure what is considered ethnographic knowledge. Yet, despite the loss of certitude of what subjects themselves can know of their experiences and of what can be represented ethnographically, queer ethnography must persist in interpretive social theorizing.
>
> *(p. 537)*

A focus on "interpretive social theorizing" signals a significant shift in thinking about how research into schooling with critical ethnography (and poststructuralism) requires moves beyond interpretative and solidifying cultural insights toward more dynamic and uncertain engagement with theory in research sites. And queer work has certainly been central to this. For Youdell, queer ethnography "brings tensions that are productive in their irresolvability" (2010, p. 88). Quinlivan likewise observes that, "[r]ather than cultivating reflexivity in order to hold on to an ontologically and epistemologically stable place, the production of a stable ethnographic self in the field is rendered impossible and limited in terms of engaging with power relations" (2013, p. 58; see also Rooke, 2009). Valocchi (2005) argues from this that queer theory has irrevocably changed the way we see gender and sexuality, and that binaries – male–female, gay–straight, feminine–masculine – have been questioned and broken down by queer approaches:

> Queer theory turns this emphasis on its head by deconstructing these binaries, foregrounding the constructed nature of the sex, gender, and sexuality

classification systems and resisting the tendency to congeal these categories into social identities. Because the binaries are revealed to be cultural constructions or ideological fictions, the reality of sexed bodies and gender and sexual identities are fraught with incoherence and instability.

(pp. 752–753)

Because the field of gender and sexuality studies is heavily engaged with poststructuralism, challenging binaries is a key refrain. While some scholars have moved toward posthumanism and new materialisms (see later), Bronwyn Davies (in Davies et al., 2020) insists that this does not have to be at the expense of poststructuralism; indeed, she points out "binaries have a powerful grip on our capacity for thought, and the rendition of poststructuralist theory and posthumanist theory as binaries is easy enough to slip into" (Davies et al., 2020, p. 24). She also argues that "[t]hough poststructuralist theorists may have dwelt primarily on the human body, they were not unaware of the power of material objects, including the materiality of texts themselves" (p. 24).

New Materialist (Feminist) Ethnography

While some new materialists have avoided the term ethnography, and sought other methodological articulations in line with their commitments to social theory, others are exploring the intersections between the two. New materialisms are diverse in theoretical approach, but have in common a commitment to attend to and analyze various materialities. Fox and Alldred (2015) note that:

New materialist ontology breaks through "the mind-matter and culture nature divides" . . . [and is] consequently also transversal to a range of social theory dualisms such as structure/agency, reason/emotion, human/non-human, animate/inanimate and inside/outside. It supplies a conception of agency not tied to human action, shifting the focus for social inquiry from an approach predicated upon humans and their bodies, examining instead how relational networks or assemblages of animate and inanimate affect and are affected.

(p. 399)

Fox and Alldred (2015) suggest new materialist research can be approached as an "assemblage". Paying attention to the materiality of the world, including the more-than-human and the intersections between people, plants, things, animals, and so forth, is possible in ethnographic inquiry. However, it relies on the researcher expanding their ontological gaze beyond the limits of anthropocentrism (for further discussion, see Chapter 3). Davies et al. (2020) assert that the challenge of new materialisms "is not to abandon the insights gained from poststructuralist work, but to open thought up to the liveliness of matter, and the ways in which matter matters" (p. 24). Subjectivity remains important in this work, even if one accepts its inherent limitations and the impossibilities of ever attempting to address it. Allen (2018) undertakes a duality in arguing that she can "attempt to unsettle humanist qualitative research at the same time as . . . describ[ing] my enactment of it" (p. 10). There are thus both tensions and potential for productive exploration when new materialisms are brought into play with ethnographic research approaches. Renold and Ringrose suggest that new materialist and posthuman research "is beginning to unsettle our understandings, through new onto-epistemologies, of the ways in which bodies, affect, objects, history, place, and discourse entangle and come to matter in and indeed make their mark on children and young people's everyday lives" (2017a, p. 633). Hickey-Moody's (2020) feminist new materialist ethnography, for example, examines the cross-faith engagement of children. She draws on a process of "intra-action", a key notion drawn from the work of Barad (2007; see Chapter 2). This approach, Hickey-Moody (2020) observes:

> [R]ests on the assumption that nothing is inherently separate from anything else, but rather, separations are temporarily enacted so one can examine something long enough to gain knowledge about it. This view of knowledge provides a framework for thinking about how culture and habits of thought can make some things visible and other things easier to ignore, or even to never see.
>
> *(p. 725)*

Hickey-Moody also draws on the notion of diffraction, which she explains as "the relationship between materials, people, and ideas" and notes that "[m]aterials have agency, they change ideas in certain ways, and they 'diffract' human agency in unexpected ways" (p. 725). She employs art-making to examine "[t]he transversal lines of making art, having a shared discussion about 'what matters' – or what might matter, what is valued, and what we believe". And she argues that this "can encourage children to link simple ideas and words learnt through rote religious education with critical practices in ways they haven't experienced" (p. 729). In so doing, Hickey-Moody doesn't seek to solve or resolve tensions and multiplicities, but, rather, to be with them, to understand them, and to think and write about how these intersect in educational contexts.

In another study, Landi (2019) undertook a critical ethnographic study with queer youth and employed new materialism and affect via the work of Deleuze and Guattari. He notes that "[i]nstead of thinking of identity as either 'natural' or 'constructed', new materialism theorises bodies as continuously produced in relation to material and social forces" (2019, p. 171). Landi employs the notions of dredging and mapping to work with research materials and present ideas related to the athletic and sexy body and queer desire. He argues that queer desire can be a productive and transformative force in schools and he calls on researchers to see schools as queer spaces (see also lisahunter, 2017). In a related paper, Landi writes with Safron (Safron & Landi, 2021) to explore affect theory and poetic inquiry to understand how diverse youth engage with fitness testing practices in schools. They note that "[a]ffects became intensities that incited us . . . [and] . . . produced intensities that encompassed our thinking, doing, and creation process from data generation to inquiry, often with little discernable distinction" (p. 6). By bringing together ethnography with critical approaches to affect, these scholars open up possibilities for exploring gender and sexuality in educational contexts.

In the second half of this chapter, we move from discussing the theoretical trajectories of critical ethnographies focused on gender and sexuality to considering how ethnographic methods open up particular kinds of inquiry for such research, and how researchers engage with some of the complexities they encounter. We begin by considering how ethnographic temporalities allow a responsive and relational approach.

Ethnographic Temporalities and Gender Sexuality

Ethnographic explorations of gender and sexuality in education contexts allow for particular kinds of research materials to emerge that may not be possible under other conditions. Because ethnographers spend significant time in research sites, and pay close attention to issues of culture, they are able to experience how their research sites change over time, how particular embodied expressions congeal or are altered, how people relate in complex ways to the places they inhabit, and how multiple one context can be. Talburt (1999) argues that ethnography's historical aim of giving voice is questionable because the positions that emerge are still received through relations of power (see also Chapter 2):

> [B]ecause identities are "seen" through established norms, they may not be "seen" at all except as they can be understood within given discursive systems. In other words, representations are created within and can perpetuate social knowledges and ignorances in a circular system.
>
> *(p. 528)*

Ethnographic temporalities – time spent in the field – can allow researchers to interrogate how norms are reinscribed and how voices are shifting and fluid. Ethnographers pay attention to how such identities articulate over time, in ways that intersect with cultures, environments, objects, and spaces, as well as within and through ethnicity, place, social class, race, and so forth. Maher and Tetreault, for example, reflected on their ethnographic approach over six years with feminist tertiary teachers in different institutions. The extended time period of the research allowed them to challenge their own ontologies, including "a set notion of the ideal feminist teacher" (1993, p. 20) and "the persistence of the rationalist positivist paradigm in our thinking and methodology" (p. 20). The latter is a significant insight during a time period when poststructuralist thinking was challenging research ontologies, and qualitative research paradigms were pulling strongly away from positivistic thinking. Maher and Tetreault (1993) concluded that:

> [P]ositionality enjoins us to take account of these relations – student and teacher, ethnographer and informant – as always occurring in a specific context, one which changes with each group of students and with each group of informants. Just as some feminist teachers continually reposition their relationships to their students, so must feminist ethnographers continually deconstruct their positions.
>
> *(p. 31)*

In this sense, the work of ethnography helps to highlight how relationalities and subjectivities change over time. Researcher subjectivity is more obviously and unavoidably a part of the research project and ethnographic temporalities require researchers to engage relationally (see Chapter 4). This is unavoidable because researchers form relationships with participants and come to see themselves as relationally implicated in the research settings. More than this, though, the researcher becomes part of the scene of research, immersed in relational engagements with people, objects, ideas, and the historicities of the context. Abidin (2020) notes that, in digital ethnography, researchers can engage in different kinds of posturing to gain the trust of and access to participants. This can be "a result of conscientiously mobilising and performing selective aspects of one's identity inscriptions" (p. 58) over time and in different contexts.

Fields' (2008) research into sexuality education in US middle schools also highlights how ethnographic temporalities allow for deep engagement with context and social histories and meaningful attention to intersectionality. Her book, *Risky lessons: Sex education and social inequality* Fields (2008), details the ethnographic fieldwork she completed at three middle schools in North Carolina between 1996 and 1998, a time when abstinence education was legislated by the state. Fields spent time in classes, interviewing students and talking with teachers, and engaging with community members. Her interest in the topic was stimulated at the time by intense debates about sex education on local radio, in newspapers, and in community meetings. A key strength of her ethnography is Fields' (2008) focus across socioeconomic groups (her schools were located in White middle-class, diverse working-class, and Black working-class communities) and her writing about how her own embodied engagement changed between those contexts. She reflected that:

> Most days I wore slacks and a blouse when doing fieldwork. Toward the end of my time in the schools, I became more relaxed and dressed more casually. One day, as I left the house, I noted that I felt more like myself

than I had in weeks of fieldwork. As Jimmy left class that afternoon, he said, "No offense, but you look like a tomboy today". Jimmy's comment marked for me how I had managed my sexuality, not only by not disclosing it verbally but also by adopting a more conventionally feminine mode of self-presentation.

(pp. 177–178)

Paying attention to how one engages as a researcher in (and becomes part of) the study is an unavoidable part of ethnographic work. Indeed, a key tenet of critical ethnography relies on researchers continuously interrogating their subjectivity and positionality (see also Chapters 2 and 4). Although such insights are possible in other research approaches, the time element of ethnography creates greater potential for reflection on bodily engagement and how it changes across time and context. Fields (2008), for example, reflected that:

> Like many ethnographers and others who do not conform to normative gender and sexual expectations, I had assessed the three schools and decided whether I would be able to come out as a lesbian and still have access to the teachers and students.

(p. 178)

Fields' ethnographic approach also allowed her to interrogate the intersection of whiteness and gender. For example, she noted that:

> I found that gender hierarchies informed my experiences as an interviewer. Though some were more reticent than others, all of the women – regardless of race – honored my request for an interview. Two men refused my requests, and during the interview all men expressed impatience for the conversation to end. Rather than celebrate whites' openness or consider the reticence of African Americans, men, and young people something to overcome in order to achieve full disclosure, I consider the participants' openness and caution. . . . Both point broadly to the ways gender, race, and power shape everyday interactions and research. More specifically, the patterns that emerged concerning who wanted to talk about sex education, who would speak with me, and how those conversations unfolded, suggest rules governing talk about race and sexuality.

(p. 178)

The possibilities of an ethnographic approach in Fields' work are summed up well in her methodological notes. There she states that her intention for the book was to "adopt a critical stance on the taken-for-granted ideas and examine the meanings and narratives that people construct about young people and sexuality" (p. 179). She goes on to observe that "[s]tories about youth and sexuality, as well as stories about sex education, are as volatile and constructed as the practices themselves" (p. 179); ethnography allowed for a dynamic engagement with the telling of those stories, and a simultaneous plotting of their volatility over time. Importantly, Fields was able to make significant observations about the cultural differences between the schools she observed, including a much more informative curriculum at the private school in comparison to the public schools (where abstinence education was enforced). Fields (2008) connected gender and sexuality with social class and racialized social relations to conclude that:

> Those students whose racial, socioeconomic, and educational privilege already positions them to claim agency in their lives have access to sex education that reinforces their claims to knowledge, pleasure, and subjectivity. Those students with less privilege, whose sexual expressions policy makers cast as the stuff of social problems, sit in abstinence-only classes that aim modestly to help them survive the onslaught that puberty heralds.
>
> *(p. 146)*

Ethnographies of gender and sexuality then often pay attention to intersections of social class, ethnicity, place, and other identity positions because the researcher engages in a lived experience of a social and cultural context, and is immersed in the politics of gender and sexuality across time and within place. Ethnographic temporalities have, thus, allowed particular kinds of insights in the field of gender and sexuality studies in education, including how young people are engaging in long-term negotiations of power relations in their own schools, and the complexities (and, often, contested nature) of these negotiations.

McGlashan's (2017) ethnographic work with queer and trans youth in schools is a good example of how gendered knowledges are worked, over time and in complex ways, by young people. McGlashan's study of a queer activist and support group in a New Zealand high school suggests that young people are now articulating greater knowledge of gender fluidity and using this knowledge to contest school settings. McGlashan's (2017) group of queer-identifying young people actively questioned heteronormativities in their school and contested power relations within the group itself. These included the power of teachers to set the tone of queer group meetings, as well as the power relations between students who identified as queer and those who identified as trans. The latter had much less stable gender identities. Because she spent over a year participating in the group, McGlashan was able to observe the subtle changes in how students dealt with (their) agency and how the control of the group shifted from being teacher-led toward a more complex dynamic of student–teacher power relations (McGlashan & Fitzpatrick, 2018). This also involved students (and the group) engaging a more public identity in the school, against the teachers' concerns for safety and privacy. Students in that project discussed their knowledge as superior to that of their teachers, and felt sorry for teachers who displayed homophobic behaviors, which they interpreted as ignorance rather than bigotry (McGlashan & Fitzpatrick, 2017; Fitzpatrick & McGlashan, 2018). At the same time, the students grappled with the difficulties of contesting power, both with teachers and with each other.

The time element of ethnography can allow the nuance of such engagements to be more fully explored. More than that, though, such studies highlight the multiplicities of sites and the importance of attending to contradictions and conundrums. Quinlivan argues that "[e]thnography lends itself to a rich engagement with the uncertain and curious complexities of everyday life and maintaining an openness towards research as an evolving and emergent 'culture in the making'" (2013, p. 57). For her, ethnography and queer theory are productive "because researching queerly in schools puts researchers inevitably in such uncomfortable places, they are [thus] well placed to develop methodological approaches that explore the uncomfortable possibility of knowing the unexpected" (p. 58). Quinlivan's (2012, 2013) ethnographic work in health education classrooms and with a queer activist support group in schools in New Zealand highlights the messy realities of schools. Spending significant time allowed Quinlivan to see the possibilities for a queer activist support group to both interrupt heternorms and also to pathologize difference. She argues that such groups inevitably "produce contradictory double binds" (p. 66). She reflects that employing "uncomfortable reflexivity" (Pillow, 2003) in her ethnography helped her "to consider the extent to which my modernist investment in the research process as an emancipatory success story sat uncomfortably with my queer intentions" (p. 67). Both these research projects show the affordances of ethnographic temporalities when researchers are engaged with theory.

Spatiality: Gender and Sexuality Across and Between Ethnographic Sites

Spatiality is also an important ethnographic concern, and gender sexuality ethnographies have been employed to compare and contrast sites. Drawing on multisite and autoethnographic materials from Finland in the 1990s, Lahelma (2014), for example, argues that two competing (and ineffective) discourses have dominated discussions of gender and education for some time. The first, she names as a "gender equality discourse", which centers on the concerns of girls and women; the second – "boy discourse" – encapsulates the moral panic about the feminization of girls in education and the so-called underachievement of boys. The latter, she points out, is problematic because, even when boys are shown to be underachieving relative to girls, this seems to make no difference to their overall success, educational opportunities, or subsequent dominance in the labor market. Lahelma argues that neither discourse has achieved very much. She claims this is because sustainable change needs to occur via a dedicated policy approach, and that gender and gender issues are complex and difficult for teachers to grasp.

She views the problem as located, at least in part, in the treatment of gender as a hard binary in that "[a]ssumptions that girls and boys are two different species are often implicitly behind" such research (p. 177). This conclusion is powerful and is possible because she was analyzing deeply across multiple sites and policy contexts. Lahelma (2014) does not name her research critical ethnography, but it is clear that her concerns are driven by feminist, poststructuralist ontologies, along with concerns with gendered relations of power, and that her methods are ethnographic. Ethnographic studies like this pay attention to spatialities and places in ways that enable certain kinds of insights, especially when places are juxtaposed or explored alongside, and in relation to, each other.

In another example, Bhana (2016) looks at articulations of gender and sexuality in primary [elementary] schools in South Africa. She uses multisite ethnography to interrogate the production of gender and sexuality in four schools, against popular discourse and claims by teachers that young children are "free" from gendered and sexual cultures. Bhana also examines contextual intersections and "explores the myriad ways in which the production of gender and sexuality is shaped by the interconnections between race, class, structural inequalities, fragile environments, and the actions of boys and girls as they navigate their gendered and sexual selves" (p. 3). This interplay – across the sites and within each site – allows comparison across the schools, balanced with deep contextual insights. As a result, the study examines how racialized discourses of boys' achievements and attitudes work differently in each setting, and how these compare across the contexts. This comparison is highly productive, as observations in one school spark conversations and observations in the other sites. The intersections of social class, race, and cultures are also highlighted as Bhana analyzes how children from "African", "Indian", "White", and "colored" backgrounds are subject to fixed notions of gender and race, many of which limit subjectivity, and explain behavior in racialized ways. For example, it is clear from Bhana's observations that dominant masculinities are celebrated in the schools. One boy in the most affluent school – Samit – is singled out by the teacher for disliking girls. The teacher explains this dislike in relation to Samit's religion and states that he is Muslim. Bhana, however, discovers that the boy is actually Hindu. Bhana also shows how girls are routinely marginalized by the masculinist practices of the boys. She demonstrates the location of such practices in wider cultural contexts and highlights how teachers position students like Samit in problematic ways. The comparison between schools allows Bhana to illustrate how gender power articulates differently as a result of the interstices of social class, location, and ethnicity.

Temporalities and space are explored in different ways through digital ethnographies.[2] Abidin and De Seta argue that "doing ethnographic research about, on, and through digital media is most often a messy, personal, highly contextual enterprise fraught with anxieties and discomfort" (2020, p. 1). Digital spaces have different temporal and spatial logics, allowing both "accelerated mediated time" (Keightley, 2012, p. 2) and access across time and place. Keller et al. (2018), for example, used ethnographic methods to explore how young women use digital media to contest rape culture. They explored both how women's experiences were digitally mediated and how social media was used as a space of activism. Using a website, a twitter handle, and an individual tweet to a group of followers, the researchers could trace online interactions across time, and then engage participants for interviews and a survey. Renold and Ringrose (2017a, 2017b) engaged digital and nondigital approaches in an activist research project into young people's sexualities, sexual regulation, and harassment in schools. Employing new materialist and posthuman theories, they mapped out the micro practices of the everyday in schools. In one part of the project, they analyzed digital tagging and Facebook exchanges and were able to explore how complex networks of relations operated to create digital sexual cultures (Renold & Ringrose, 2017b).

Understanding Nuance

Ethnographic temporalities also allow researchers to gain insight into how gender works in nuanced ways at the level of culture. Mary Jane Kehily (2002) reports on her ethnographic fieldwork conducted in schools in England during the 1990s, and also reflects on the key work of earlier educational ethnographies – Willis' (1977) ethnography of working-class boys and McRobbie's (1978) study of working-class girls (see also Chapter 3). Conducting research almost 20 years later in the same geographical area (England's midlands), she observes:

> In the post-Fordist era it appeared that the young people in my study were hardly "learning to labour" [Willis] or preparing for marriage and motherhood [McRobbie]. Their futures in the workplace and the home were less certain and not so clearly defined. The materiality of young people's lives pose many big questions for schools concerning the nature and purpose of education in the present period and the relationship between school and society in the face of global change. The role of the school and its relationship to the local economy is seemingly less obvious as local industries and long-term manual work decline. At the same time, multinational chains in the retail and service sector, together with new forms of "flexible" employment, have expanded.
>
> *(p. 3)*

As a result of these changes, Kehily asks research questions that can only be answered ethnographically, and which clearly have a critical orientation:

> How has economic change impacted upon the lives of young women and men in school? What are the implications for versions of masculinity and femininity? Is there a new, emergent sex-gender order?
>
> *(p. 3)*

Kehily draws powerful insights from this work, and reflects methodologically that "things look different, depending on where you are looking from" (p. 5). This is important because, unlike studies that see the researcher go into and then out of a site (e.g., a school), critical ethnography (like any ethnography) requires time and multiple, recursive engagements with participants (see Chapter 2). This kind of relational engagement makes it clear that all contexts are changing, inconsistent, and contradictory, and that cultures play out ultimately in subtle and differentiated ways. As a result, she argues that "text produced by ethnographic fieldwork can be viewed and interpreted as a form of social practice" (p. 5). This is important because, by definition, ethnographic research materials decentralize the concept of the knowing subject, placing all utterances and happenings within social and political (and physical) contexts. In this sense, Kehily is able to draw on extensive evidence to show how, over time, the school site is constitutive of gender and sexual identities, and so produces heterosexualities in particular ways. A clear example of this is in her descriptions of a sexuality education teacher, "Mrs Evans". Kehily gives a detailed overview of this teacher's various commitments – to a version of female empowerment, encapsulated in the right to "say no" to male advances, and to her boldness in making sure students had open access to information about sex – coupled with her Christian views about abstinence and delaying sexual relationships. The intertwining of these various commitments was made apparent over the course of the year through Mrs Evans' teaching, actions within the school, and interviews with her.

In a study on health education in Australian schools, Leahy (2014) explored how nuanced pedagogical interactions between teachers and students worked to reinforce discourses of young people being at risk in a range of contexts. By spending over 80 hours in classrooms, Leahy (2014) was able to draw important links between quite different topics to show how disgust and shame worked in tandem with notions of risk in terms of health and sexuality. She argues that:

> One of the recurring features throughout health education pedagogical assemblages is the presence of and recruitment of affect, by both teachers and students as they educate and are educated. For example, in the party excerpt . . . shame, regret and embarrassment were considered to be the most potent risks. In fact, the risk of contracting an STI or becoming pregnant, that had been a part of the previous brainstorm, was usurped by the privileging of the constellation of 'affective' risky possibilities.
>
> *(p. 178)*

The ethnographic approach created the possibility for such an analyses to pay attention to notions of affect and their repeated articulation over time.

C.J. Pascoe's (2007) ethnographic study of masculinity in a working-class high school in the United States is another example of how ethnographic methods enable nuanced and relational understandings of how gender plays out in complex ways. The time Pascoe spends in the school, and the relationships she builds with students, allows evidential statements to be made that reflect long-term engagement and observations of cultural context, rather than the contingencies of one-off observations or interviews. For example: "through extensive fieldwork and interviewing I discovered that, for boys, achieving a masculine identity entails the repeated repudiation of the spectre of failed masculinity" (p. 5). She further observes:

> From what I saw during my research, African American boys were more likely to be punished by school authorities for engaging in these masculinizing practices. Though homophobic taunts and assertion of heterosexuality shore up a masculine identity for boys, the relationship between sexuality and masculinity looks different when masculinity occurs outside male bodies. For girls, challenging heterosexual identities often solidifies a more masculine identity. These gendering processes are encoded at multiple levels: institutional, interactional, and individual.
>
> *(p. 5)*

This statement is based on 18 months of engagement with the school, and many staff and students. This length of time allowed Pascoe to offer the following theoretical insight: "I conclude by suggesting that close attention to sexuality highlights masculinity as a process rather than a social identity associated with specific bodies" (p. 5). Likewise, Youdell's (2005) ethnographic study of gender articulations at a South London high school shows how complex gender expression can be over time, and how the heterosexual matrix (Butler, 1999) – what Youdell (2005) calls the sex-gender-sexuality constellation – shifts in complex ways, even within one school site. She analyzes students' bodily practices in assemblies, in classrooms, and with other students. Her ethnographic analyses elucidate how gender and sexuality are "contingent, provisional and fragile" (p. 254). Such analyses get to the minutiae of gendered moments of expression, nuances that might not be evident through other methodological approaches.

These varied examples highlight how ethnographic temporalities and spatialities have extended work in gender and sexuality and allowed for certain kinds of messy and contradictory analyses to emerge. This is evident in the attention to, and importance placed on, theory in this work, including being at the forefront of academic developments. Feminist analyses and methodological practices and, more recently, queer and new materialist ethnographies, have been influential within and beyond feminist educational research. In many of these developments, critical ethnography (broadly defined) has been at the intersection of gender and sexuality studies with education, thus proving to be a productive fulcrum for both fields in important and significant ways.

Notes

1. For example, see the special issue of *Sexualities* on Trans Genealogies, 2019, *volume 22*(1–2).
2. The term digital ethnography is used here but others use terms such as cyber ethnography, online ethnography, netography, and virtual ethnography. For further discussion see: Abidin and De Seta (2020); Pink et al. (2016).

References

Abidin, C. (2020). Somewhere between here and there: Negotiating researcher visibility in a digital ethnography of the influencer industry. *Journal of Digital Social Research*, *2*(1), 56–76.

Abidin, C., & De Seta, G. (2020). Private messages from the field: Confessions on digital ethnography and its discomforts. *Journal of Digital Social Research*, 2(1), 1–19.

Aggleton, P., Cover, R., Leahy, D., Marshall, D., & Rasmussen, M. L. (2019). Youth, sexuality and sexual citizenship: An introduction. In P. Aggleton, R. Cover, D. Leahy, D. Marshall, & M. L. Rasmussen (Eds.), *Youth, sexuality and sexual citizenship* (pp. 1–16). Routledge.

Ahmed, S. (1999). Phantasies of becoming (the other). *European Journal of Cultural Studies*, *2*(1), 47–63. https://doi.org/10.1177/136754949900200103

Albury, K. (2013). Young people, media and sexual learning: Rethinking representation. *Sex Education*, *13*(sup1), S32–S44.

Albury, K., & Byron, P. (2018). Taking off the risk goggles: Exploring the intersection of young people's sexual and digital citizenship in sexual health promotion. In P. Aggleton R. Cover, D. Leahy, D. Marshall, & M. L. Rasmussen (Eds.), *Youth, sexuality and sexual citizenship* (pp. 168–183). Routledge.

Allen, L. (2005). 'Say everything': Exploring young people's suggestions for improving sexuality education. *Sex Education*, *5*(4), 389–404. https://doi.org/10.1080/14681810500278493

Allen, L. (2007a). Doing 'it' differently: Relinquishing the disease and pregnancy prevention focus in sexuality education. *British Journal of Sociology of Education*, *28*(5), 575–588. https://doi.org/10.1080/01425690701505367

Allen, L. (2007b). Denying the sexual subject: Schools' regulation of student sexuality. *British Educational Research Journal*, *33*(2), 221–234. https://doi.org/10.1080/01411920701208282

Allen, L. (2018). *Sexuality education and new materialism: Queer things*. Palgrave Macmillan.

Allen, L., & Rasmussen, M. L. (Eds.). (2017). *The Palgrave handbook of sexuality education*. London: Springer Nature.

Allen, L., Rasmussen, M. L., & Quinlivan, K. (Eds.). (2013). *The politics of pleasure in sexuality education: Pleasure bound*. Routledge. https://doi.org/10.4324/9780203069141

Barad, K. (2007). *Meeting the universe halfway: Quantum physics and the entanglement of matter and meaning*. Duke University Press.

Bhana, D. (2016). *Gender and childhood sexuality in primary school*. Springer.

Braidotti, R. (2019). *Posthuman knowledge*. Polity Press.

Butler, J. (1999). *Gender Trouble: Feminism and the subversion of identity*. Routledge

Carmody, M. (2015). More than plumbing: Sexuality education. In *Sex, Ethics, and Young People* (pp. 59–82). Palgrave Macmillan.

Clark, T. C., Fleming, T., Bullen, P., Denny, S., Crengle, S., Dyson, B., Fortune, S., Lucassen, M., Peiris-John, R., Robinson, E., Rossen, F., Sheridan, J., Teevale, T., & Utter, J.

(2013). *Youth'12 overview: The health and wellbeing of New Zealand secondary school students in 2012*. The University of Auckland.

Connell, R. (1995). *Masculinities*. University of California Press.

Davies, B., Diaz-Diaz, C., & Semenec, P. (2020). Interview with Bronwyn Davies. In C. Diaz-Diaz & P. Semenec (Eds.), *Posthumanist and new materialist methodologies: Research after the child* (pp. 21–32). Springer.

Davis, D-A., & Craven, C. (2016). *Feminist ethnography: Thinking through methodologies, challenges, and possibilities*. Rowman & Littlefield.

Desmond, M. (2014). Relational ethnography. *Theory and Society, 43*(5), 547–579.

Evers, C. W., Albury, K., Byron, P., & Crawford, K. (2013). Young people, social media, social network sites and sexual health communication in Australia: "This is funny, you should watch it". *International Journal of Communication* (Online), 263. https://ijoc.org/index.php/ijoc/article/view/1106/853

Fields, J. (2008). *Risky lessons: Sex education and social inequality*. Rutgers University Press.

Fine, M. (1994). Dis-stance and other stances: Negotiations of power inside feminist research. *Power and Method: Political Activism and Educational Research*, 13–35.

Fitzpatrick, K., & McGlashan, H. (2018). "Some teachers are homophobic because, you know, they just don't know any better": Students reimagining power relations in schools. In P. Aggleton, R. Cover, D. Leahy, D. Marshall, & M. L. Rasmussen (Eds.), *Youth, sexuality and sexual citizenship* (pp. 263–277). New York: Routledge.

Foucault, M. (1978). *The history of sexuality*. Vintage Books.

Fox, N. J., & Alldred, P. (2015). Inside the research-assemblage: New materialism and the micropolitics of social inquiry. *Sociological Research Online, 20*(2), 6. doi:10.5153/sro.3578

Gilbert, J. (2014). *Sexuality in school: The limits of education*. University of Minnesota Press.

Graham, K., Treharne, G. J., & Nairn, K. (2017). Using Foucault's theory of disciplinary power to critically examine the construction of gender in secondary schools. *Social and Personality Psychology Compass, 11*(2), e12302.

Hammersley, M. (1992). *What's wrong with ethnography? Methodological explorations*. Routledge.

Haraway, D. (2006). A cyborg manifesto: Science, technology, and socialist-feminism in the late 20th century. In J. Weiss, J. Nolan, J. Hunsinger, & P. Trifonas (Eds.), *The international handbook of virtual learning environments* (pp. 117–158). Springer.

Haraway, D. J. (1989). *Primate visions: Gender, race, and nature in the world of modern science*. Psychology Press.

Hickey-Moody, A. C. (2020). New materialism, ethnography, and socially engaged practice: Space-time folds and the agency of matter. *Qualitative Inquiry, 26*(7), 724–732.

Hillier, L., Jones, T., Monagle, M., Overton, N., Gahan, L., Blackman, J., & Mitchell, A. (2010). *Writing themselves in 3: The third national study on the sexual health and wellbeing of same-sex attracted and gender questioning young people*. Australian Research Centre in Sex, Health and Society.

Jones, T. (2013). How sex education research methodologies frame GLBTIQ students. *Sex Education, 13*(6), 687–701.

Kehily, M. J. (2002). *Sexuality, gender and schooling: Shifting agendas in social learning*. Taylor and Francis.

Keightley, E. (2012). Introduction: Time, media, modernity. In *Time, media and modernity* (pp. 1–22). Palgrave Macmillan.

Keller, J., Mendes, K., & Ringrose, J. (2018). Speaking 'unspeakable things': Documenting digital feminist responses to rape culture. *Journal of Gender Studies, 27*(1), 22–36.

Kosciw, J., Greytak, E., Diaz, E., & Bartkiewicz, M. (2009). *The 2009 National School Climate Survey. The experiences of lesbian, gay, bisexual and transgender youth in our nation's schools*. GLSEN.

Kristeva, J. (1982). *Powers of horror: An essay on abjection* (L. S. Roudiez, Trans.). Columbia University Press.

Kristeva, J. (1990). The adolescent novel. In J. Fletcher & A. Benjamin (Eds.), *Abjection, melancholia, and love: The work of Julia Kristeva* (pp. 8–23). Routledge.

Kristeva, J. (2000). *The sense and non-sense of revolt.* Columbia.

Lahelma, E. (2014). Troubling discourses on gender and education. *Educational Research, 56*(2), 171–183. https://doi.org/10.1080/00131881.2014.898913

Landi, D. (2019). Queer men, affect, and physical education. *Qualitative Research in Sport, Exercise and Health, 11*(2), 168–187.

Lather, P. (1998). Critical pedagogies and its complicities: A praxis of stuck places. *Educational Theory, 48*(4), 487–497.

Lather, P. (2007). *Getting lost: Feminist efforts toward a double(d) science.* SUNY Press. http://muse.jhu.edu/books/9780791480267

Lather, P. (2012). *Getting lost: Feminist efforts toward a double (d) science.* Suny Press.

Leahy, D. (2014). Assembling a health [y] subject: Risky and shameful pedagogies in health education. *Critical Public Health, 24*(2), 171–181.

lisahunter. 2017. What a queer space is HPE, or is it yet? Queer theory, sexualities and pedagogy. *Sport, Education and Society, 24*(1), 1–12.

Madison, D. S. (2009). Crazy patriotism and angry (post) Black women. *Communication and Critical/Cultural Studies, 6*(3), 321–326.

Madison, D. S. (2019). *Critical ethnography: Method, ethics, and performance* (3rd ed.). Sage.

Maher, F. A., & Tetreault, M. K. T. (1993). Doing feminist ethnography: Lessons from feminist classrooms. *International Journal of Qualitative Studies in Education, 6*(1), 19–32. https://doi.org/10.1080/0951839930060103

McGlashan, H., & Fitzpatrick, K. (2017). LGBTQ youth activism and school: Challenging sexuality and gender norms. *Health Education, 117*(5), 485–497. https://doi.org/10.1108/HE-10-2016-0053

McGlashan, H., & Fitzpatrick, K. (2018). 'I use any pronouns, and I'm questioning everything else': Transgender students contesting homogeneity. *Sex Education, 18*(3), 239–252, https://doi.org/10.1080/14681811.2017.1419949

McRobbie, A. (1978). Working class girls and the culture of femininity. In Centre for Contemporary Cultural Studies (Ed.), *Women take issue: Aspects of women's subordination* (p. 96). Hutchison & Co.

McRobbie, A. (1991). *Feminism and youth culture.* MacMillan.

Miller, D. A. (1988). *The novel and the police.* University of California Press.

Naples, N. A. (1996). A feminist revisiting of the insider/outsider debate: The "outsider phenomenon" in rural Iowa. *Qualitative Sociology, 19*(1), 83–106. doi:10.1007/BF02393249

Ollis, D., Coll, L., & Harrison, L. (2019). Negotiating sexuality education with young people: Ethical pitfalls and provocations. *American Journal of Sexuality Education, 14*(2), 186–202. https://doi.org/10.1080/15546128.2018.1548317

Pascoe, C. J. (2007). *Dude you're a fag: Masculinity and sexuality in high school.* University of California Press.

Pillow, W. S. (2003). Confession, catharsis or cure? Rethinking the uses of reflexivity as methodological power in qualitative research. *International Journal of Qualitative Studies in Education, 16*(2), 175–196.

Pink, S., Horst, H., Postill, J., Hjorth, L., Lewis, T., & Tacchi, J. (2016). *Digital ethnography: Principles and practice.* Sage.

Quinlivan, K. (2012). Emotional provocations: Attending to the materiality of queer pedagogies in a high school classroom. *Sex Education, 12*(5), 511–522.

Quinlivan, K. (2013). The methodological im/possibilities of researching sexuality education in schools: Working queer conundrums. *Sex Education, 13*(sup1), S56–S69.

Ragonese, M., Bowman, C. P., & Tolman, D. L. (2017). Sex education, youth, and advocacy: Sexual literacy, critical media, and intergenerational sex education(s). In L. Allen & M. L. Rasmussen (Eds.), *The Palgrave handbook of sexuality education* (pp. 301–325). Palgrave Macmillan.

Rasmussen, M. L., Cover, R., Aggleton, P., & Marshall, D. (2016). Sexuality, gender, citizenship and social justice: Education's queer relations. In A Peterson, R. Hattam, M. Zembylas, & J. Arthur (Eds.), *The Palgrave international handbook of education for citizenship and social justice* (pp. 73–96). Palgrave Macmillan.

Renold, E., & Ringrose, J. (2017a). Pin-balling and boners: The posthuman phallus and intra-activist sexuality assemblages in secondary school. In L. Allen & M. L. Rasmussen (Eds.), *The Palgrave handbook of sexuality education* (pp. 631–653). Palgrave Macmillan.

Renold, E., & Ringrose, J. (2017b). Selfies and relfies: Phallic tagging and posthuman participations in teen digital sexuality assemblages. *Educational Philosophy and Theory, 49*(11), 1066–1079.

Riggs, D. W., & Bartholomaeus, C. (2018). Transgender young people's narratives of intimacy and sexual health: Implications for sexuality education. *Sex Education, 18*(4), 376–390.

Ringrose, J. (2012). *Postfeminist education? Girls and the sexual politics of schooling.* Routledge.

Robinson, K. H., & Davies, C. (2017). Sexuality education in early childhood. In L. Allen & M. L. Rasmussen (Eds.), *The Palgrave handbook of sexuality education* (pp. 217–242). Palgrave Macmillan.

Rooke, A. (2009). Queer in the field: On emotions, temporality, and performativity in ethnography. *Journal of Lesbian Studies, 13*(2), 149–160.

Safron, C., & Landi, D. (2021). Beyond the BEEPs: Affect, FitnessGram®, and diverse youth. *Sport, Education and Society*, 1–15.

Sedgwick, E. K. (1990). *Epistemology of the closet.* University of California Press.

Shipley, H. (2017). Teaching sexuality, teaching religion: Sexuality education and religion in Canada. In L. Allen & M. L. Rasmussen (Eds.), *The Palgrave handbook of sexuality education* (pp. 157–176). Palgrave Macmillan.

Talburt, S. (1999). Open secrets and problems of queer ethnography: Readings from a religious studies classroom. *International Journal of Qualitative Studies in Education, 12*(5), 525–539. https://doi.org/10.1080/095183999235935

Tedlock, B. (2000). Ethnography and ethnographic representation. In N. K. Denzin & Y. S. Lincoln (Eds.), *Handbook of qualitative research* (2nd ed., pp. 455–486). Sage.

Valocchi, S. (2005). Not yet queer enough: The lessons of queer theory for the sociology of gender and sexuality. *Gender and Society, 19*(6), 750–770. https://doi.org/10.1177/0891243205280294

Willis, P. (1977). *Learning to labor: How working class kids get working class jobs.* Columbia University Press.

Youdell, D. (2005). Sex-gender-sexuality: How sex, gender and sexuality constellations are constituted in secondary schools. *Gender and Education, 17*(3), 249–270. https://doi.org/09540250500145148

Youdell, D. (2010). Queer outings: Uncomfortable stories about the subjects of post-structural school ethnography. *International Journal of Qualitative Studies in Education, 23*(1), 87–100. https://doi.org/10.1080/09518390903447168

8

GETTING LOST, FINDING YOUR WAY, ENDING A PROJECT[1]

This final chapter draws on Patti Lather's notion of "getting lost" to reflect on the ends of critical ethnographic projects, how we might consider ceasing fieldwork and the notion of loss and lost projects.

All ethnographers are lost. We lose our way in the very beginning: in the entangled forest of questions and concerns, at the intersection of emotions, in the demands of fieldwork, in searching for "proper" academic questions. We are lost in the deep mud of the field, and then, in the writing and rewriting, in the maze of analysis, in ontological uncertainty. We get lost on purpose but are no less anxious to find the way out. Searching for the path is exhausting; feeling lost is both distressing and invigorating. Fieldwork may even be – as Crapanzano and Vincent (1977) noted, long before anxiety gained its current complex meanings – intensely anxiety-inducing. Ethnographic work is permeated by uncertainty, doubt, and blindness. An ethnographer feels fatigue, break through, tension, excitement, alienation, responsibility, and, ultimately, loss. We remain intensely aware of the ontological and existential difficulties of our projects, even while we immerse ourselves in the messy relationalities of the theory-field, and how these co-constitute each other (see Chapter 3).

In this, it is tempting to try to find order, to write clean and coherent narratives, to give in to the reproduction of what Pitt and Britzman (2003) call "lovely knowledge", which is simply a reinscription and reinforcement of prior assumptions about the project and the research. Instead, they encourage researchers to seek "difficult knowledge", knowledge of the kind that grapples with breakdowns and challenges assumptions, knowledge that courts disruption, that resists secure claims (Lather, 2007). Within all this mess, an ethnographer has to make decisions about when to begin and end a project. This seems

DOI: 10.4324/9781315208510-8

a pragmatic decision, but it is far more esoteric. Jeffrey and Troman (2004) note that:

> Ethnographic projects are never finished, only left, with their accounts considered provisional and tentative. The total length of a research project may be defined by the researcher/s themselves indicating its closure. Alternatively, some projects are developed throughout the whole of a researcher's life; an ethnography may become a long, episodic narrative.
>
> *(p. 538)*

At the end of a project (if we know it is the end, or if we are forced to end it), the ethnographer is faced with the choice to leave (or leave off researching) – a decision that may entail grief and relief – or to continue. Continuation, as Jeffrey and Troman (2004) note, may require revisiting and returning many times to the ethnographic materials or to the field. Similarly, a researcher may leave with no intention of returning and then be called back: by people, by lingering questions, or by a desire for comparison between times and places and theories. Iversen (2009) notes that leaving has ethical consequences, especially when relationships are significant. Nevertheless, "ethnographic projects are never finished" (Jeffrey & Troman, 2004, p. 538) because researchers live them, and the project is thus written into the body. Ethnographers continue to carry the people, places, and events as memories long after the fieldwork is complete, and these, indeed, might continue to engage us, both physically and digitally. Ethnographic materials lead multiple lives; they continue alternative existences in the ethnographic writing, and in the memory of the ethnographer and the retelling of their stories, and in how they are subsequently reread, cited, quoted, and revisited.

All ethnographies both exist and do not exist simultaneously. A project is always partial and unfulfilled, begging for further inquiry and, at the end, always denied completion, fullness, the whole story. Aspects of ethnographic inquiry are lost even in the process of fieldwork, and in their retellings. We can never be in all places and listening to all conversations; we cannot follow all the possible leads we would like to (because of time, energy, and focus); and we cannot continue a project forever. When we do finish, we are then faced with various crises of representation, with losing our way in the materials, and having to face the question of how to deal with the interplay of voices in our writing: authorial voice, the voices of participants, and the voices of theory. With reference to her book, *Getting lost*, Patti Lather advocates for an approach that "delineates the openendedness of practical action as a structure of praxis and ethics without foundations in a context of demands for practices with more to answer to in terms of the complexities of language and the world" (2007, p. 3). She notes that it is difficult to accept the challenges of poststructuralist theory – especially the contention that language, at best, allows only partial and power-laden representation, and that subjectivities are made by the contexts they inhabit. At the same time, Lather (2007) challenges researchers to work at and expose injustice, while being simultaneously uncertain and open to being wrong.

In this chapter, Katie draw on the notion of loss and of being lost in ethnographic work and also reflect on the edges and the end of ethnographies. In this, I argue that all ethnographies are lost ethnographies, because there are inevitably missed moments, things we turn away from, and endings of various kinds. Ethnography always feels like unfinished business. Using my school-based ethnographic work as a springboard, I wonder where the edges of ethnographic work are, where our responsibilities lie for continuing or stopping, and how we might know when it is time to stop. I reflect in detail on what was lost in stopping a particular project when I did, and what remains lost in refusing to follow it up (some 15 years later).

Ethnographic Re-encounters

When I think about my first major ethnographic project (Fitzpatrick, 2013), I feel a sense of wistfulness and a lingering sadness. Is it regret? I don't think so, but something of loss lingers at the edges of my memory. The research was an intense fieldwork experience over the 2007 school year with a group of students (16–17 years old) and their teacher. The latter was a gifted practitioner with a passion for unconventional pedagogical approaches, and a deeply held commitment to social justice for the mostly working-class, Indigenous, and migrant students he was working with. His pedagogy was not one of loss, it was laced with playfulness, fun, laughter, and a healthy ability to poke fun at the absurdity of schooling (Fitzpatrick & Russell, 2015). When I was in his classes, I reflect now – with more than a hint of nostalgia – I could lose myself in play, in learning, and in my interactions with the sassy, smart, observant, and irreverent teenagers. But this memory is only one telling. I also – if I force myself – remember the boredom of hanging out at a high school, the way I had to drag myself out of bed in the mornings to go, and how self-conscious I was being a researcher (rather than a teacher). I remember how useless I felt and how uncertain I was about getting anything good, useful, or focused. I didn't know if I was asking the right questions; I didn't know what I was missing. Wetherell (2012) argues that we need to pay more attention to emotion in research. She notes that "an emotion is not an object inside the self but is a relation to others, a response to a situation and to the world" (p. 24). Willis (2012) likewise argues that researchers should open up rather than suppress emotion in their writing. Emotions are interwoven in projects and evident in the body of the ethnographer. These projects are impossible to leave and are never finished, partly because we carry the emotions of the project with us, and partly because ethnographers are voracious observers of people and places. These are always changing, and we thus remain intensely interested in their ongoing social dramas.

Ending a Project

My first critical ethnographic research project was a school-based ethnography of youth in health education and physical education classes in Aotearoa New Zealand. In 2007, the year that I undertook the ethnographic fieldwork, the students were 17–18 years old – in their final years of high school – and (almost) all identified as Indigenous Māori and/or Pacific Island (Samoan, Tongan, Niuean, Cook Islands Māori). Of the latter, some were new or first-generation migrants, while others came from families that had been in Aotearoa New Zealand for generations. Their identities not only centered on ethnicity and culture but were also located in a place called South Auckland – a suburb stereotyped in public discourse as being poor, brown, and gang-ridden (Loto et al., 2006). Needless to say, the young people rejected these assumptions about their home, while also engaging in a kind of organic analysis of how places carry particular meanings relative to other sites. They knew the stereotypes were unfair and they compared their suburb to others. Most were proud of their place, some held intentions to leave. All these young people had ambitions: dreams of elite sport, career aspirations, and study plans. As a group, they were wholly unaware of the inequities of social class, and naïve about how difficult it would be for them to achieve the kinds of economic and social mobility they sought. It was clear to me that these difficulties were unlikely to be a result of either their efforts or abilities, but more likely connected to persistent social class and racialized barriers. These included economic pressures at home; a lack of the resources and support that middle-class youth enjoyed; family responsibilities, including health problems, exacerbated by poverty; and logistical difficulties (e.g., of traveling to sites of higher education, of paying student fees). Nevertheless, the students still had an unwavering and deep-seated belief in meritocracy, and they ascribed failure to "not working hard enough".

I was reluctant to shatter this perception, partly because I didn't want to engage in deficit thinking, and partly because of my own assumption that it gets even harder to succeed if belief in success is taken away. For example, one of the young people in this study, Ben, told me a great deal about his life and his family. Describing his close relationship with his brother – who was on the run from the police at the time – he disclosed his ambition to become a lawyer because he thought his family needed one. I helped him get into university after he left school and secured him a place in the university's student accommodation. I stayed in touch, found him a mentor, and met up for coffee on campus. But he dropped out because of the expense, cultural dislocation, and guilt. Guilt that he wasn't earning money for his family. By now, he would be in his early 30s, and I wonder where he is and what he is doing. I'd like to ask him if my analysis was wrong, and I'm interested in how he views his life now. Harriet was another young person I formed a close relationship with. Before we lost touch, she had joined the navy and had a child. She had been accepted into the navy in 2009 for the sailor training program. She didn't think she would get into the officer program, and she didn't ever try. She was adamant that the navy was pro-equity because she was treated exactly the same as the men. I also wonder where she is now.

This ethnographic project initially spanned the 2007 school year but I followed up with some students, like the two discussed earlier, in the year immediately post-school to see what they did. I stopped after that for two reasons. The first was that it was more difficult to keep in touch with the participants after they left school. A few moved to Australia and others to different parts of Auckland. Second, I needed to "move on" and write up the research, and the participants were also moving on with their lives. They seemed less interested in the study and I perceived that they had less desire to talk to me about their lives. A few seemed to actively avoid keeping in touch, but I wasn't sure why, or if I was just being overly sensitive. I certainly felt guilty that I couldn't help them more in achieving their goals, given my own privilege. I also wondered whether some students were embarrassed looking back on what they disclosed to me about their lives – their older selves looking back with disdain on their then naïvety and openness. But this could just be my interpretation. I had no reason to believe they even remembered half the things they told me a year or more before.

In that project, of course, things were also lost along the way. Paris (2014) encourages "refusing research" as an ethical choice to not write about something, to resist romanticizing and objectification. Ethnographers make such choices all the time as we think about the effects of representation, or writing about incidents, criminal activity, or moral decisions (see Chapters 4 and 5). There were a great many things in that project that I did not write about because I knew it would make the youth themselves, their families, or the school vulnerable to attack, to increased stereotypes, and even to arrest. The latter was unlikely, but I was still not willing to risk it. I also left out what I saw as the more problematic consequences of schooling. While highlighting the difference that good teaching made to the hopes, dreams, and expectations of working-class Māori and Pacific students, I left out other observations of bad or incompetent teaching. I did not pursue observations about the inefficiencies of schooling that frame boredom and dislocation, and I talked little about the physical discomforts (and even health issues) that schooling spaces engender.

I did not write about these because of my ethical responsibility to uphold the trust of the school and because – having previously worked as a teacher in such schools myself – I know the vulnerability of schools and teachers who work, often in extreme circumstances, to serve low socioeconomic communities. I have seen some of the very best teachers in those schools, I know they often work harder than their colleagues in middle-class schools because they work at the margins, at the intersections of poverty, racism, and social class disadvantage (Kincheloe, 2007). This is not a deficit narrative because I also believe that these schools provide some of the very richest learning experiences for young people, precisely because of those challenges and because of the diversity of their communities. Even so, poverty is brutal, and it severely limits potential.

But it is even more complex than this. Lather reminds us that getting lost is also to embrace "that which shakes any assured ontology of the 'real', of presence and absence, a postcritical logic of haunting and undecidables" (2007, p. 6). She argues that "such aporetic suspension is ethical practice in disenchanted times" (p. 6). Consequently, I need to keep interrogating my assumptions and conclusions about the critical ethnography and the only way to do it is to go back. I am curious to know what has happened to the students, to see how their aspirations have played out for them, now some 15 years later; to hear their adult selves disrupt, challenge, and contest the assumptions of their teenage years and my own at the time about the limits of (their) possibility. This moment might be lost in my fear that my analysis is correct. Will I find stories of sadness and ongoing marginality, or will their current narratives surprise and disrupt my analysis? Importantly, what responsibility do I have to tell or to not tell such stories? Is this moment also lost in my fear that they will not want to talk to me again?

Falling Off the Edges

I reflect next on where the edges of ethnography lie in spatial terms and employ Harvey's (2006) tripartite categorization of space. While acknowledging that space can be viewed in many ways, Harvey (2006) views space as simultaneously absolute, relative, and relational:

> If we regard space as an absolute it becomes a "thing in itself" with an existence independent of matter. It then possesses a structure which we can use to pigeonhole or individuate phenomena. The view of relative space proposes that it be understood as a relationship between objects, which exists only because objects exist and relate to each other. There is another sense in which space can be viewed as relative and I choose to call this relational space – space regarded . . . as being contained in objects in the sense that an object can be said to exist only insofar as it contains and represents within itself relationships to other objects.
>
> *(p. 121)*

An ethnographic project can also be thought of as absolute, relative, and relational. While ethnographies are famously slippery, the textual products of the study have absolute qualities. People's words, theoretical analyses, and published articles have an absolute quality as material objects produced at a particular point in time. There are, of course, potentially many different absolute artifacts that result (in my study, there were photos, maps, notes, messages, voice recordings, transcripts, etc.). Any ethnography is also relative to other kinds of research; it exists in its difference (to, e.g., quantitative methods, interview research, and case studies).

The spaces between these define their difference. All research is also relative to not conducting a study at all. And ethnographic research is deeply relational, it depends on the relationships we form with others in the field and is reflected in our commitments to ongoing connections and reciprocity (see Chapters 2 and 4). A particular ethnography is also relational in that it signifies, echoes, contests, and evokes other ethnographic studies in different times and places.

These spatial metaphors suggest that ethnographic projects have edges: limits to their relativity, limited performative qualities. The limitations perhaps lie in where we perceive the edges to be. What about the aspects of ethnography that are lost even in the telling, in what is pursued (or not) during fieldwork? Ward and Winstanley (2003) use the visual art term "negative space" to think about how silences are constructed in research. They explain it as follows:

> In order to capture this concept, we have borrowed a term from the vocabulary of two-dimensional visual language in practical art: negative space. Positive space is the space occupied by the drawing object and negative space is the space behind the object or between two objects. . . . In practical art, it is often the practice not only to draw the composition, but also to draw the negative spaces which force an awareness of the composition as a whole.
>
> *(p. 1263)*

The concept of negative space draws attention to what is in the background of ethnographic research; what impacts on the shape of the things that are in focus. For example, in my project, I focused on one class of students, whom I watched, interviewed, and talked with in classes. But what went unnoticed in the negative spaces? I barely attended to the physical environment of the study, writing in only a cursory way about the effects of the physical classrooms, gyms, and the wider school environment. As I explained earlier, I chose to ignore some aspects of the cultures of schooling. This was to preserve my relationships at the school, and to not exacerbate the dominant deficit perspectives of schools in low socio-economic and ethnically diverse communities. What made the study possible at all was the institution of schooling, brought into focus by the negative space of not-schooling. Not only the missing thousands of young people not in school, but also the missing notion that we might not have schools at all. Lather notes that "the necessary exclusion is the very organizer of whatever insight might be made and critical texts always turn back on the very things they denounce/renounce" (2007, p. vii).

While I am critical of the effects of schooling, I did not countenance what the lives of these young people might look like without school. Maybe this is also the edges of the space where I am afraid to go. It is hard to imagine, invested as I am in the work of education (and institutions), that un-schooling might be worth methodological pursuit. This possibility was also lost. Lather reminds us that "getting lost functions as a paradox. It is a means of critiquing a certain confidence that research must muster in the audit culture" (2007, p. 12). She suggests that getting lost might be "a metaphor for a new generation of postcritical work" (p. 12). In this, considering the lost elements at the edges of our projects might also help us to understand what frames the absolute products of our research, including audit cultures, a push for confident arguments and certainty.

Walking Away, Refusing Research, Knowing When to Stop

Iversen (2009) observes that most methodological attention is paid to issues of access, engaging participants, and the planning of ethnographic projects. Relatively little attention has been paid to leaving the field or "getting out" at the end of an ethnography. Indeed, even knowing where the end might or should be is tricky. Iversen (2009) notes that:

> The discursive evolution of the "researched" from "subject" to "informant" to "respondent", and for some to "collaborator" and other forms of relational mutuality, necessitates full attention not only to how ethnographic research begins and is conducted, but also to how contact ends such that disengagement is more mutual as well.
>
> *(p. 23)*

After my ethnographic project, I had really wanted to follow the students from school into their post-school lives. As discussed earlier, I did this for the first year but then it dropped off. It didn't happen for many ethical, emotional, and practical reasons. This was partly because the young people were at a key transition moment in their lives, leaving school and considering what options they had. In this, they faced the hard realities of life outside of school: the costs of living, the costs of study, the realities of the job market. Many did not have the luxury of family members being able to support them to study at a tertiary level. And therein lies an ethical conundrum. From the relatively safe haven of their penultimate year of school, I had asked the students about their dreams and future goals. A year and half later they then had to leave school and enact those goals (or not). At this point, some withdrew from the study (simply by not answering emails). I wonder now, with hindsight, if they felt like they had let me down, and I wonder now about the ethics of researching their lives at a time they could enact little control over their financial situations and life choices. Others, however, kept in close touch for several years. One student, Malia, invited me to her 21st birthday party and she proudly introduced "the university lecturer" to her parents. They thanked me for mentoring her and keeping her "on track". I haven't heard from her now for many years; maybe I should get back in touch?

The final reflection I have to offer here concerns deciding to not go ahead or to pull out, pull back, or resign from a project. This is rarely discussed but, I suspect, happens often. I wonder what might be possible if I were to return to this project now, 15 years later. What might be lost or gained from returning and what might be lost or gained if I didn't. As I have hinted earlier, this project was very emotional for me. I formed intense relationships with these young people at a key time in their lives. I am curious to understand their choices, how their lives have played out since, and how they understand this.

Consistent with my critical approach, I'd like to conduct a social class analysis of what happened, comparing their tightly held aspirations with what happened next. In some ways, this potentially important social class analysis is exactly what is stopping me from pursuing this project – from deciding that this project is, perhaps, not yet complete. I am hopeful that their lives will tell a much more complex and nuanced story, but I'm fearful that many have been subject to various forms of social reproduction. In my critical ethnographic analysis, I employed the work of Bourdieu, alongside others, to understand the intersection of social class and place in the lives of these students. My overwhelming conclusion aligned with a Bourdieusian view about social reproduction, which suggests that social "equality" is an illusion: "Those who talk of equality of opportunity forget that social games . . . are not fair games. Without being, strictly speaking, rigged, the competition resembles a handicap race that had lasted for generations" (Bourdieu, 2000 pp. 214–215). It was clear to me at the time that this assertion held up: the work, study, and career opportunities available to these young people were so much more circumscribed than those available to their middle-class contemporaries.

In this critical ethnographic study, I also employed postcolonial theory and drew on the spatial metaphor of the margins to understand the experiences of these young people. Bhabha (1994) argues that, in postcolonial societies, the subjectivities of the colonized are split, fractured, and conflicted. Rather than this split necessarily being problematic, Bhabha (1994) argues that it "is the sign of the productivity of colonial power, its shifting forces and fixities, it is the name for the strategic reversal of the process of domination through disavowal" (p. 159). Moments of splitting were evident in how the young people in the study played with the power relations of schooling and with notions of authority.

These stories are, of course, partial. Lather suggests we might lose simplistic assumptions, and instead adopt "research approaches that no longer confidently assume that we are 'in the know'" (2007, p. 4). While I remain unsure about re-encountering this project, it might be a way to let go of certainty and require me to climb out of the hole of my own analyses. Berard (2006) reminds us that what we conclude about social problems, such as inequities, are partly a function of focusing on those issues in the first place and fundamentally a reflection of ontology. Perhaps I need new theoretical approaches to understand this project 15 years on? What would happen if I revisited my own analyses with different theories, opening up to new theorizing that pays more attention to materialities or to "cosmic intensities" (Braidotti, 2013, p. 166)? Britzman (2003) notes that:

> Poststructuralist theories raise critical concerns about what it is that structures meanings, practices, and bodies, about why certain practices become intelligible, valorized, or deemed as traditions while other practices become discounted, impossible, or unimaginable. For poststructuralists, representation is always in crisis, knowledge is constitutive of power, and agency is the constitutive effect, and not the originator, of situated practices and histories.
>
> *(pp. 245–246)*

All ethnographic accounts are partial and relational, located within our ethico-onto-epistemologies, and disrupted by the field. We write through these in the mess of the theory-field nexus and form texts that have a life of their own. In critical ethnographic research, we do this to highlight issues of injustice and, even while we continue to be uncertain, we also hope to highlight inequities and challenge their bases.

Getting Lost (Ethnographically)

This chapter has discussed what it means to be lost in ethnography and to lose the ethnographic study at the end. It has reflected on what is lost at the edges and at the end of ethnographic work, including the reasons we stop researching and the reasons we do not subsequently follow up. Researching with young people in schools requires delicacy and ethical sensibilities. In forming relationships with youth at key transition points (in this case between school and leaving school) we are observing, as well as engaging in, a kind of boundary crossing: between youth and adult, between researcher and mentor, between ethnographer and confidant. When we gain the trust of young people and invite them to share their aspirations with us, it is difficult for both parties to face the realities of what those aspirations come up against; especially at the intersection of social class and ethnicity.

All ethnographic work is emotional, and getting to the edge, to the end, is an affective as well as practical decision, one with embodied and relational consequences. Bourdieusian theory – which has been so influential in my work (Fitzpatrick & May, 2015) – suggests that because we conduct ethnographic projects over time, they get written into our bodies (our habitus) in lasting ways. Even while leaving the field, we inevitably carry the project with us. Leaving then is an embodied continuation of the ethnography. Projects are never finished or entirely lost, even while aspects disappear over the edge, are hidden in the negative space, or appear blurry at the edges of perception.

This raises questions about how we continue to write about the self and our participants through changing circumstances. How do we continue to write about participants as they were, and as they are, changing over time? How might our theoretical analyses be more responsive to changing times while avoiding getting stuck (Lather, 2007)? The notion of being lost, of losing, of forgetting, of losing the way is also somewhat liberating. All ethnographies are lost in the sense that we can never quite pin down or adequately transcribe experience, the culture of the field, the richness and diversity of participants, and our (shifting) relationships with them. Lather calls this "getting lost at the limits of representation" (2007, p. 1). She reminds us also that: "At its simplest, getting lost is something other to commanding, controlling, mastery. At its most complex, in a Lacanian register, we spend our lives with language trying to make it register what we have lost, longing for lost wholeness" (p. 11).

It's easy to get lost in an ethnographic research project, and it might even be a requirement of good research. And yet, there are also some key moments in some projects that we lose, lay aside, or walk away from. Being lost is, however, the point. All ethnographies are lost. Insights are lost at the edges and in the negative spaces, and there are inevitable losses in stopping a project. Re-encounters are always a possibility, but we can never go back.

Note

1. An earlier version of this chapter was published as: Fitzpatrick, K. (2019). The edges and the end: on stopping an ethnographic project, on losing the way. In R. J. Smith & S. Delamont (Eds), *The lost ethnographies: Methodological insights from projects that never were* (Studies in Qualitative Methodology). Emerald (pp. 45–56).

References

Berard, T. J. (2006). From concepts to methods: On the observability of inequality. *Journal of Contemporary Ethnography, 35*(3), 236–256.

Bhabha, H. (1994). *The location of culture*. Routledge.

Bourdieu, P. (2000). *Pascalian meditations* (R. Nice, Trans.). Polity Press.

Braidotti, R. (2013). *The posthuman*. Polity Press.

Britzman, D. P. (2003). *Practice makes practice: A critical study of learning to teach* (Rev. ed.). State University of New York Press.

Crapanzano, V. (1977). On the writing of ethnography. *Dialectical Anthropology, 2*(1–4), 69–73.

Fitzpatrick, K. (2013). *Critical pedagogy, physical education and urban schooling*. Peter Lang.

Fitzpatrick, K., & May, S. (2015). Doing critical educational ethnography with Bourdieu. In M. Murphy & C. Costa (Eds.), *Theory as method in research: On Bourdieu, social theory and education* (pp. 101–114). Routledge.

Fitzpatrick, K., & Russell, D. (2015). On being critical in health and physical education. *Physical Education and Sport Pedagogy, 20*(2), 159–173. https://doi.org/10.1080/17408 989.2013.837436

Harvey, D. (2006). *Spaces of global capitalism: Towards a theory of uneven geographical development*. Verso.

Iversen, R. R. (2009). Getting out' in ethnography: A seldom told story. *Qualitative Social Work, 8*(1), 9–26. https://doi.org/10.1177/1473325008100423

Jeffrey, B., & Troman, G. (2004). Time for ethnography. *British Educational Research Journal, 30*(4), 535–548. https://doi.org/10.1080/0141192042000237220

Kincheloe, J. (2007). City kids – not the kind of students you'd want to teach. In J. Kincheloe & K. Hayes (Eds.), *Teaching city kids: Understanding and appreciating them* (pp. 3–38). Peter Lang.

Lather, P. (2007). *Getting lost: Feminist efforts toward a double(d) science.* SUNY Press. http://muse.jhu.edu/books/9780791480267

Loto, R., Hodgetts, D., Chamberlain, K., Nikora, L. W., Karapu, R., & Barnett, A. (2006). Pasifika in the news: The portrayal of pacific peoples in the New Zealand press. *Journal of Community and Applied Social Psychology, 16*(2), 100–118.

Paris, D., & Winn, M. T. (Eds.). (2014). *Humanizing research: Decolonizing qualitative inquiry with youth and communities.* Sage.

Pitt, A., & Britzman, D. (2003). Speculations on qualities of difficult knowledge in teaching and learning: An experiment in psychoanalytic research. *International Journal of Qualitative Studies in Education, 16*(6), 755–776. https://doi.org/10.1080/095183903 10001632135

Ward, J., & Winstanley, D. (2003). The absent presence: Negative space within discourse and the construction of minority sexual identity in the workplace. *Human Relations, 56*(10), 1255–1280. https://doi.org/10.1177/00187267035610005

Wetherell, M. (2012). *Affect and emotion: A new social science understanding.* Sage.

Willis, A. (2012). Constructing a story to live by: Ethics, emotions and academic practice in the context of climate change. *Emotion, Space and Society, 5*, 52–59.

INDEX